£12-50

This book is to be returned on
the last date stamped below

30. MAY 1986

-3 OCT. 1986   -6. OCT. 1987   2 1 MAY 2003

11. DEC. 1986   14.

14. JUN 91

25. MAR 83

07. OCT 88   1 4 JAN 1994

2 8 APR 1995

3 1 MAY 1995

Sexual stigma

International Library of Sociology

Founded by Karl Mannheim

Editor: John Rex, University of Warwick

Arbor Scientiae
Arbor Vitae

A catalogue of the books available in the **International Library of Sociology** and other series of Social Science books published by Routledge & Kegan Paul will be found at the end of this volume.

Sexual stigma:
an interactionist account

Kenneth Plummer
Department of Sociology
University of Essex

Routledge & Kegan Paul
London and Boston

First published in 1975
by Routledge & Kegan Paul Ltd
Broadway House, 68–74 Carter Lane,
London EC4V 5EL and
9 Park Street,
Boston, Mass. 02108, USA
Set in 10/11 Times Roman
and printed in Great Britain by
Butler & Tanner Ltd, Frome and London
© Kenneth Plummer 1975
No part of this book may be reproduced in
any form without permission from the
publisher, except for the quotation of brief
passages in criticism

ISBN 0 7100 8060 3

Contents

v

Acknowledgments

This book, derived from a Ph.D. thesis submitted to the University of London in Spring 1973, may be seen as the end product of a series of interactive encounters with a host of 'significant others' over a long period of time. Only a few of these, rather invidiously, can be singled out for special thanks.

First, there have been a number of groups who have helped me at various stages. The Social Science Research Council provided me with a year's grant; Enfield College of Technology (now Middlesex Polytechnic) provided me with a sabbatical term and a most useful library service; the Albany Trust gave me much help in the early days of field work; and latterly the Gay Liberation Front served as an important – if transitory – stimulant for me to remember ideas that could easily have got lost in the welter of interactionist subjectivism. A major debt is to the homosexual community which greatly assisted me in the gathering of materials for part 3 of this book: I hope I have not betrayed its authenticity.

Second, there are a number of people who made the book possible. Stan Cohen stimulated my initial interest in the field of deviance; David Downes guided me through the early days of my research; Michael Schofield kindled my enthusiasm for 'sex research'; and John Gagnon provided a critical reading of the entire manuscript. Kay Templeman was responsible for typing the finished product, and Peter Hopkins of Routledge was an encouragement throughout. Two other people need special thanks. Paul Rock supervised the thesis in its later stages and provided me with detailed criticisms: I hope his theoretical influence will be apparent. Peter Urbach proved to be my sternest critic; and while he will disagree with much of what I have written, his influence nevertheless remains considerable.

ACKNOWLEDGMENTS

Third, personal thanks must go to my parents and my close friends – without whom, nothing could have been written.

Finally, the author and publisher would like to thank D. Sonenschein and the *Journal of Sex Research* for permission to reproduce Table 6.

Enfield
November 1973

part one

Problems and perspectives

Reality, then, in this distinctively human world, is not a hard,
immutable thing but is fragile and adjudicated – a thing to be
debated, compromised and legislated. Those who most succeed
in this world are those who are most persuasive and effective in
having their interpretations ratified as true reality. Those who
do not are relegated to the fringes of the human world, are
executed as heretics or traitors, ridiculed as crackpots, or
locked up as lunatics.

(McCall and Simmons, 1966: 42)

We can, and I think must, look upon human life as chiefly
a vast interpretative process in which people, singly and
collectively, guide themselves by defining the objects, events,
and situations which they encounter . . . . Any scheme designed
to analyse human group life in its general character has to fit
this process of interpretation.

(Blumer, 1969)

1 Introduction: the problem of sexuality in sociology

Sociologists have failed to study a most important aspect of human social conduct: that of sexuality. Given the prolific outpouring of popular materials on this subject, and given too the folklore that sociologists are men paid thousands of pounds to find their way to the nearest whorehouse, it is a surprise to discover that few sociologists have shown any interest in this field.

The main roads to a knowledge of sexuality lie in the work of Freud, Kinsey and Masters – there were few students before them, and most subsequent work bears the imprint of one or other.[1] Yet although they were not immune from social explanation, they were not sociologists. Freud's interest rested with the innermost emotional development of individuals, Kinsey's lay with the taxonomic classification of behavioural variations, and Masters was engrossed in problems of physiology – a clinician, a zoologist and a gynaecologist respectively.

Those few 'sociologists' who have explored sexuality have done so from viewpoints divorced from sociology. Thus, the pioneer works of Westermarck, Malinowski and Sumner roamed so far from home shores to merit the label 'anthropological', while the work of W. I. Thomas on gender variation roamed so far from the sociological perspective to merit the label 'psychological'. Likewise, the work of men like Marcuse and Reich must be seen as essentially metatheoretical excursions, and at the other extreme, the studies conducted by Schofield, Gorer, Dickinson and others must be seen as social surveys and not sociology. These latter studies of social book-keeping – of who does what with whom, how often and where – are the ones most frequently tagged 'sociology': but their authors have rarely been sociologists interested in theory and working in sociological contexts. Dickinson was a medical man, Davis a social worker, Hamilton a psychoanalyst, and Bromley and Britten were

3

journalists. Most of the studies commonly regarded as sociological simply do not meet the criteria of that discipline.

Why has such a neglect within sociology come about?[2] One popular answer is simply that sexuality is a 'taboo' area, in which the practical problems of research are much greater than in other fields. In addition to the problem of getting respondents to talk about such sensitive areas, there are problems of infringing the law, of personal attacks and abuse, of difficulties in authorities co-operating and of public censure (Farberow, 1963: 28; Christenson, 1971: ch. 7; Pomeroy, 1972). Now while there may be some 'special problems' attached to sex research, I agree with Hooker's remark that 'Many of these problems are in no sense unique to the problem area. To treat them as unique or special is to obscure the real issue' (Hooker, 1963: 44). This 'real issue' is that of scientific integrity – that all good scientific work is difficult. It is not enough to account for the neglect of sex research in terms of practical problems because all scientific work has these if performed seriously.[3]

A more fruitful approach to understanding this neglect comes from the sociology of knowledge. As Reiss has hinted, the neglect of sex research has little to do with fieldwork problems and a lot to do with the low place accorded to sex research in the academic hierarchy (Reiss, 1967: 4). Sociologists, fund-granting agencies, publishers and public may all mirror the attitude of a society which devalues and casts suspicion on sex by adopting the same stance towards sex researchers. The person who elects to work in the field of sex becomes morally suspect. If this is true, a change in sexual attitudes in the broader society may be accompanied by the increased output of sex researchers.

The need for a sociology of sex

Whatever the reasons may be for this neglect of sex research in the past, the sociologist continues to ignore it at the peril of both society and his discipline.

On the one hand there is a pressing, practical need for greater understanding of sexual matters in order to resolve both the 'personal problems and public issues' that surround it (Mills, 1970: ch. 1).[4] There is undoubtedly much personal sexual suffering in this society – most of it untapped, and much of it agonizing to the individuals concerned. There are also undoubtedly huge moral and political debates concerning sexuality in this society – the future of marriage, sex education, pornography and censorship, birth control, sexism and feminism, abortion and sex offences, 'permissiveness' and so forth. All these problems are surrounded by such a veil of emotion, dogma, ignorance and blind prejudice that informed debate and humane help remain scarce, while personal suffering and public confusion remain abundant. While in other areas of life, the search for understanding through research is seen as a *sine qua non* of progress, in sexual matters it is decried as irrelevant, dehumanizing and pernicious.[5] I am sure however that such research is shunned at great cost.

On the other hand, the sociological analysis of sexuality should also be seen as a worthy subject in its own right and as an important contributor to general sociological theory. Quite apart from the need to describe and explain the multifaceted nature of sexuality for its own sake, such study also touches upon all those matters that have been of a central and lasting concern to sociologists: the problems of the nature of sociological explanation, order, change and meaning. Theorizing about sexuality would thus have a pay-off in understanding such problems.

First, then, it may clarify the nature of sociological explanation. The problems in such an enterprise become most acute when one examines a phenomenon that is generally considered to be individualistic (organic, psychological). Durkheim's choice of suicide – an 'intensely personal act' – to demonstrate how social phenomena may be explained socially was hardly fortuitous. Likewise, with sexuality a subject is provided which is generally assumed to be a biological invariant with psychological consequences. Yet of all the biological properties of human life, sexuality is one of the most malleable and culturally variable. As Simon and Gagnon (1969: 734) write:

> Undeniably, sexuality is rooted in biological processes, capacities and even needs. But admitting this in no way provides for a greater degree of biological determinism than is true of other areas of corresponding interaction. Indeed, the reverse may be true: the sexual area may be precisely the realm wherein the superordinate position of the socio-cultural over the biological is most complete.

Such a statement gains support from those anthropological, historical and social research materials which indicate that the forms that sexual experiences take are socially organized as well as distributed. This does not deny the role of biological processes in understanding sexuality; on the contrary, the task is to develop detailed studies of the interrelationship between biological invariants of sexual experience and the socially organized forms that it takes. Sociological imperialism is as dangerous as biological tyranny. The problem, however, in developing theories about sexuality that attempt to integrate individual and social factors before an adequate understanding is arrived at of each component part, is the tendency for the field to become merely an eclectic hotchpotch of correlations

5

where genuine theoretical understanding is overlooked. Such, at least, appears to be the plight of the indisciplinary approach to criminology in England, and it would be a pity if the eclectic discipline of 'sexology' moved in the same direction, as it appears to be doing in the United States. The sociological task requires that the sociologist demonstrates the social nature of sexuality while remaining sensitive to the boundaries imposed by biology and psychology.

A second central problem for sociologists is that of order and control, and sexuality is sometimes seen as playing an important part in this order. Either it is argued that through sexuality our social order is channelled, or it is argued that through social order our sexuality is channelled. These two views pose empirically divergent interpretations of sex.

The first view – that sexuality canalizes order – is heavily rooted in the Freudian and biological imagery of an all-powerful 'natural' erupting sexual drive which serves as a shaping influence in the social world. There is both a 'right-wing' and a 'left-wing' version of this view. The former holds that the all-powerful demon of sex needs strong societal regulation for order to be maintained, any chink in the armoury of control leading to rapid moral decay, sexual anarchy and the decline of civilization. In the academic literature such a view is found in the writings of Unwin (1934) and Sorokin (1956) and in the contemporary moral crusades in England of Whitehouse and Longford (Longford, 1972). The 'left-wing' view holds that the powerful drive could be a means of creative self-fulfilment if it was not twisted and repressed by an oppressive state for its own ends: the State regulates the powerful drive through the family in order to rigidify the personality system and render it subservient to the needs of the rulers. In the academic literature such a view is found in the writings of Marcuse (1969) and Reich (1969), and more popularly in the contemporary ideologies of the Gay and Women's Liberation Movements (Altman, 1971; Milligan, 1973). While the right wing sees sexuality as the demon within and the left wing sees sexuality as the great liberator, both credit sexuality with enormous – almost mystical – powers in contributing to social order. Sex becomes the central force upon which civilizations are built up and empires crashed down.

While such views see sexuality as shaping social order, some other theorists suggest that it is society which shapes and orders the sexual experience. In no society does sexuality exist in an inchoate, unstructured form; rather it becomes welded into a system of typifications which render it routinely experienced. As Gagnon and Simon remark (1968a: 121):

All too often the sexual impulse is conceived as a beast held in check only by the application of immense societal sanctions, and much that is both destructive and creative in the human experience is believed to arise from the tension between biological impulse and social contract. Thus the act of freeing the sexual impulse is thought of by some persons as increasing human freedom and by others as creating the conditions for social collapse. In this sense, we have overlooked the meanings and power of sexual acts, and what is likely to be discovered is that the significance of sexuality is exactly in proportion to its perceived significance; that is without the imagery of power and danger, the sexual impulse is no more potent than any other biological component.

This approach leads to a third problem of concern to most sociologists – that of 'meaning'. Indeed, for some it is the central problem of sociology: 'We must take the problem of objectively determining the social meanings of actions to the actors as the fundamental problems of sociology' (Douglas, 1971b: 38). In the sociology of sex, such meanings have not usually been a focus of analysis: rather the sociologist has set about his tasks assuming the everyday, common-sense definitions of sex as given. In his social book-keeping, he has assumed the meanings of sex, orgasm, love and the like; in his cross-cultural comparisons, he has assumed the comparability of 'masturbation', 'homosexuality' and the like; in his metatheorizing, he has taken a series of biological assumptions about man's sexuality and used them as a basis for his theorizing. Throughout the question of how an individual gives meaning to his sexuality has been evaded.

A fourth problem faced by most sociologists – past and present – is that of social change. A number of controversies exist here. First, there is the empirical problem of the nature of sexual change in recent times – some sociologists seeing little change in behaviour patterns over the past fifty years but much change in attitudes (Reiss, 1967; Gagnon and Simon, 1972), others seeing change in behaviour (Christensen and Gregg, 1970) and others envisaging astounding changes occurring or about to occur (Toffler, 1973). Second, there is the theoretical problem of explaining change – some seeing sexuality as a powerful source of change (especially through birth control), while others see sexual changes as the outcome of other societal changes. Third, there is the controversy over the consequences of changing sexuality – some seeing change as leading to the moral decline of society, others seeing it as liberating, and others seeing it as suffering from 'overkill' and saturation. Understanding sexuality as it is linked to social change will tell us a great deal not only about sexuality, but more importantly perhaps about social change.

For sociologists, then, there already exist a series of latent debates surrounding the key issues of sociological theory. On the problem of sociological explanation, some stress sexuality as a biological invariant while others stress its social malleability. On the problem of order, some see it as causal – as a powerful force in shaping society; while others see it as caused – as shaped by social situations. On the problem of meaning, some see it as unproblematic – assuming the meaning of sexuality to be invariable and absolute; while others see it as a social contract relative to time and place. And on the problem of change, some see it as the one great constant over time, others see it as miraculously undergoing rapid change; some see it as precipitating great changes, while others see it as being caused by other changes. In sum, while the sociology of sex may touch upon many great problems of social theory, the answers that have been given so far to these problems can only be seen as a theoretical sea of confusion. It is then from this 'sea of confusion' as well as the 'pressing practical problems' that a need for serious sociological work on matters sexual arises.

Some immediate tasks

Having rejected the view that the sociology of sex is a trivial, titillating indulgence far removed from central sociological concerns, and having been made aware of the paucity of serious work in this field, the sociologist is confronted with a field of seemingly infinite research possibilities. There is simply so much that needs to be done, and so little to build upon. Among the most pressing immediate tasks in building up a serious sociology of sex are the formulation of consistent sociological perspectives, the clarification of the questions that need to be asked through research, and the codification of existing research findings. Without perspectives, work will remain eclectic and unsophisticatedly empirical. Without the formulation of questions, there is no direction or purpose and the field will remain a grand jumble. And without sorting out the existing important findings, and placing them in developed frameworks, work will remain non-cumulative. These are obvious enough points, but points which have not been taken too seriously in the sociology of sex.

This book attempts to address these problems within one limited area of sexual analysis, that of 'deviance' or 'differentiation'. Although deviance can never be understood by divorcing the consensually acceptable from the privately variable, in this book my emphasis is placed upon understanding all those patterns of sexual conduct that occur outside of heterosexual coitus in wedlock. Calling such activities 'deviant' is indeed problematic, and as the argument unfolds it will be apparent that I prefer the terms 'differentiation' and 'variation', while simultaneously acknowledging that some forms of variation by virtue of being stigmatizable are usefully conceived of by sociologists as 'deviance'. Some kinds of sexual experience take on distinctive properties as a consequence of being stigmatizing.

The structure of the book is simple. In chapter 2, I spell out the theoretical perspective which informs this book, and show its applications for both the study of sexuality and the study of deviance. In part 2, I develop a framework for the analysis of sexual deviance, showing the kinds of questions that need detailed examination and reviewing the existing findings around the problems. Part 3 then serves as a more specific 'case study' – showing the relevance of the approach and framework to one area that is publicly acknowledged as deviant in this society: that of the contemporary male homosexual experience. Throughout I am concerned with opening up the field in a systematic way for further exploration: scarcely a paragraph has gone by in the writing of this book where I have not felt the need for an expansion of the argument to chapter or even book length. Such is the plight of any student who elects to work in a comparatively undeveloped field of inquiry. Hopefully this situation will soon be rectified.

2 Deviance, sexuality and the interactionist perspective

The starting point of any sociological inquiry must be with the formulation of a theoretical perspective. Yet surprisingly, the study of sex by sociologists has in the main been conducted without explicit reference to theorizing. As Sagarin (1971a : 407) notes, 'The sociology of sex is largely bereft of any association with the great founders and theoreticians of sociology. There is a need for a theoretical framework, or many such frameworks, within which to study this field.' This book is an attempt to utilize one such framework, and to apply it to the conceptual field of deviance. The theoretical perspective developed here is that of interactionism, and in this chapter I propose to provide a brief outline of the theory and the implications it has for the analysis of deviance and sexuality.

Interactionism introduced

Unnamed, unsystematized and unpublicized during its formative years at Chicago during the first decades of this century, symbolic interactionism has become one of the dominant strands in sociological work – its major theoretical rival being that of functionalism. During the early years it emerged through both the pragmatic philosophizing of Dewey and Mead and the ethnographic fieldwork into the problems of the city conducted by Park, Burgess and Faris among others. Although there are now many varieties of interactionist thought (Petras and Meltzer, 1973), Herbert Blumer has captured its mood in three basic postulates: 'human beings act towards things on the basis of the meanings that the things have for them'; 'the meaning of such things is derived from, or arises out of, the social interaction that one has with one's fellows'; 'these meanings are handled in and modified through an interpretative process by the person in dealing with the things he encounters' (Blumer,

10

1969: 2). Locked within these postulates, I have detected three foci of interactionism which will organize the discussion to follow.[1] These suggest the world may be seen as a subjective reality, as a process and as interactive. The first directs the student to study the 'inner' side of life, to look at meanings and to analyse the ways in which the world is socially constructed. The second directs him to study the emergent and constantly changing nature of social life. While the third suggests that the individual is best constantly studied in conjunction with some significant others, or in collective action.

1 The world as a subjective, symbolic reality

'The most important thing about a man's situation', write McCall and Simmons (1966: 39–40), 'is that he lives simultaneously in two very different worlds. In the first place he is a mammal of quite ordinary properties, yet at the same time he lives in a symbolic universe.' Thus, on one level, man is an organism with needs, drives, physiological responses and capacities bound into an environment by geography, history and political groups and confronting objects that exist independently of him – the worlds studied by the biologist, psychologist and the structural sociologist. But at another level – the level which concerns the symbolic interactionist – man is the inhabitant and creator of a symbolic world in which the existence of language, symbols and gestures enables him to attach meanings to objects and actions in everyday life, to interpret the world around him, and to daily create social life. It is this symbolic world of meanings – both manmade and the maker of man – which marks him off from the non-human world. Man's ability to make, modify and manipulate symbols is the distinctive feature that makes him truly human and social. As Lindesmith and Strauss comment (1968: 7):

> The central position [of symbolic interactionism] is that the features of human behaviour that distinguish it from the behaviour of other animals are derived from the fact that man is a symbol manipulator, the only symbol manipulating animal and the only animal whose social groupings depend upon and are pervaded by complex symbolic processes.

Within this symbolic world both 'objects' and 'action' emerge. 'Objects' are human constructs and not self-existing entities with intrinsic natures – meanings do not reside within objects, nor within the psychological elements in the person, but rather emerge out of the process of interpretation by which definitions of objects are created and used. 'Meanings arise out of interaction and not the other way around' (Douglas, 1971a: 295). 'Objects' may therefore vary in

11

their meanings according to the definitional processes of persons: a 'pornographic book' is not the same 'object' in the worlds of schoolboys, priests, moral crusaders, 'sex fiends', anxious parents, printers and newsagents. In each of these cases, the meanings that emerge from a situation involving a 'pornographic book' are likely to vary. The object itself does not possess 'meaning', but rather the meanings arise through interaction, and remain constantly negotiable.

'Action' is behaviour to which a subjective meaning is attached, and a major concern of the interactionist is to understand social phenomena from the point of view of specified actors. This concern is taken most seriously by the phenomenological sociologists who view their prime tasks as describing the content of consciousness and showing the processes by which it is constituted. Such a viewpoint sees the world as devoid of absolute, inviolable meanings – and sees man as experiencing an ongoing struggle to make his life meaningful. Clearly, behind this notion of a 'meaningless-world-made-meaningful' lurks the spectre of solipsism and idealism, serious charges that are frequently levied against the interactionist (Lichtman, 1970; Hindess, 1973). For the interactionist seems to say that we can only take seriously the world of personal meanings, and that concomitantly there can only be personal truth. We can describe 'sexuality' or 'deviancy' from the point of view of some actor, but we cannot hope to find a transpersonal, objective truth about such phenomena. All knowledge then becomes relativized and the scientific enterprise is rendered as 'absurd'.

Now if these serious charges can be made to stick, interactionism must be relegated to an epistemological quagmire. For all theories that do not at least hold out hope for 'objective knowledge' must in the end lead to intellectual anarchy. These are serious epistemological problems, and I tread somewhat lightly around them in this book. My convictions – which I must argue in detail elsewhere – may however be simply listed as follows:

1 The world is without inherent, intrinsic meaning and man is constantly charged with the task of imposing meaning upon it.

2 The interactionist's preoccupation intellectually is with understanding this process of 'meaning creation'.

3 This position can easily lead to an extreme subjectivism and relativism, but these positions are epistemologically indefensible; and must be rejected.

4 Standards have to be arrived at – themselves the symbolic constructions of man – which enable one to 'judge' one set of meanings as 'better' than another.

5 For the interactionist, these standards may be *internal* to this theory or *external* to it. Internal standards are derived from the

social worlds that he is studying (that is, the rules the actor uses to construct his own reality, or the rules abroad in the objective reality in which he is enmeshed). External standards are derived from outside of the worlds being studied – in particular from the philosophy of science (which entails a commitment to 'science'), or from various political and moral stances.

6   Internal standards allow only a limited situational objectivity; external standards allow for a broader transituational objectivity.

7   The problem of 'external standards' is the most serious epistemological problem that can be encountered. Without holding one, all knowledge becomes trivialized.

I will return to these central problems at various points throughout this book, though it would be absurd to make any claims about their resolution.[2]

2   The world as process

From such a conceptualization of meanings, the empirical world of man comes to be seen as a state of flux. Human beings act towards others and objects on the basis of the meanings that such things have for them, but meanings are constantly being modified and constructed through interaction. Thus, if the first focus directs the student away from the objective world to the world of subjective meanings, the second directs him away from the usual concerns with stable or fixed psychological and sociological attributes and moves him towards a concern with processes by which social reality is constantly constructed by people in everyday life. Rather than viewing behaviour as a simple 'release' from a pre-existing psychological structure (such as drives, personalities, emotions or attitudes) or as a consequence of an external coercion by social 'facts' (cultures, structures, organizations, roles, power), the interactionist focuses upon emergence and negotiation – the processes by which social action (in groups, organizations or societies) is constantly being constructed, modified, selected, checked, suspended, terminated and recommenced in everyday life. Such processes occur both in episodic encounters and in longer-lasting socialization processes over the life history.

Thus, first, whenever a person enters any social encounter (and effectively he does this every waking minute of the day), many processes come into immediate play. Together they constitute a massive scheme for interpretation, for making sense of the situation in which he is placed. Before he does anything, the person has to indicate to himself what he is expected to do, how he would like to be seen, what 'meanings' the 'objects' in his path have, what meanings the other actors in the situation are attributing to him and their selves and so forth.

Cumulatively, and borrowing a phrase from W. I. Thomas, this may be called the 'definition of the situation'. At the outset of any interactive encounter, then, between Ego and Alter, Ego has to imaginatively construct a guiding set of meanings which will serve as the initial basis of any behavioural movements or gestures that he makes. Once a gesture is made, it immediately signifies to Alter what Ego is going to do; it immediately signifies what Alter is expected to do; and it signifies the joint action that is to arise by the articulation of the acts of both. Meaning has been tentatively constructed, social action has commenced and the task of the encounter may be undertaken. No matter how speedily and implicitly, such phenomena are an ever-present, all-pervasive feature of human social life. The interactionist takes this processual picture as his main field of inquiry. Aside from the importance of process in the minutiae of everyday interaction, it is also central to the entire life span – serving as one solid foundation for socialization and offering a different picture to that given by behavioural psychologists, Freudians and functional sociologists, where emphasis is placed upon internalization and introjection rather than interaction. As McCall and Simmons (1966: 203) have written: 'The life history of an individual is a reflexive sequence of interactions in which any given interaction is influenced by the sum of past interactions and in turn influence the sum of future interactions.'

Rather than seeing socialization as a 'printed circuit' in which men are programmed to behave in the 'right way', where they blanketly absorb the values of society, the interactionist charts the daydreaming and the questioning, the funnelling and the digging, the adopting of now this stance and now that stance, the recurrent problems and the turning-points by which social life becomes truly social. Most useful in this perspective of shift and sway, is the concept of the 'career' – usually used to depict the recurrent problems encountered over time by people occupying a similar status in society. Thus rather than considering the 'student nurse' as simply learning and accepting the belief system of the nursing profession in a direct and simple way, the researcher may chart her recurrent problems and her resolutions to them, showing how problems are resolved and how further contradictions and anxieties emerge to be resolved from this (F. Davis, 1968). Whether one is looking at interactive encounters or socialization, the focus is always placed upon the processes involved and never the given structure or personality. Human interaction thus comes to be seen as a positive shaping process in its own right rather than simply emanating from pre-existing psychological or sociological structures.

Such a picture is underscored by certain philosophical assumptions about the nature of man and freedom – that man is characterized by an 'essential openness of personality structure', that there is a 'freedom of action',[3] and rightly gives rise to a view of the world as being in a constant Heraclitean flux, where men are always negotiating situations, and where reality is precarious and emergent. At its most extreme, it creates an imagery of a disorderly world where men are constantly going back to first principles, making decisions and tangling with the myriad problems that lie in their daily path, each one having to be faced and resolved in its own right. Clearly, such a picture is as bizarre as it is false, and the interactionists themselves recognize this to be so. For the world does not appear to be in an endless flux; there is some measure of order; and in most circumstances it is perfectly possible to routinely predict what other men are going to do. When I give my ticket to a ticket-collector I expect him to clip my ticket, not my nose. If such is the case, then why do the interactionists focus upon process and mergence, and why do they ignore the existence of structure and stability? In short, they argue that while, analytically, all social life is everywhere and always emergent, problematic and socially created (and this is their central concern), it is also restrained by certain boundaries to interaction and the presence of certain recurrent and habitualized features of interaction.

The boundaries to interaction have been discussed in a brief but important chapter in McCall and Simmons's *Identities and Interactions*. They suggest that some of these limits are 'intrinsic' to the 'logical and ecological nature of man's world', and that others are 'extrinsic' – arising from 'accidental features'. In discussing the intrinsic features, the authors suggest that the basic question of interaction analysis involves asking, '*Who* come together to engage in *what* social acts *when* and *where*?' and argue that the choice of any one of these four key variables (who – what – when – where?) inevitably entails answers to the others because of their invariable intrinsic interrelatedness. The selection of a given year (say 1066) immediately precludes the possibility of my living in America (where?), watching television (what?) or knowing about Kant (who?). More importantly, extrinsic restraints are derived from the wider cultural, social, biological or personality systems. Thus to be born a woman or a disabled person is to immediately restrict oneself in the range of action possibilities (although, of course, precisely what these restrictions will be are dependent upon the socially constructed meanings of femininity and disability); to be born into a slum immediately sets limits to the interaction possibilities available (although, of course, there is always a potential for eliminating these restrictive barriers); to be born in a particular historical period will

15

likewise narrow the range of choices or perceived choices. Such boundaries only demonstrate the limits to the kinds of interaction that may take place, and they often require the analyst to resort to other types of theories (historical, political, etc.) in order to explain them. However, interactionists themselves have developed a range of concepts and ideas which attempt to cope with some of these problems of stability.

Among these concepts are those of *self-lodging, commitment* and *perspective.* Self-lodging is discussed by Denzin, who shows that while identification processes have to be negotiated at the outset, they may over time become recurrent and established and consequentially (while still having to be 'constructed' constantly) non-problematic to the actor; the self becomes lodged in a structure rather than remaining free-floating. Empirical indicators of self-lodging include personal names, styles of speech, modes of dress, special gestures and body movements – all of which provide recurrent clues as to how individuals are going to behave (Denzin, 1969: 924). The concepts of 'commitment' and 'perspective' are found in the work of Becker (1971), 'perspective' being used to locate recurrent solutions to recurrent problems and 'commitment' to depict an investment of energy in particular lines of action which make it increasingly costly to follow alternative paths.

While concepts like 'perspective' and 'commitment' are formed from symbolic interactionism, strong similarities exist between them and the concepts used by the closely aligned phenomenologists such as Schutz's 'world-taken-for-granted view' and Scheler's 'relatively natural conception of the world'.[4] Phenomenology, like interactionism, also views the world as an emergent process, but stabilizes it within the context of 'world-taken-for-granted' and 'thinking-as-usual' views. Of these Schutz (1962: vol. 2, 96) writes:

> Thinking-as-usual may be maintained only as long as some basic assumptions hold true, namely: (1) that life and especially social life will continue to be the same as it has been so far; that is to say, that the same problems requiring the same solutions will recur and that therefore our former experiences will suffice for mastering future situations; (2) that we may rely on the knowledge handed down to us by parents, teachers, governments, traditions, habits etc. even if we do not understand its origins and its real meaning. (3) that in the ordinary course of affairs it is sufficient to know something about the general type or style of events that we may encounter in our life world in order to manage and control them; and (4) that neither the systems of recipes and schemes of interpretation and expression nor the underlying basic assumptions just mentioned are our

private affair, but that they are likewise accepted and applied by our fellow men.

Such views are inevitably only partial, incomplete and contradictory – and hence may often be seen as problematic in themselves. Nevertheless, they are a particularly fruitful source for understanding the routinization of the otherwise problematic and emergent world.[5]

3   The world as interaction

A basic though obvious premise of the perspective is that individuals are never considered in isolation from interactive partners – actual or ideal, real or imaginary. In contrast to all individualistic theories, interactionists suggest that it is not possible to understand the distinctly human aspects of social life unless one constantly questions the part played by others in influencing and shaping an individual's action.

The importance of 'otherness' can be found in key concepts of interactionism like 'self', 'role', 'reference group' and 'collective action'. Here I will make only a few observations on 'self' and 'role'. The notion of 'self' has several divergent meanings (Gordon and Gergen, 1968), but the cornerstone of interactionist thought is that derived from Mead and discussed by Blumer (1969). The basic insight is that the human being is capable of becoming an object to himself. The 'self' is a reflexive process in which the two constituent parts – the 'I' and the 'Me' – are in constant interaction with each other in a wider social context (Mead, 1934: 175):

> The 'I' is the response of the organism to the attitudes of the others; the 'Me' is the organised set of attitudes of others which one assumes. The attitudes of the others constitute the organised 'Me', and then one reacts towards that as an 'I'.

Any human activity involves an individual not only intentionally initiating action, but also imaginatively reconstructing the anticipated responses of others to that action. It is the former which is called the 'I' and which is the source of 'freedom' in individual action, and it is the latter, which is the 'Me', which also gives interaction some stability. Much of Mead's analysis was concerned with the processes by which selves emerged in social situations, especially in early childhood. Mead suggests that individuals become capable of designating and indicating objects and actions to themselves, a mechanism is evolved by which individuals may form and guide their conduct in everyday life. It is the existence of the 'self' which provides a constant link between the individual and the society, and which serves as the basic unit of interaction analysis. To sum up and express the idea crudely: 'You're never alone with a self.'

17

Another concept that is central to interactionist thought and which highlights again the importance of 'otherness' is that of 'role', although it is widely used by sociologists who are not in sympathy with the postulates of interactionism. Such theorists follow in the tradition of Linton, not Mead, and it will be useful initially to distinguish what they say – because at crucial points it is the opposite of the kind of role theory used by interactionists.

To such theorists, such as Parsons and Merton, whom I will call structuralists, a role is fundamentally a set of expectations held towards the occupant of a particular social status or position such as a doctor or schoolteacher. The concept of role here is used in a structural sense to describe a pattern of expectations associated with a given position in society, and often – though not always – finds itself describing a society in which there is a fundamental harmony and consensus as to what people are supposed to do in any given role. Thus, for example, when Parsons discusses the 'sick role', he delineates four features of it that exist in an ideal form; the discussion may then range around the conflicts and the strains and the divergencies from this 'ideal role pattern'. But if one questions the existence of any kind of consensus of expectations attributed to given social positions, then Parsons's position becomes at the best merely a heuristic device and at the worst a distortion of reality (Parsons, 1951: ch. 10). But the notion of consensus is not really what bothers the interactionist in his usage of the term, although it is true that on occasions such a perspective has been called 'a refinement of conformity theory' (Turner, 1962: 37). Rather he is concerned with the tendency to produce a mechanical, overdetermined, overscripted, static conception of roles that blatantly works against the empirically observable dynamic process of role-taking, role-making, role distance and role identification. In the words of Dahrendorf, such a picture is 'pale, incomplete, strange, artificial man'. He is not a truly social being but a scientific abstraction (Dahrendorf, 1968).

The focus of the interactionist perspective on roles starts out from the notion of men in everyday life busily constructing images of how they expect others to act in given positions (role-taking), evolving notions of how they themselves expect to act in a given position (role-making) and also imaginatively viewing themselves as they like to think of themselves being and acting in a given position (role identity). No 'role structures' pre-exist that men simply 'fit into', like some huge waxwork effigy. There may be many culturally derived cues for interpreting roles, but the actual process of role construction is an emergent, unstable, constantly negotiated activity.

The distinction between these two branches of role theory is often considered under the contrasting names of 'structural role theorists' and 'dramaturgical role theorists', but such a distinction does not

18

neatly correspond to the kind of distinction made above (Heiss, 1968). Dramaturgy – usually attributed to Goffman – can be as deterministic, mechanistic and rigid as structural analysis: instead of working within the framework of mutual expectations, the analyst works within the framework of an assumed and reified consensual script, in which all the actors are fully versed in the parts that they are to play. If the dramaturgical analogy is to be used by the interactionist, it should adopt a view of drama as improvisation rather than classical drama – for only then can he remain faithful to the emergent nature of social reality.[6]

In summary, then, interactionism is a sociological perspective which highlights the ongoing construction of symbolic social worlds by men in interaction with each other. It is this approach which informs the rest of this book.[7]

Deviancy and the interactionist perspective

As an area of study, deviance has traditionally been the province of the criminologist who (in England at any rate) has been dominated by pragmatism, positivism, reformism and an interdisciplinary stance which excludes and misunderstands sociology (Cohen, 1974). Yet in recent years, there has been a considerable expansion of interest in the area by sociologists. Indeed, in America first and latterly in England, deviance has become one of the major areas of development within sociology (Douglas, 1970a: 3). The impetus for this growth has been a full-scale critique of criminological orthodoxies and a desire to return deviancy analysis to the arena of sociological theory from which it had become largely disconnected.[8] (See Debro, 1970: 165; Matza, 1969.) Rejecting individualism, scientism, absolutism, correctionalism and the pathologizing of the earlier approaches, a number of important debates surrounding such issues as 'a value-free social science', the sociology of law, and the links between political sociology and deviance were re-opened. Box (1971b: 403), summarizing Matza's argument on this, puts it very succinctly: 'The perspective has shifted from one which viewed [deviance] as a *simple pathology* in need of *correction*, to another which views it as *complex diversity* we should *appreciate*.'

This critique, and the studies that have flowed from it, undoubtedly enriched the field of criminology, and has been eulogistically called the 'New Deviance Perspective' and the 'New Criminology'. Yet it is important to note that while these theorists may have been united in their opposition to conventional criminology, they were not united in what they stood for. And while they may have appeared to be saying something new, their ideas can be traced back to well-established theoretical positions. What once appeared to be a new

19

deviance paradigm, now emerges as a number of theoretically conflicting positions each with its own historical lineage. At the very
least, it is possible to detect four strands of theorizing which these
sociologists have drawn upon: functionalism, with its roots in
Durkheim; interactionism, with its roots in Chicago and Mead;
conflict theory, with its roots in Marx and Engels; and phenomenology, with its roots partly in Weber and more fully in Husserl and
Schutz.[9]

Of all these strands, it is interactionism which has been most
clearly identified with the recent growth of sociological work. This
may in part be due to a rising interest in problems of labelling, a
problem which interactionists are well able to cope with;[10] and it
may in part be due to the symbolic identification of Howard S.
Becker with the 'New Deviancy'. Yet Becker's symbolic role should
not be taken to indicate that he actually originated the newer deviancy approaches. Indeed, there were many significant accounts
before him. In the 1920s Mead had written about stigma and identity
(Mead, 1928), while the Chicago Ecologists had started their detailed
ethnographic work of 'deviant life styles' for which they are now
rightly famous. In the 1930s, Sutherland developed his learning
theory of deviance (Sutherland and Cressey, 1966), Tannenbaum his
idea of the dramatization of evil (Tannenbaum, 1938) and Waller
in his studies of social problems had suggested that: 'Social problems
are not solved because people do not want to solve them. Solving
social problems would necessitate a change in the organizational
mores' (Waller, 1936: 928).[11] Later, the study by Lindesmith on
opiate addiction set the mode of analysis of deviancy which must
have shaped Becker's own work, for the two studies bear a close
resemblance theoretically and methodologically (Lindesmith, 1947).
There was then an ongoing tradition long before Becker's writings
which had strong affinities with the interactionist approach to deviance.[12] To talk of interactionism as a new approach to deviancy
is to be blind to history.

In what follows, I wish to return to the foci of interactionism
raised earlier in order to show their relevance for the study of deviance. In sum, deviancy is seen as a subjective reality, as a process
and as a consequence of societal and self-reactions.

Deviancy as reaction

The crucial analytic variable in the interactionist perspective on deviancy is the existence of individuals or groups in society who define
certain behaviour as deviant and act towards it in stigmatizing ways.
Deviancy cannot be understood adequately by simply considering
the attributes of a person considered deviant; rather one always has

20

to consider the 'deviant' in relationship to those groups and individuals who define him so. One cannot be understood without the other – they constitute the two halves of any deviant action. As the classic interactionist study puts it (Becker, 1963: 9):

> Social groups create deviance by making the rules whose infraction constitutes deviance, and by applying those rules to particular people and labelling them as outsiders. From this point of view, deviance is not a quality of the act the person commits, but rather a consequence of the application by others of rules and sanctions to an 'offender'. The deviant is one to whom that label has successfully been applied; deviant behaviour is behaviour that people so label.

Such studies are concerned with outlining the origins and nature of 'societal reactions' – be they those of official control agents, moral entrepreneurs, informal groups or dyadic partners – and assessing the impact and consequences of such 'reactions' upon the creation and transformation of deviancy. Instead of assuming that deviance leads to 'reactions' and control, an alternative route – that control and reactions lead to deviancy – is taken (Lemert, 1967: v). This is not to say that 'reactions' create the behaviour in the first place (though on occasions they may even do that); it is simply to stress that the existence of 'reactions' alters the nature and shape of those experiences to which the label of deviancy becomes attributed. It is this awareness of the role that 'reactions' play in 'creating' deviancy, that has led to an increasing concern with the political nature of deviancy. Deviancy becomes one form of conflict situation, in which norms and laws are seen as the product of economic, moral and political conflicts, and encounters between 'deviants' and 'controllers' are 'exchanges' between groups with differential access to power. The study of deviancy thus becomes a sub-branch of political sociology. As Lyman and Scott comment: 'The so-called "labelling" school of deviance is in effect a school engaged in a "political sociology" ' (Lyman and Scott, 1970: 218).[13]

It should be noted that it is not an argument of interactionism that specific people actually have to react towards a deviant for 'labelling' to be successful: it is often sufficient for the individual to simply react towards himself. 'Self-indication' and 'self-reaction', then, may be just as analytically important as societal reactions. Thus, for example, a person who experiences a homosexual feeling does not have to be hounded out of town, sent to prison, or treated by a psychiatrist to come to see himself as a homosexual – he may quite simply 'indicate' to himself, through the 'interpretation' of the given feeling and the accompanying awareness of the societal hostility, that he is a homosexual.

21

This is a very important point, frequently misunderstood. Several recent critiques of interactionism have started from the premise that the theory is concerned with the reactions of control agents to deviants, and have then been able to demonstrate that (1) many deviant patterns become well established without such official reactions (Mankoff, 1971; Clinard, 1972), and that (2) some deviant patterns remain unaffected by highly 'degrading' formal reactions (Williams and Weinberg, 1971). Such criticisms gloss over the crucial dimension of self-reaction, by which individuals may process themselves as deviant in the absence of official reactors and neutralize deviant stigmas imputed by others to them. It could be argued that such an approach makes interactionism a very woolly theory indeed; and indeed it may well be that it is not a theory at all. Rather, it constitutes a perspective, or an orientational system which directs the researcher to key problem areas. But to miss the central role of self-labelling is to do a great disservice to the perspective. Emphasis on the 'self-reactions' must be seen as endemic in the reactions approach (Spitzer and Denzin, 1968: 462; Lorber, 1967).[14]

Indeed, it is partially this neglect of self-reactions which has led to another spurious criticism of the theory. For some critics have argued that interactionism overemphasizes the role of control agencies and leads to a deterministic account of deviance, by which 'People go about minding their own business, and then – "wham" – bad society comes along and slaps them with a stigmatised label. Forced into the role of deviant, the individual has little choice but to be deviant' (Akers, 1968: 463).

Again this is a travesty. To take a theory that is sensitive to self, consciousness and intentionality[15] and render it as a new determinism of societal reactions could only be possible if the initial theory was totally misunderstood in the first place (Schervish, 1973). As Rock (1973: 66) comments:

> It is possible to use a definitional perspective without arguing that deviants are instantaneously brought into being by single and cataclysmic acts of labelling or that properties of deviation are merely imputed . . . deviation is an all permeating phenomenon which lends force to any serious decision involving some detachment from routine activity. It is rarely an alien label which strikes the unprepared innocent from afar. The process of becoming deviant is a vastly more complex negotiation of identities and consequences which takes place in an endless series of mundane contexts. . . . Instead of there being a great gulf between labeller and labelled, conceptions of deviance are woven into the very fabric of everyday life and minutely affect behaviour which is not officially monitored. . . .

22

Whilst official rituals lend clarity and authority to moral passages, there is abundant deviation which develops without any formal intervention by official agencies.

If I labour this point, it is for two reasons. First, even the most sophisticated critique of 'labelling theory' (that of Taylor, Walton and Young, 1973) seems to have fallen foul of this interpretation. And, second, in much of what follows, I will be arguing that in looking at sexual deviance it is not official labelling that matters, but rather the self-labelling that takes its cues from an externalized, reified stigma label.[16]

Another point of importance is that the sociological task itself may come to be seen as one prop of the 'societal reaction'. It is after all through the writings of social scientists of all shades that many of the key penological and social policies emerge – the Freudian literature, for example, heavily influenced the types of reaction accorded to the 'mentally ill' and converted the rhetoric used to describe homosexuality into one of 'sickness'. Thus, the interactionist approach of *necessity* must involve the scientist being critically aware of the part that he may be playing in changing or supporting the societal reaction and of the consequences that this may have for the deviant. Indeed, as several observers have noted, the very use of the concept of 'deviance' serves to cast apart those groups so designated (Lofland, 1969: 9; Szasz, 1971: xxv).

Deviance as a subjective reality

Most accounts of deviance until recently have assumed that the norms in a society were part of an absolute reality, were objectively given, and were consequentially unproblematic. Following from this, the central area of inquiry in much deviancy research has centred around the 'deviant' – attempting to explain why and how some individuals should have come to violate these stable and unproblematic norms.[17] In the study of drug use, for example, Young (1971) has suggested how researchers traditionally assume a unanimity of values – a moral consensus – by which drugs come to be seen as a kind of universal evil or immorality and how this has remained an unstated, tacit assumption in the background of their research. In order to explain how any person can come to violate the absolutist norm against drug use, theories are evolved which attribute a 'pathology', an 'inauthenticity' and a lack of personal integrity to the drug user. Assuming that the norms governing drug use embody a universal wisdom, rationality and meaning, those who violate the norm can only be described as behaving in a meaningless way: the pot smoker comes to be seen as acting in an irrational way devoid of meaning. Such a mode of analysis can only survive for as long as there is an assumption that there is an absolute reality that exists independent of individual personally constructed meanings – a reality that is both necessary and unproblematic. The existence of such an absolute reality is thoroughly challenged by the ideas of phenomenology, by which reality is largely seen as residing in consciousness and arising through specific situated interactions. Deviance in this view is a social construction and takes on variant meanings according to the situation and the individuals interacting. It is not something well defined upon which most members may agree; rather, it is something fragile which has to be negotiated. Every social situation is bounded by implicit rules that differ greatly from the 'formal' rules that sociologists traditionally have studied, and whenever such rules are violated – and this may be constantly taking place – deviancy definitions become a strong possibility. Ethnomethodologists and phenomenological sociologists have suggested that the analysis of the ways in which such tacit rules and meanings are situationally constructed are central not only to deviance analysis, but also to the sociological task. It is not possible to understand deviancy without first attempting to understand what the members' definitions of deviancy actually are in specific situations. Far from seeing deviancy as objectively given, then, the interactionist sees it as subjectively problematic (Rubington and Weinberg, 1968: 1–6).

From this relativistic conception of deviancy, several consequences of interest can be mentioned. First, it has resulted in a series of studies which simply aim to locate the world of deviancy as it is phenomenally experienced by the deviant in his natural *milieu*. Goffman's mental patents, Polsky's pool-room hustlers, and Humphreys's 'tearoom trade' are recent examples of an orientation which began in the Chicago studies of Shaw, and has continued to provide rich insights into personally constructed deviant realities (Shaw, 1930; Goffman, 1961a; Polsky, 1967; Humphreys, 1970).

A second consequence is the more recent emergence of studies that attempt to demonstrate the presence, emergence and consequences of 'typifications of deviancy' – notably by control agents such as the courts, the police and the psychiatrist. Such studies aim to locate the subjective reality of agents of control, of trying to see how those employed in 'deviance work' routinely employ certain tacit meanings which may differ markedly from the assumed, abstract meanings supposedly held in the imagery of an absolutist society.

A third consequence has been studies of the relationship between 'deviancy' and 'meaning': no longer can it merely be assumed that deviant activity is 'meaningless', rather it can be seen as yet another form of human conduct in which meanings may be constructed,

24

rationalizations evolved and 'accounts' given. Studies may thus be made of these 'accounting procedures' (Layman and Scott, 1970; Taylor, 1972).

A fourth consequence has been the emergence of studies which consider the ramifications of seeing deviancy as a form of stigma symbol, as a symbol which, if appropriately interpreted either by society or the deviant himself, may result in profound changes in self-conception. Schwartz and Skolnick, for example, have depicted the consequences of a legal stigma for individuals in society and Edgerton has explored some of the consequences of the mentally retarded being seen as a stigmatized group (Becker, 1964; Edgerton, 1967).

A fifth consequence has been the broadening of scope of appropriate areas for deviancy analysis. For, clearly, central to the subjectivist notion of deviancy is the idea that deviance is ambiguous (Schur, 1971: 24). The world once seen as composed of two types of people – the good and the bad, the normal and the abnormal, the black and the white – now becomes a potpourri of variegated stigma labels which are available for application under a wide variety of situations. Conceptually, then, it is just as valid to ask how deviancy comes to be attributed by a husband to a wife in their marital relationship as it is to ask about the more conventional categories of criminals (Denzin, 1970).

Finally the relativization of deviancy has led to an increasing awareness among sociologists of 'the problem of values'. While this debate is far from being resolved, the problem has been aired in an important way by Becker, Gouldner and others – and no sociologist who works in the area of deviancy can afford to ignore the manner in which values potentially enter his work at every stage. In the past, much 'social problem' writing has taken for granted the feasibility and desirability of 'being objective' and 'being value-free', but much of this has subsequently been shown to work from a 'professional ideology of objectivity' which mystifies the points at which values enter (Mills, 1943; Liazos, 1972). The elimination of such mystification is a crucial step which many of the more recent studies of deviancy have taken.

While the relativizing of deviance has a number of important and valuable contributions to make, the enterprise is not without its dangers. Most especially, it can send one hurtling into the relativist collapse by which it becomes possible to argue that anything is deviant and anything goes. If I choose to call homicide and rape 'normal', while tagging routine conversations and sleeping as deviant – then that is my relativistic right. But clearly, such a position leads to nonsense that is far from helpful in understanding the problems of deviance, and critics have rightly pointed this out (Liazos, 1972; Gibbs, 1972; Taylor, Walton and Young, 1973). This extreme relativism is a view that I wish to avoid throughout this book.

To do this, a simple distinction must be made between 'societal deviance' and 'situational deviance'. The former is that conduct described as deviant in the public, abstract and reified values systems which all societies must have – even though individual actors may dissent from them, and even though such systems need not be clear, non-contradictory, or without competition. The latter is that conduct which emerges as deviant in interpersonal encounters. The former – while relative cross culturally – is perceived as absolute by most members of a society and possesses moral authority; while the latter is capable of considerable relativity. The former thereby sets constraints on what can be called deviant in any given society, though these constraints are far from being rigid and fixed.

Thus, for example, on an interpersonal, situational level, individuals may choose to call homosexuality 'normal' and heterosexuality 'deviant' according to the norms and rules which regulate their activities. Knowing the norms of that group becomes important. But to suggest that this group is utterly unaware that 'abstract society' generally considers homosexuality to be odd is to suggest that groups function as atomized units divorced from larger social contexts. Groups may reject societal definitions, but they cannot wish them away or remain unaware of them. You cannot steal, murder, rape, be blind, deaf or mentally ill without being aware that you are violating some publicly held norms. In this sense, societal deviance remains absolute.

Deviance as process

Schur (1969b: 310) has written that:

> Very likely the single concept or theme most central to the
> writings is that of *process*. The societal reaction conception is
> pre-eminently a dynamic one. It insists that deviant behaviour
> can be understood only in terms of constantly changing states
> reflecting complex interaction processes, that it is quite
> misleading to treat it as a static condition. It is more interested
> in the 'social history' and ramifying effects of deviant behaviour
> than in the basic 'characteristics' of deviating acts or actors.

With process as a pivotal feature of the interactionist approach to deviancy, the interest in 'given structures' and 'static conditions' becomes strictly limited. Rather than explaining deviancy in terms of a simple cause–effect model, where a strain in the social structure (anomie) or malfunctioning within the family irrevocably thrusts an individual into deviance, the interactionist builds up a sequential and cumulative portrait of the processes involved in becoming deviant. Rather than focusing on the problem of what motivates an individual to behave deviantly, the concern rests with charting the recurrent contingencies that individuals encounter through which they gradually build up commitments to deviance, or retreat from and modify such commitments. Nobody becomes deviant 'all at once', and it is thus with the processes of *becoming* deviant that interactionists are centrally concerned.[18]

In approaching deviancy through a series of changing and interacting 'contingencies' and 'careers', Lemert makes the crucial distinction between primary and secondary deviance. This analytic distinction is used to highlight the contrasts between the original and the effective causes of deviance, between the deviancy as it arises casually in the first instance and the deviancy as it becomes stabilized and organized for the individual subsequently through the development of self- and societal reactions. Lemert (1967: 40) puts it thus:

> *Primary Deviation* as contrasted with secondary, is polygenetic, arising out of a variety of social, cultural, psychological and physiological factors, either in adventitious or recurring combinations. While it may be socially recognised and defined as undesirable, primary deviation has only marginal implications for the status and psychic structure of the person concerned. . . .
>
> *Secondary Deviation* refers to a special class of socially defined responses which people make to problems created by the societal reaction to their deviance. These problems are essentially moral problems which resolve around stigmatisation, punishments, segregation and social control. Their general effect is to differentiate the symbolic and interactional environment to which the person responds so that early or adult socialisation is categorically affected. They become central facts of existence for those experiencing them, shattering psychic structure, producing specialised organisation of social roles and self-regarding attitudes . . . the secondary deviant, as opposed to his actions, is a person whose life and identity are organised around the facts of deviance.

Understanding deviance, then, is largely a matter of understanding the movement from primary to secondary deviance – with the conditions under which this happens, with the stages through which it passes, and with the dynamics of its occurrence.

A number of other processes are involved in deviancy analysis. In particular, the entire process of social control may be viewed sequentially. Thus the interactionist studies the building up of moral crusades; the emergence of laws, norms, 'problems' and stereotypes, the construction of control agencies, and their day to day functioning; the processes of designating behaviour as deviant and applying such designations successfully, the maintenance and transformation of deviancy definitions over time. Once again, the interactionist does not simply view norms, laws and stereotypes as givens or explain them by reference to static antecedents; rather he focuses upon the processes of their emergence, modification, stabilization and termination. Deviancy arises against a backdrop of perpetual change.[19]

Yet another area of process analysis is that of the interactive encounters of deviant groups in the day to day world. In a perceptive paper, Lofland (1970) has suggested that much interactionist work has been concerned with the analysis of *strategies* by which individuals cope with problematic situations, and such strategic analysis has frequently been used in deviancy research. Thus, for example, strategies have been noted for 'passing as normal' (Goffman, 1963a), legitimating one's deviance (Sykes and Matza, 1957; Henslin, 1971c), disavowing deviance (Davis, 1961) and negotiating realities (Scheff, 1968). Whether through the deviant actor, the control agent or the encounters of everyday life, process analysis is at the heart of interactionist studies of deviance.

A concluding comment: Over the past decade or so, the interactionist theory of deviance has moved from an underdog position in sociology supported by only a few 'radical scholars' to an overdog position where it can be seen as a new orthodoxy in sociology. As with any orthodoxy, it has recently become the object of much criticism (Gibbs, 1972; Bordua, 1967a; Gouldner, 1970, 1973; Gove, 1970; Mankoff, 1971; Bandyopadhay, 1971; Filmer *et al.*, 1972; Scott and Douglas, 1972; Kitsuse, 1972; Davis, 1972; Taylor, Walton and Young, 1973; Schervish, 1973; Liazos, 1972). Before these criticisms gather momentum, as they surely will, I have tried in this chapter to move to the defence of this 'new orthodoxy'. I have done this by suggesting that (1) the interactionist approach to deviance is not merely a fad but represents a continuity with intellectual positions developing in America from the 1920s onwards; that (2) its growth has resulted in a fruitful outpouring of research; and that (3) many of the criticisms of the perspective are founded upon misconceptions of it. I believe that the conception of deviancy as interactive, processual and subjectively problematic are well-argued theoretical positions from which there can be no easy retreat. It is these positions which underline the remainder of this book.

The interactionist approach to sexuality

The interactionist approach to sexuality takes as one of its fundamental concerns the problematic and socially constructed nature of sexual meanings. In doing this it stands in marked contrast to those accounts of sexuality that assume man's sexuality as able to 'translate itself into a kind of universal knowing or wisdom . . . the assumption that sexuality possesses a magical ability that allows biological drives to seek direct expression in psycho-social and social areas in ways that we do not expect in other biologically rooted behaviour' (Simon and Gagnon, 1969: 735). Such accounts assume a 'magical ability' that is commonly recognized and experienced as similar by society's members. Commonsense and research definitions alike frequently assume that 'everybody-knows-what-sex-is', that 'sex-as-we-know-it' exists independently of its social construction, and that when members talk about 'sex' the categories used are not problematic to the users. But such assumptions cannot be taken-for-granted by the interactionist: for him they become the central data.[20]

The model to be used here thus starts out from an 'open-ended' conception of man, in which he is only marginally restrained in his daily life by the tyranny of biological processes, and then sets about analysing the ways in which sexual meanings are constructed, modified, negotiated, negated and constrained in cojoint action with others. Kuhn, writing in a critique of the reductionist Kinsey approach to sexuality, summed up some of the key points of an interactionist perspective long ago (Kuhn, 1954: 123):

> Sex acts, sexual objects, sexual partners (human or otherwise) like all other objects towards which human beings behave are *social objects*; that is they have meanings because meanings are assigned to them by the groups of which human beings are members for there is nothing in the physiology of man which gives any dependable clue as to what pattern of activity will be followed toward them. The meanings of these social objects are mediated to the individual by means of language just as in the case of all other social objects. That the communicators which involve these definitions are frequently – at least in our society – surreptitious and characterised by a huge degree of innuendo does not in any wise diminish the truth of this assertion. In short, the sexual motives which human beings have are derived from the social roles they play; like all other motives these would not be possible were not the actions physiologically possible, but the physiology does not supply the motives, designate the partners, invest the objects with preformed passion, nor even dictate the objectives to be achieved.

29

Drawing from the previous discussion on interactionism, it will be apparent that the interests of clinicians are very different from those of interactionists. Where the clinician highlights man's physiology, interactionism stresses his consciousness and symbol-manipulating ability: 'drives' become subservient to 'meanings'. Where the clinician highlights fairly permanent sexual structures awaiting 'release', the interactionist analyses the often precarious, always emergent task of constructing and modifying sexual meanings: determinism becomes subservient to man's intentionality and points of choice. Where the clinician views sexuality as an independent variable, the interactionist sees it as a dependent variable – one shaped through cojoint action: the social context becomes central for comprehending sexuality as it is commonly experienced in everyday life.

Such a perspective, potentially most illuminating, has been hampered by a lack of empirical research. There are few studies that have inquired into the content of sexual meanings; and knowledge of their forms, nature and range is virtually non-existent. Similarly, little is known about the sources used for building up sexual meanings, and only fractionally more about the learning process involved in the transmission of them. Nor are there studies that attempt to define the boundaries for constructing sexual meanings – can it really be assumed that man is infinitely plastic, or are there limits to his capacity to develop sexual meanings? Are there deeply regulative rules of sexuality? How are meanings negated, normalized and manipulated in social contexts? Why does any given actor come to hold his particular definition of sexuality and not another? In the absence of detailed information on these points, the following brief discussion is only exploratory and suggestive of a massive research programme.

The nature of sexual meanings

The fundamental axiom of the interactionist approach is simply put: *nothing is sexual but naming makes it so. Sexuality is a social construction learnt in interaction with others.* This is not, of course, to deny the existence of genitals, copulation or orgasms as biological and universal 'facts'; it is simply to assert the sociological commonplace that these things do not have 'sexual meanings' in their own right: these have to be bestowed upon them through social encounters. The 'mind' has to define something as 'sexual' before it is sexual in its consequences. As a simple illustration of this, two extreme cases may be cited: the first involves a woman lying naked while a man fingers her vagina, the second involves a boy watching a football match. If one was asked as an external observer to define which situation was sexual – by 'universalist, commonsense' definitions – there would be little to query. The first was sexual, the second was not. However, if one ignored the purely behavioural aspects and focused upon the meanings that the actors give to the situation, quite a different picture may emerge. For the man fingering the woman may be shown to be a doctor involved in a vaginal examination; and both actors may have produced clear definitions of the situation as being a medical one (Emerson, 1970; Henslin and Biggs, 1971); while the boy watching the football match may be busily involved in defining the boys playing football as sexual objects, imagining them in sexual acts, and interpreting internal sensations as sexual ones.

This is a very simple example, and there are some obvious difficulties with it – for example, in a vaginal examination members have to work hard to neutralize the 'sexual' elements and thus it may well be that whenever genitals come into a situation, actors associate them with sex unless they can neutralize such meanings away.[21] These real problems notwithstanding, the example could be multiplied many times to make the general point that sexual meanings have to be negotiated and are often problematic.

When a child plays with its genitals, is this 'sexual'? When a person excretes is this sexual? When a man kisses another man publicly, is this sexual? When a couple are naked together, is this sexual? When a girl takes her clothes off in public, is this sexual? When a lavatory attendant wipes down a toilet seat, is this sexual? When a boy has an erection climbing a tree, is this sexual? When a morgue attendant touches a dead body, is this sexual? When a social worker assists her client, is this sexual? When a man and woman copulate out of curiosity or out of duty, is this sexual? The list could be considerably extended; but the point I hope is made. Most of the situations above could be defined as sexual by members; they need not be. Sexual meanings are not universal absolutes, but ambiguous and problematic categories.

A few instances of this problematic nature may be developed here. Thus, for example, a child playing with its genitals may often be linked in adults' minds with sexual experiences it remains unaware of: one of Freud's errors was to equate the sexual meanings constructed by adult men with those of children. What for man may assume the proportion of a learnt sensation of sexual excitement may for the child initially resemble no more than simple bodily play and exploration. There can be little doubt that children both do 'sexual things' (Broderick, 1966) and have 'sexual things' done to them (Gagnon, 1965a); but this does not mean that they automatically 'feel' and 'recognize' these experiences in the ways that adults do. Genital play and indecent assault may both be experienced by the child in a totally 'non-sexual' way, because the child has not yet been fully socialized into the motives and feelings that adults routinely come to associate with sexuality: thus the child is merely 'playing', 'being attacked' or 'playing with an adult'. Whatever meanings people come to associate with sexuality, they are always learnt and constructed meanings (Mills, 1940).

This error is also made when considering the sexuality of other cultures and other historical epochs. It cannot be assumed – it is a task for research – that the ancient Greeks' experience of homosexuality was in any way at all like that which we call homosexuality today (Eglinton, 1971), or that the Eskimos' form of wife-exchange can be likened to the contemporary 'wife-swapping, swinging' scene in America (Bartell, 1971). Such assumptions are frequently and quite unjustifiably made in many discussions of sexuality – both lay and academic. Homosexuals, for example, who make a claim to their homosexuality on the grounds that 'the ancient Greeks did it' really highlight the danger of this kind of approach. That sexual meanings change quite dramatically can be found by any brief review of photographic pornography over the past hundred years or so. Positions, postures, 'sexy dress' and so forth change quite rapidly – so as to render what was once 'highly sexy' even ten years ago, almost comic, and certainly not 'sexy'. Further, the gamut of sexual meanings in our culture has probably changed dramatically since the advent of Freudian symbolism: a tree used to be a tree, now it is a phallic symbol.

The social sources of sexual meanings

Rather than sexuality determining our social being – as many writers suggest, especially Freudian ones – it is the other way round: social meanings determine and affect our sexuality. Sexuality has no meaning other than that given to it in social situations. The forms and the contents of sexual meanings are another cultural variable, and why certain meanings are learnt and not others is problematic. One important implication of this perspective is the need to analyse sexual activity in our culture for its social origins, the ways in which social experiences become translated into sexual ones. Much sexual behaviour may have 'non-sexual' sources: the health-food faddist may take sex at prescribed regular intervals in the same way as health foods and for the same purpose; the married couple may regularly have sexual activity because they believe the other expects it of them, even when neither wants it; the prostitute employs sex as a means of earning a living – as does the stripper;[22] the man may seek a flow of regular sexual partners in the belief that this may sustain his public image of masculinity; and the student may masturbate out of habit or out of an association with tension-reduction. In each case, sexual experiences are constructed from social motives and settings. Gagnon and Simon (1968b: 28) in one discussion on homosexuality in the prison setting suggest that:

> What is occurring in the prison situation for both males and females is not a problem of sexual release, but rather the use of sexual relationships in the service of creating a community of relationships for satisfying needs for which the prison community fails to provide in any other forms. For the male prisoner homosexuality serves as a source of affection, as a source of validation for masculinity, or a source of protection from the problems of institutional life.

. Here sex is not merely a 'release' used to structure experiences; rather, the 'sexual world' is itself fashioned by the social needs of the individual. These needs may be centred around the quest for relationships, for validation of gender, or as part of an occupational task. I deal with some of the non-sexual sources of homosexuality in chapter 7.

The range of sexual meanings[23]

The ambiguity, relativity and modifiability of each individual actor's socially constructed sexual meanings leads to a seemingly infinite potentiality for the bestowal of such meanings on any object. Having dispensed tentatively with an 'absolute' essentialist definition of sexuality, it is necessary to explore the range of sexual meanings held by actors. In this section my aim is to highlight some of the meanings found in this culture (though there can obviously be no claim to exhaustiveness or systematization in this),[24] while in a subsequent section my aim will be to explain some of the constraints placed upon their construction.

Some current sexual meanings: Presumably, largely as a heritage of the Judaeo-Christian culture, one of the most commonsensical and publicly acknowledged sexual meanings is the *utilitarian one of procreation*: sex is linked intrinsically to processes of child production. Yet, strangely, while this may be a publicly verbalized meaning, it may be statistically the least important and most defunct meaning to actors. Indeed, in some cultures – the Trobrianders studied by Malinowski, for example – it is possible for members to make no mental connection between acts of copulation and procreation (Malinowski, 1929). While it remains a task for research, a suspicion should be voiced that 'sex-as-a-means-of-having-children' as a privatized sexual meaning is statistically unusual. Some recent

33

writers[25] have noted this by distinguishing between procreative and non-procreative sex, suggesting a move in contemporary patterns away from the former towards the latter. In fact, I suspect that throughout history and across cultures it has been rare for individual actors to hold private 'utilitarian' sexual meanings (even when verbalizing them publicly).[26] This view stands in contrast to the 'global, commonsense' views that sexuality, procreation and the family unit are intrinsically linked; and leads to a view which sees sexuality as autonomous from these realms, and open to a wider range of meanings. Some of these I wish to look at briefly.

Perhaps the most significant of these is the *erotic meaning of sexuality*, summed up in everyday language as 'being turned on', 'feeling randy' and 'feeling sexy'. It is a meaning of 'pleasure' constructed to interpret sensations of internal physiological (usually genital) changes 'triggered off' by some stimulus in the outer world. These stimuli seem to have an infinite range; this is most likely to be a member of the opposite sex – but there are many other possibilities. Items of clothing, particular kinds of 'action', books, music, animals and so forth may all trigger erotic meanings for some actors under some situations. Some actors may find a wide range of stimuli which 'turn them on', while others may find few or even none. The research problem here is to analyse how sexual meanings of this kind become attached to variant objects.

Such meanings are generally associated with overt behavioural forms such as masturbation, coitus and orgasm; but they need not be. Further, they are likely to include a number of related components – some 'erotic meanings' are tinged with meanings of 'dirt and filth', others with 'guilt and shame', others with 'danger and excitement', others with 'power and assertiveness'. Moreover such meanings may well be manipulated differently by different socio-economic groupings – if Bernstein's thesis is right, it may well be that middle-class groups are susceptible to a wider range of stimuli for interpretation because of their greater ability at manipulating symbols generally.

These are all issues that need detailed consideration, and I am not arguing that 'erotic meanings' are capable of being captured and bottled in a one-dimensional way. I am merely hinting at one broad category which itself displays a wide range.

Another range of meanings that may be linked with sexuality (and which are themselves clearly linked with the erotic ones described above) could be called *romantic meanings*, caught in phrases like 'he's dreamy', 'I'm in love', 'he gives me goose-pimples'.[27] Such meanings may be publicly declared and announced or they may be secretly pondered upon. This latter category seems to correspond with the privatized sexual meanings discussed by Zetterberg (1966), who suggests the prevalence of a neglected stratification dimension – privatized feelings of emotional overcomeness, demonstrates how their existence may vary in different social contexts and explores some of the dynamics involved in such stratification. According to Zetterberg, most actors may be seen as possessing an erotic ranking – 'the secretly kept probability that he can induce an emotional overcomeness among persons of the opposite sex' – and much tacit interaction in everyday life may be viewed in terms of a secretive ranking and estimating process. An important component of the meanings that Zetterberg discusses flows from their privatized and secretive nature. Making such meanings public dramatically alters the nature of the social relationship; the secret and romantic longing for Johnny becomes a ritualized courtship once the secret is broken and an encounter embarked upon (cf. Aubert, 1965: 201).

A third range of meanings may be seen as linked with *matters of gender*. The very word 'sex' is frequently used as a synonym for 'gender', yet the meaning of sex here, while linked with the others, cannot be equated with them. Garfinkle's discussion of Agnes the hermaphrodite confronted with problems of passing as a 'normal-sexed person' is perhaps the clearest example of research that attempts to stipulate and discuss the socially constructed nature of sexual meanings. For most members of society, sexuality exists as a matter of objective, institutionalized, taken-for-granted knowledge – as a 'natural phenomenon'. Agnes also perceives the world in this way, but through her peculiar location in the social structure as a person of dubious gender identity, she is confronted regularly with situations in which her gender becomes problematic. She thus comes to possess 'uncommonsense knowledge of social structures' through her position as a passing deviant. It is just this kind of knowledge which the researcher needs to possess in the whole spectrum of sexual meanings, and just this kind of knowledge that he currently lacks (Garfinkle, 1967: ch. 5). Apart from analysing some of the problematic situations of passing, which are confronted by Agnes – her management of beach attire, dating, sharing flats with girl friends, visiting hospitals – Garfinkle also presents a ten-point statement on the properties of 'natural, normal sexed persons . . . from the standpoint of adult members of our society'. While there are question marks hanging over his methods, studies of meanings similar to this are crucial to advancing our knowledge in this field.

One further range of sexual meanings could be termed *symbolic*. Here sexuality is seen as a symbol or as being manifested in a symbolic form – it does not have to be seen as procreative, provoke inner feelings of 'sexiness', highlight gender differences, or be infused with notions of love, though it can of course be linked to any of these. Such symbolism may take many forms. In the past it has often

35

been associated with religion and worship, and a number of objects from the male phallus to snakes and food were given a sexual meaning (Ellis and Abarbanel, 1961). Sometimes it has been associated with 'nature' (Watts, 1958). And, since Freud especially, some sexual meanings have become located in a truly diverse range of secular activities from hard work to stealing. While much of this symbolic work may be linked explicitly with the previous categories, some of it exists quite independently of it.

Now these five broad categories – utilitarian, erotic, romantic, gender and symbolic – highlight variations and contrasts in what can be taken for granted in daily used sexual meanings. Such meanings often overlap with each other – a gender meaning may provide many clues as to appropriate erotic and romantic meanings (Kagan, 1964; Simon and Gagnon, 1969), the boy seeing sexuality as linked to aggression and the girl to romance. Further, this brief discussion has not attempted to cover all possible sexual meanings. Two more come to mind from the pages of the journal *Social Problems*: an article (Foote, 1954) suggests that sex is assuming the meaning of 'play', and a later article (Lewis and Brissett, 1967), which, after reviewing marriage manuals, concludes that sex has become 'an activity permeated with the qualities of work'. Many other categories could be added to the above, and in the long run of course it will not be sufficient to simply list the categories of sexual meanings that people construct; analyses will have to be made of the rules used for constructing such meanings and organizing sexual life.

The constraints on sexual meanings

The picture which has so far emerged, and which underlies the interactionist approach to sexuality, is one in which human sexuality is capable of exceptional flexibility and variety and in which man possesses considerable ability at manipulating and developing a wide range of sexual meanings and symbols. Certainly there is growing historical and cross-cultural evidence of the enormous range, in intensity, incidence, and content, of man's (and woman's) sexuality between groups and cultures. This malleability will thus be taken as axiomatic throughout the book.

But the interactionist's commitment to flexibility and open-endedness should not be taken to imply, as I have commented earlier, a total freedom from constraints. Man may possess a potential for the manipulation of sexual meanings but at many points his 'choice' becomes narrowed, routinized and restricted by a number of factors. It is the task of the interactionist to study these constraints, just as much as it is his task to study the emergent and creative aspects of social life. I cannot deal at any length with such large issues requiring detailed interdisciplinary analysis, but will raise briefly three sets of variables that merit consideration in any discussion of the constraints placed upon man's sexual plasticity. These three variables are (a) biological, (b) cultural and (c) interactive.

a   *Biological constraints:*   An important distinction to make here is between those biological explanations of sexuality which mystify by using obscure reified notions such as 'sexual drives', 'sexual instincts' and 'libido', and those more tangible medical accounts which explore the role of hormones, brain structures, nervous systems, sexual morphology and genetics in the development of sexuality. While the former hinder interactionist understanding, the latter aid it.

The most general biological explanation of sexuality resides in notions of 'instinct'. Now the history of social science can, in one sense, be seen as an ongoing struggle to rescue man from such explanations which constantly reduce him to the level of animals and which constantly stress his instincts as the basis for his action. At one time, every form of human behaviour could be interpreted by evoking the notion of an instinct, but today this status is reserved for a very limited range of man's social activities, with sex to the fore. Now the central point about man's social life – as contrasted with sub-human species – is that it is a symbolic life. This means that man's sexual feelings constantly have to be placed in the context of his symbolic interpretation of them: he does not just act on the basis of biological forces pushing him from within to behave in certain ways; rather he constantly sets about interpreting inner feelings, and making sense of the world around him. To talk of man as having a sexual instinct is a crude reification of a complex symbolic process: rather he has a biological capacity (in the same way as he may have a biological capacity for aggression or cognitive development) which is capable of great variation as he moves and manipulates his symbolic environment. The notion of a drive or instinct builds into the whole idea of sexuality a strength to control human life that I suspect it simply cannot have. It is partly for this reason that a number of psychologists have recently preferred the concept of 'appetite', or 'capacity' to depict the overall biological basis of sexuality (Hardy, 1964; Whalen, 1966; Wright, 1970). Such a concept captures the malleability of sexuality so essential to the interactionist viewpoint.

Many biologists do not simply talk of an instinct – rather they perceive it as a high-pressure drive constituting a closed energy system subject to the laws of the conservation of energy. Such a position is clearly to the fore in Freud's conception of the personality as a complex, intricate but closed energy system in which the libido

37

serves as one great source of energy, which if not channelled into sexual activity will be channelled elsewhere. It is also to be found in Reich's discovery of 'orgone energy', capable of being measured in the orgone accumulator and appearing as a pale blue liquid! Sociologists such as Davis and Polsky also seem to view sexuality as a powerful drive.

The belief, in its crudest terms, suggests that the sexual energy is an absolute force which, if not allowed to manifest itself in its 'natural' state, will break out into other areas of life. Two key concepts here are *repression* and *sublimation*. Thus if 'absolute sexuality' does not develop 'naturally', the energy may be *repressed* – in which case deviations and neuroses are likely to occur through the damning up of libidinal energy; or *sublimation* may arise – in which case, libidinal energy may become the source of extra energy in work, especially in such benevolent occupations as nursing, teaching and social work. There are other mechanisms by which the energy may be diverted from its original sexual goal. Freud and others thereby encourage a search for the underlying sexual basis of much social behaviour – one becomes very sceptical of the apparently sexless person and imputes to him all manner of sublimation techniques. Now the concepts of sublimation (along with its recent counterpart 'repressive desublimation'), repression and the libido are all unproven assumptions, which have been absorbed into the 'taken-for-granted' notions of sexuality. They remain 'hypotheses', not 'facts', and if one looks for evidence, there is little that does not hinge around polemics. Two simple hypotheses may be deduced from the broad assumption of an energy system: (1) if a man has little sexual outlet, he must be repressing or sublimating his desires in some manner – and consequently, most likely, exhibiting some form of neurosis; (2) if a man has much sexual outlet, his energy must be sapped away from other things – he is unlikely to be creative, active, or productive. In the first case, one wonders what the man can be doing with his sexuality, where it is being sapped to; and, in the second, one becomes concerned with the man's ability to perform well in other spheres of life. For both hypotheses, there is little evidence. The work of Kinsey, however, does suggest that individuals with a high degree of sexual activity can be 'of considerable significance socially' – one of his most sexually active respondents was a 'scholarly and skilled lawyer' who 'averaged over thirty [orgasms] a week for thirty years' (Kinsey, 1948: 195); and others have suggested that 'no genuine tissue or biological needs' are generated by a lack of sexual activity (Beech, in Wright, 1970: 233). The whole area then is one open for empirical debate.

The scepticism which interactionists pour upon mystificatory 'instincts' becomes much less pronounced when applied to specific biological mechanisms such as hormones and nervous systems. These must of course be viewed in relationship with interpretative processes – a hormone may provide a sensation, but it cannot in itself provide a meaning – but the fact that they play a central role is not denied. Simon and Gagnon (1969: 13), interactionists who work harder than most to discredit instinct theorists, comment:

> There is much evidence that the early male sexual impulses – initially through masturbation – are linked to physiological changes, to high hormonal inputs during puberty. This produces an organism that, to put it simply, is more easily turned on. Male adolescents report frequent erections, often without apparent stimulation of any kind. Even so, though there is greater biological sensitisation and hence masturbation is more likely, the meanings, organisation, and continuance of this activity still tends to be subordinate to social and psychological factors.

Here the authors refer specifically to 'hormonal input', but other biological factors could also serve as the basis for the social organiza-tion of meanings. The nervous system, for example, may provide internal sensations that are innately pleasurable – but the actor has to 'learn' to ascribe meaning to these sensations. The external sexual morphology similarly provides a series of 'cues' as to appropriate gender behaviour, but the actor has to build up appropriate inter-pretative responses. In each case, a biological foundation provides a source for building up appropriate sexual meanings. But the biological foundation in itself tells us little about the meanings bestowed. And, in cases where there may be cultural confusions about appropriate meanings, or cases where there are biological anomalies not capable of immediate translation, the problematic nature of sexual meanings becomes more apparent.

b *Cultural constraints:*   While there may be important restrictions placed upon man's sexual capacity by biological factors, cultural constraints are clearly more significant from the point of view of sociologists. As Berger and Luckmann (1967: 67) say:

> While man possesses sexual drives that are comparable to those of the other higher mammals, human sexuality is characterised by a very high degree of pliability. It is not only relatively independent of temporal rhythms, it is pliable both in the objects towards which it may be directed and in its modalities of expression. Ethnological evidence shows that, in sexual matters, man is capable of almost anything. . . . At the same time, of course, human sexuality is directed, sometimes rigidly structured, in every particular culture. Every culture has a distinctive

sexual configuration, with its own specialised patterns of sexual conduct and its own 'anthropological' assumptions in the sexual area. The empirical relativity of these configurations, their immense variety, and luxurious inventiveness, indicate that they are the products of man's own socio-cultural formations rather than of a biologically fixed human nature.

Man, then, is born into a pre-existing 'sexual world' with its own laws, norms, values, meanings, typifications on the cultural level, and its own relationships on the structural level. This 'world' exists independently of any specific actor, confronts him as massively real, and exerts a tacit power over him. The implications of this statement will be taken up in chapter 3, although here it must be cautioned that I do not propose to substitute a reified cultural determinism for a reified biological determinism. The constraints exist but they are not of a simple, direct nature. As will be shown in chapter 3, each society develops its own configuration of sexual meanings, but actors do not rudely encounter them. Rather, they are built up by actors in a highly intricate interactive process over the life span. An important set of constraints on sexual manipulation will thus be the interactive ones.

c *Interactive constraints:* Central to interactionism is a sensitivity to the potentially enormous range of sexual meanings available to an actor and an awareness of their constantly negotiated character. Yet it remains an unreal picture if adequate weight is not also given to the constraints that are built into action through day to day encounters over the life span. Such constraints serve to narrow down, restrict, routinize and order the range of sexual meanings experienced by an individual. They may be such as to almost totally eliminate any sexual meanings from an actor's world – as in the portrait given of an Irish island called Inis Beag (Messenger, 1971). They may be such as to sensitize an individual to an almost inexhaustible supply of sexual meanings – as in the case in the 'culture of civility' of San Francisco (Becker and Horowitz, 1970). But, whichever extreme, the sexual world of an individual is never totally emergent – it is also constrained, partially by biology, partially by 'culture', but centrally by interaction itself.

I have discussed the constraining features of interaction in chapter 1. While it is a stimulating picture to imagine man facing each new interactive encounter as if for the first time and evolving new solutions and new meanings, I stressed that this was absurd and false. Through interaction he builds up *commitments, perspectives, 'world-taken-for-granted views'* and a *stable self-conception,* all of which lend a precarious stability to his social world. Such interactive constraints also play a key part in the stabilization of his sexual world. He faces 'problematic sexual situations' and evolves 'perspectives'; he becomes attached to the values of some groups and not others; he comes to view himself as a particular kind of 'sexual being' (or 'non-sexual' being); and he develops a rudimentary, dimly sensed world-view of sexuality. All of these remain subject to constant modification as he encounters new experiences, and faces 'turning points'. But they also serve to restrict his perceived range of alternative choices.[28]

Conclusion

This chapter has outlined some of the problems that an interactionist approach to sexuality raises. What are the kinds of sexual meanings available? How are they constructed? What constraints are placed upon them? These and other questions constitute a large, almost completely unexplored, research programme; and the comments made in this chapter have only been exploratory and suggestive of some paths that could be taken.

A few of these paths will be taken up in the remaining sections of this book. Having explored the relevance of interactionism to the areas of sexuality and deviance, it is now possible to turn to the more central purpose: the analysis of sexual deviation. Part 2 will thus explore the general applicability of interactionism to this area, and part 3 will consider its relevance to one particular problem area, homosexuality.

part two

Building an interactionist account of sexual deviance

Sexual roles are constructed within the same general precariousness that marks the entire social fabric. Cross cultural comparisons of sexual conduct bring home to us powerfully the near-infinite flexibility that men are capable of in organising their lives in this area. What is normality and maturity in one culture is pathology and regression in another.

(Berger, 1966: 180)

There is no form of sexual activity that is not deviant at some time, in some social location, in some specified relationships, or with some partners. Truly, one can say that sexual deviance covers a multitude of sins. As a consequence of this variety, sexual deviance as a category includes behaviours that call forth societal responses that range from tacit encouragement to almost incalculable ferocity. It is important therefore that the term 'sexual deviation' should be approached somewhat less globally.

(Gagnon and Simon, 1968a: 107)

3 The social context of sexual deviation

While sociologists have ignored sexuality, others certainly have not: in the field of sexual deviance especially, there exists an abundant and growing literature. Yet tragically, from so much effort comes so little understanding and so little progress. Apart from the lurid and the sensational, the main contributors to this field have been clinicians; and the standard of their work has often been on the margins of scientific acceptability. At their very worst, they are riddled with simple inaccuracies, smothered in ideological invective, and worryingly injurious to the population under study. But for the possible harm that they do, they should not be taken seriously (e.g. Reuben, 1971). But at their best, they are paralysed by the limitations of their paradigm (e.g. Allen, 1969). They divorce the 'pervert' from his cultural context, locate him in a rhetoric of pathology, seek to explain his behaviour with reference to psycho-logistic factors residing firmly 'within him', and present individual-istic programmes for prevention and cure. As such, these studies epitomize the difficulties that mainstream criminology is generally encountering (cf. Matza, 1969; Cohen, 1974; Taylor, Walton and Young, 1973).

From this profuse clinical literature, little progress has been made.[1] What is required is an opening up of the field so as to encompass a broader range of problems and research programmes.[2] At the least, any adequate theory of deviance should deal with three areas: *actions*, *reactions* and *interactions*. For a sociological account of sexual deviance, questions need to be asked about the causes, characteristics and consequences[3] of (a) the general process of 'becoming sexually different' (action), (b) the general process of 'sexual problem definition' (reactions) and (c) the interplay between sexual experiences in a society and the reactions towards them as deviant (interaction). In the past, theories of sexual deviance have

45

ignored the last two questions and have dealt only selectively with the first problem. In this chapter, I propose to look at the first two areas; and in chapter 4, to consider their interaction. Throughout my theoretical guidelines will be taken from interactionism,[4] and my task will be defined as that of an assembler – assembling existing sociological materials into an orderly but entirely unfinished statement.[5]

The social reality of sexuality

No adequate understanding of sexual deviance is possible without a detailed analysis of the society in which such deviation arises. Definitions of sexuality and deviancy differ widely from culture to culture and within the same culture, plainly having considerable consequences for the nature of the sexual experience. Yet despite this well-documented observation, most explanations of sexual deviance ignore the fundamentally social nature of the phenomenon. The discussion that follows therefore enters several areas that need considerable sociological work – namely a description of the characteristics of the contemporary socially constructed sexual realities, and a consideration of some theories used to explain such realities.

The characteristics of sexual realities

If one does not regard the social world as phenomenologically constituted – and most studies do not – then it is a comparatively easy (though still neglected) task to describe the sexual belief system of that world. Look at the laws; look at the institutions such as the family; study the stereotypes given in the media; measure the attitudes of the societal members – perform all these tasks with scientific precision and one will be able to record the contemporary sexual world. There may be technical difficulties in describing this world, but it is in principle readily available for discovery and on hand for research.

Such is clearly not the case with the interactionist perspective. For its concern with the social world as intersubjective, emergent and negotiated renders sexual meanings as fundamentally problematic, an argument developed in part 1. The emphasis moves away from global statements about sexual norms to situated analyses of negotiated meanings.

Both these perspectives will bring with them different foci and accounts of reality; one simply records and taps what already exists 'out there' in the 'factual' social world, while the other patiently immerses itself in the microcosms of everyday interaction. The two perspectives may not be entirely incompatible, as the recent work by Berger and Luckmann potentially demonstrates.[6] These authors posit a dialectical relationship between the externally coercive, reified and objectified society, and the ever-changing, emergent, historical forces of men in action, suggesting that (Berger and Luckmann, 1967: 78–9):

> The objectivity of the institutional world, however massive it may appear to the individual, is a humanly produced, constructed objectivity . . . despite the objectivity that marks the world in human experience, it does not thereby acquire an ontological status apart from the human experience that produced it. . . . [Here is] the paradox that man is capable of producing a world that he then experiences as something other than a human product . . . the relationship between man, the producer, and the social world, his product, is and remains a dialectical one. That is man and his social world interact with each other. The product acts back upon the producer. Externalisation and objectivation are moments in a continuing dialectical process. The third moment in this process . . . is internalisation. . . . It is already possible to see the fundamental relationship of these three dialectical moments in social reality. Each of them corresponds to an essential characterisation of the social world. Society is a human product. Society is an objective reality. Man is a social product.

Their argument is ahistorical and non-empirical, but could be directly applied to everything taken as sexual 'knowledge' in any society. Starting with individual actors in historical situations (as one possible 'dialectical moment'), the manner in which sexual meanings are constructed may be depicted. But such 'knowledge' rapidly becomes institutionalized, routinized and sedimented into a package of 'objectively given' meanings; it becomes possible to provide analyses of this seemingly stable and abstract sexual belief system as it arises at one moment in the dialectical process. At this moment, and only fleetingly, it *might* be possible to 'bottle' some of the elements of this objectified world. As soon as one does this, however, one is at the very least reifying, and it is probable that a whole bundle of other phenomenological sins will be committed. Finally, the analysis may turn back to the actor once more to consider the ways in which he partially internalizes this 'objective world' into his inner subjectively felt world, while simultaneously retaining his potential for modifying and changing the sexual world in which he finds himself. These dialectical moments are only analytically capable of separation, for the sexual reality is constantly being modified and altered in the light of these intertwining processes.

47

For the analysts, the task of darting to and fro, between a world of 'objective, global realities' and a world of 'micro intersubjective realities' is indeed a formidable one. Nobody has yet accomplished such a task, which remains a key problem for sociologists.

In what follows I wish to look first at some features of the sexual world as it is apprehended as an objective reality, and then turn to the sexual world as an intersubjective one. Their complex interconnection *will* remain a research problem.

Sexuality as an 'objective reality': Man is born into a sexual world composed of institutions and legitimations which are apprehended as an objective reality. Among institutions are the family, and gender, providing routine patterns of sexuality through their mere existence; the legal and normative system, providing explicit statements about how people ought to behave sexually; imagery, providing controlling portraits of both 'normal' and 'aberrant' sexuality; belief systems – attitudes and opinions – providing clues as to 'what everybody thinks' about sexuality; and language – providing a rhetoric which through its mere existence gives structure to the sexual world. All of these institutions are accompanied by legitimations – implicit and explicit – drawn from theology, philosophy, history, science, folk wisdom and so forth, all of which serve to justify the existing order, and to make it appear 'sensible' and 'logical'.

This sexual world has the properties of Durkheimian 'social facts': it is external, coercive and possesses both moral authority and historicity (Berger and Luckmann, 1967: 77–8):

> It has a history that antedates the individual's birth and is not
> accessible to his biographical recollection. It was there before
> he was born, and it will be there after his death. The history
> itself . . . has the characteristic of objectivity. The individual's
> biography is apprehended as an episode located within the
> objective history of the society. The institutions as historical and
> objective facticities confront the individual as undeniable facts.
> The institutions are there, external to him, persistent with the
> reality whether he likes it or not. He cannot wish them away.

While this apparently autonomous domain may not be wished away there is no need for such a posture to collapse into extreme determinism (Douglas, 1971b: 190). Actors may be able to modify it, or attempt to deny its legitimacy, or may remain unaware of it. But in looking at the sexual life of man, it is impossible to deny the apparent facticity of abstract sexual meanings which impose constraints.

The sociologist needs to look in detail at this 'objective reality', in order to understand the backdrop of normality against which deviancy is enacted. Rape, voyeurism, striptease and transvestism only make sense as 'deviance' against an assumed 'natural order' locked into an 'objective reality'. Such realities contain elements explicitly directed against 'deviants' (e.g. sex laws, stereotypes of 'sex fiends', sickness language, institutionalized discrimination, 'queer-bashing', etc.), and elements which may only indirectly create deviance categories (e.g. the gender system, the romantic-love ideology, familism, etc.). These may be termed the direct and indirect reactions, and both need examination in the analysis of sexual deviance.

In a simple society, considerable consensus may be displayed on the content of the objective sexual reality. But as a society becomes increasingly large-scale and differentiated, the content is likely to become more ambiguous, shifting and pluralistic. This is not to deny that there may be areas where there are 'wider community standards' at hand,[7] nor that certain institutional forms such as the family may be more or less universally apprehended as objective (Berger and Kellner, 1964); but to stress that the acknowledgment of such abstract and seemingly consensual meanings may be accompanied by much individual dissent. Yet while many people may dislike the family system, they cannot wish such an arrangement away, nor reasonably ignore its tacit power.

Such an arena of consensus cannot be sharply delineated. Indeed, *in this culture at this time*,[8] the arena of consensus has been rendered increasingly ambiguous, relativist, contradictory, variable and subject to constant change. While such a portrait may be inaccurate as a description of what is concretely taking place, it is certainly accurate as a portrait of what is being presented as plausible. The symbolic presentations of the academic, lay and underground media are generating a plausibility structure[9] where sexual meanings are no longer certain, constant, clear, contained and consensual; they have instead become the subject of massive variety, ambiguity and change (Scott and Franklin, 1973). Such a portrait may not reflect what is actually happening in society, but may create the conditions for such occurrences.

There is then not simply one unified objective reality that confronts members of a society; rather the situation is one of pluralistic sexual realities containing conflicts,[10] contradictions,[11] and open to constant change[12] within a broad arena of consensus.[13] Such an observation has been widely documented.[14] In particular a number of empirical studies have begun the task of documenting the plurality of sexual realities among a variety of groups such as the lower class (Rainwater, 1966); the Negro slum (Hammond and Ladner, 1969); the affluent (Cuber and Harroff, 1965); the taxi-cab driver (Henslin, 1971b); the mentally retarded (Edgerton, 1967); the aged (Rubin, 1965), to give only a few examples. In each of these groups, the tolerance and expectations of varying kinds of sexual experience are objectivated in varying ways. What is important about the drift of the argument presented above is that it gradually leads back to the intersubjective world of groups and situations. There may well be transituational and abstract rules and meanings which are drawn upon by members in constructing their sexual world[15] but the fundamental nature of their personal world is an emergent, situated, negotiated one where considerable variation becomes possible.

Sexuality as intersubjective realities: The movement back down from the abstract, global reactions found in the reified, objectivated reality, to the emergent, situated reaction found in the intersubjective world of everyday life is a crucial one for the comprehension of sexual deviance. For put more concretely, it is not global laws, universal norms, omnipresent law-enforcement agencies or media stereotypes which 'react' against deviants: rather it is individual people, sensitive to certain abstract rules and constraints, who negotiate their reactions with deviants in face-to-face encounters (Douglas, 1971b: 189, *et seq.*). Often what goes firmly against the law may be tolerated or condoned in certain interpersonal contexts. Often what an individual may verbally attack as sinful and wrong, is tacitly accepted and enacted in the secrecy of the home. Often what are publicly regarded as valid stereotypes of deviants are negated by actors in the 'specific instance of a deviant at hand'. The 'deviant', of course, may see the global and abstract rules as all-constraining, and in that sense they are extremely important for analysis. But in his day to day world, he is as much concerned with what people actually say and do to him as with these global meanings.

These problems of the discrepancy between public and private rules are not new. They are caught in Allport's notion of 'pluralistic ignorance', and Williams's notion of the 'patterned evasion of norms'. Pluralistic ignorance highlights the manner in which an individual incorrectly believes that 'everybody else' in a group sub- scribes to a particular rule or value whereas secretly he does not: thus, while it seemed that in Kinsey's America 'everybody' believed that sex experience should be restricted to the missionary position inside marriage, the real situation was that very few people actually behaved that way while believing that others did. There may not just be pluralistic ignorance about sexual experiences, but also about societal reactions. Some people may publicly subscribe to objectified notions of 'homosexual hatred' while in interpersonal encounters react favourably or stoically to those met (Allport, 1924).

Williams's notion has similar implications, highlighting how patterns of behaviour arise which remain unpunished even though contradicting well-established public rules. Again, as Kinsey pointed out, the laws in America concerned with sexuality if strictly enforced would result in 95 per cent of the population being incarcerated. That they are not implies huge rule-violation that flies in the face of the objectified constraints mentioned in the previous section. What both these concepts successfully highlight, then, are the discrepancies that arise between the publicly objectified rules and the emergent, privatized meanings (Williams, 1960).[16]

The reactions analysed from this perspective are hence those of situated and negotiated meanings. If one wants to understand the nature of reactions to sexual deviants, one must study these reactions *in situ*. The audience's reaction to a stripper, the mother's reaction to a child-molester, the queer-basher's reaction to the homosexual, the wife's reaction to her husband's anilingus or the more general instances of a Women's Institute meeting discussing the problems of pornography and a community's reaction to the proposal to open a homosexual bar are all areas of study. The key task is to see how 'reactions' to sexual deviants are built up and negotiated in ordinary contexts.

These definitions of deviance will vary greatly, and these variations once again raise the thorny but often oversimplified problem of whether there exists a consensus or a dissensus over such definitions. Clearly though, the problem is raised on a more sophisticated level: it is no longer merely a matter of whether or not members of a society agree or disagree with 'packets' of 'objectified' unidimensional and unidirectional norms. Rather, rules may now be seen as multi-tiered (rules at one level may conflict with rules at another), and consensus may now be defined in terms of co-orientation and inter-subjectivity, rather than simple agreement (agreement between two actors on a given statement may not be matched by an understanding of their agreement or an understanding of this misunderstanding).[17] Given such an observation, it is no wonder that interactionists find the world vastly more problematic than many other branches of social theory. A helpful distinction to make within this debate is that of 'deep' and 'surface' rules – a distinction provided by the ethno-methodologists (Cicourel, 1973; Filmer *et al.*, 1972: 148). Most (non-phenomenological) sociology concerns itself with the surface rules, the objectified rules located in the previous section and which may well contain contradictions and considerable variance. Pluralism and conflict over deviancy definitions may thus run rampant in such a world. On the other hand, much phenomenological sociology has a goal of locating the tacit, shared understandings, the basic or deeply regulative rules that may cut across the surface divisions of pluralism, which regulate day to day, face to face interaction. While there may well be many surface and interpersonal discrepancies (as well as agreements), sustained interaction in the world is predicated upon certain fundamental rules which need locating by the analyst.[18]

In the sexual sphere, Garfinkle's study of Agnes – already described – attempts to locate the deeply regulative rules of 'normal sexed people', rules which are not only adhered to by 'normals' but also by the practical accomplishments of hermaphrodite Agnes trying to be like a 'normal sexed' person (Garfinkle, 1967: ch. 5). Garfinkle's list of properties of such deep rules is in many ways a curiosity piece which typifies some of the problems of ethnomethodological work: for how can Garfinkle claim to locate gender rules shared by 'adult members of our society' on the basis of one 'gender freak'? Still, the issue remains an important one, and the difficult research question is that of how to arrive at such phenomena. Other interesting starts in this direction have been provided in the work of Weinberg on nudism and Emerson and Henslin on gynaecological and vaginal examinations, where emergent rules about managing naked genitals in two-sex situations implied perhaps the existence of some basic rule linking genitals to sexuality (Weinberg, 1965; 1970c; Emerson, 1970; Henslin and Biggs, 1971; Vivona and Gomillion, 1972).

The emergence of sexual realities

While a description of the constitution of the sexual world is an important preliminary task in the analysis of societal reactions, an account of its origins is the task to be ultimately accomplished. There is a need to know why some of society's members react hostilely to *some* child-molesters, homosexuals, transvestites, prostitutes, etc. In the above remark I stressed *some* because, from what has just preceded, it is clear that there may not be a universal consensual condemnation of these experiences, but only a condemnation in certain situated contexts. In the past, most theories that purport to explain society's hostility have been too absolutist in producing law-like statements which provide an embarrassment of riches. They overpredict the amount of hostility to be found. Among examples of such general theories of the regulation of sexual deviants are the functional theory of sexual norms provided by Davis (1971) and Polsky (1967), the matrist/patrist theory of incest and homosexual hostility provided by Taylor (1965a) and the 'authoritarian family' theory provided by Reich (1969). They render the response to deviants as absolute, determined and automatic. But such is not the case.

The emergence of sexual realities may usefully be traced by considering the two areas raised in the previous section: society as an 'objective reality' and society as 'intersubjective'. In the former, the central focus must be historical analysis, which is certainly not incompatible with interactionism, even though it may raise difficulties.[19] In the latter, the central focus is on the emergent properties of everyday interactions.[20]

a *Emergence of objective realities:* The contemporaneous 'objective sexual reality' – with all its areas of consensus, contradictions and conflict – can be fruitfully viewed as the latest product of a long line of unfolding interactive situations: the top of an accumulated heap of both planned and not so planned historical incidents.[21] The contemporary sexual reality for example contains divergent strands from the Judaeo-Christian tradition, evangelical religions, jurisprudence, laws, power struggles over economic and status factors, philosophical debates, organizational dilemmas, public-opinion polls, moral crusaders, medical theories and psychiatric theories, not to mention large chunks of everyday interaction over hundreds of years. It would be nice to posit in such strands a unity, a logic, a system, but it is at least as reasonable to see the contemporary sexual reality that partially constrains its members as not having any underlying order. Of course, as Berger and Luckmann observe, members may impose upon their world 'a quality of logic' in order to explain 'why things are as they are' (Berger and Luckmann, 1967: 82), but such socially constructed 'canopies of legitimation' may not mirror the 'truth' of the world.

Clearly, if the objective sexual reality that members are born into is going to be explained, detailed historical analyses of key strands of that reality are required. For example, in that most concrete of areas, law, detailed historical accounts would need to be provided of the manner in which such laws emerged, were sustained, modified and removed from the statute books. Recent trends in the sociology of law have moved to more analyses of this kind, most of them demonstrating the role of conflicting interests in the emergence of laws (Chambliss, 1969: pt 1). Sutherland's analysis of the role played by psychiatrists in the 'diffusion of sexual psychopath laws' in some American states during the late 1940s stands as a classic of this kind of important yet limited analysis (Sutherland, 1950a; 1950b).

Law, of course, is one area close to the formal channels of power and a conflict theory of competing interests – latent and manifest[22] – may have much to offer in such analyses. Yet it would be unwise to put forward an entirely monolithic theory even in this case: some laws might be largely consequences of organizational dilemmas (Dickson, 1968), and others may be very largely fortuitous – as I later suggest the Labouchère Amendment in 1885 could be. There is a great deal of difference between seeing laws as the direct expression of key interest groups in society, and seeing laws as the end-product of long interactive processes in which various members and groups gnaw and nibble, negotiate and modify – and where the end-products can be seen as only partially, and maybe dimly, serving certain interest groups in society. Yet, clearly, power and interests are always important factors for consideration.

b *Emergence of intersubjective realities:* The 'reality' located above sets both constraints and cues to many members of society, and hence serves to fashion members' situated reactions to deviants. Likewise, in the long run, their own day to day reactions may contribute to the objective reality of successive generations. The dialectical process returns to a central place in the analysis.

A chief concern of the interactionist lies with the ways members build up 'reactions' in specific situations. Such reactions must be seen as the negotiated outcomes of interactive encounters, where abstract rules (objective realities), significant others, and prior commitments and perspectives play their parts. The global abstract rules and the personal prior commitments allow for a high degree of regularity and predictability in reactions across situations, but the presence of significant others gives each context its problematic nature. A hypothetical example may serve as illustrative of this process of constructing reactions. An actor, Johnny, is a working-class adolescent and he is reacting to the phenomenon of homosexuality. Assuming that he has no strong psychological need for using homosexuals as scapegoats (and that hence the personality variables are insignificant in this example), it may be predicted that for most of his functioning in the wide-awake world he will give little consideration to the issue of homosexuality. What dim and remote 'views' he may have on the subject will largely be gleaned from the abstract provided in the 'objective' reality into which he is born. Since these rules are not always clear, and sometimes contradictory, he may not necessarily be exposed to the view that all homosexuals are evil or sick. It is likely however that he will be, given certain broad consensual features of the objectivated elements of homosexual reactions. So Johnny's dim and partial knowledge of homosexuality is that it is an oddity committed by effeminate men who are sick. If it remains insignificant in his experiences, it is unlikely to be incorporated into his more stable self – his commitments and perspectives; although other parts of his life, particularly his experiences with girls, may well lead to a well-defined commitment to heterosexuality which incorporates elements of homosexual hostility by default. This then is Johnny, but out of specific contexts.

Placed in different contexts where homosexuality is an issue, his reaction may be highly variable, emergent and explosive. It may be relatively stable. The determinants of this would be the balance between his commitments to the abstract rules, and the significant others in the context. In any context, his reaction may be seen as partially a consequence of his anticipation of others' responses and the projection of his own self. The negotiated interaction may also be heavily influenced by power (Scheff, 1968). Consider the following very simple possible contexts, all hypothetical:

1 Mother asks him what he thinks of homosexuals. Johnny responds by drawing from the dim knowledge he has gleaned from the objectivated and abstract rules; that is, homosexuals are sick people requiring pity.

2 Fellow school peers talk about 'queers' derogatively. Johnny sees the boys as a valuable reference group, and wishes to belong to them. Concurs with their abuse of homosexuals.

3 Stranger attempts to solicit him for homosexual purposes while alone. Johnny responds with desire to project appropriate self as a non-homosexual. From abstract rules, he is dimly aware that homosexuals are effeminate, and to demonstrate his non-homosexuality means to demonstrate his masculinity. For him, this is intrinsically linked with aggression. Abuses the homosexual.

4 Best friend at school tells Johnny of his homosexuality. As a good friend, wishes to project self of 'staying loyal', etc. Says he finds homosexuals just like everybody else, or that friend is different from all the others.

Such simple illustrative examples are exhaustive neither in scope nor analysis, but hopefully they suggest the potential variability and modifiability of intersubjective reactions towards homosexuals. The kind of response that Johnny would make to an interviewer involved in social research could be used as a fifth example.

So it is with the emergence of these complex, situated reactions that much future work needs to be concerned. An important factor in such analyses is that of power – where the power of one interactant over another may have important consequences for the reaction outcome. While this is important on the level of routine day to day life, it is especially significant in understanding the work of crusading groups such as moral entrepreneurs who campaign for the control of pornography (Zurcher et al., 1971) and moral provocateurs who campaign for Gay Liberation (Teal, 1971); and in the relationship of control agencies, such as police, courts and psychiatrists, towards deviants.

In summary, this section has posed key questions that need asking in order to understand the reactions which arise in society against sexual 'deviants'. Viewing the world either as an 'objective' reality or as an 'intersubjective' one (but hopefully in a dialectical relationship), there is both a descriptive and explanatory task ahead.

These tasks will require (a) surface descriptions of the contradictions, changes and variations contained in the norms, images, accounts, attitudes and institutions of the 'objective' sexual world, (b) deep descriptions of the situated reactions to deviants, (c) historical analyses of the emergence of 'objectified reactions' in the contemporary sexual reality and (d) processual accounts of constructing personal reactions towards deviants.

Becoming sexually different

Without an adequate understanding of the general process of sexual socialization, little progress can be made in understanding the more limited case of becoming sexually deviant. For since no sexual experience is 'absolutely deviant', it follows that a distinction needs to be drawn between explanations of that experience *per se* and explanations of its 'deviant' properties. It is a central argument of this book that sexual experiences are likely to be altered in their form as a consequence of being susceptible to deviancy labels. It is one thing to explain why an actor comes to give sexual meanings to acts of violence, and another to explain what the possible consequences are of having 'deviant labels' thrust upon such meanings.

Since an interactionist account of the process of becoming sexual has been hinted at previously these strands can be drawn together here:

1 Man is born with a varying biological capacity for 'sexual experience', including a physiological capacity to respond to any sufficient stimulus (Kinsey *et al.*, 1953: 44). While there may be biological constraints, he is essentially characterized by plasticity and 'world-openness' (Berger and Luckmann, 1967: 65).

2 Man is born into an historically created 'objective reality', which contains a socially constructed series of 'sexual' meanings. Such a reality may contain vast contradictions and variations, but is confronted initially as a 'natural order'.

3 The process of becoming sexual is, like all distinctly human and social activities, a learning process. It is not simply the unfolding of biological tendencies, though these may set constraints. Psychodynamic theories concerned with the emotional precondition for sexual development (introjection and identification) (Freud, 1962); behavioural theories concerned with the conditioning of sexual experiences (Hardy, 1964; Whalen, 1966, Eysenck, 1972); and ethological theories concerned with the imprinting of sexual experiences at critical periods (Harlow, 1965) may all constitute part of this complex learning sequence.

4 Whatever may be the variable biological, psychodynamic,

behavioural and ethological reasons why individuals are led to certain kinds of 'sexual experiences' and not others, an interactional learning account is required in order to show how such experiences are interpreted as sexual. Sexual meanings are built up in interaction with significant others, and with the aid of the abstract meanings lodged in the 'objective reality'. Interactional learning involves the arts of symbolic gestures, language manipulation and role-taking; is a two-way process of internalization and modification; and occurs throughout the life span.[23] Such a management of 'sexual meanings' over time may be referred to as an 'erotic career'.[24]

5 While such learnt sexual meanings are always emergent and problematic in one sense, they need not be seen as being in a Heraclitean flux. Clearly, stable sexuality is possible because of the emergence of attachments, the development of perspectives and commitments, and the formulation of dimly understood 'world views'.

This summary clearly awaits detailed, critical research exploration, for most studies ignore the crucial issue raised above: that of learning sexual meanings. They tend instead to concentrate upon overt, observable acts capable of quantification.[25] While I cannot develop this problem in detail, the important work of Gagnon and Simon does serve as a useful starting-point (Gagnon, 1965a; Simon and Gagnon, 1969; Gagnon and Simon, 1973).

In their models (and they utilize data and experiences gained when they were at the Kinsey Institute as well as data from a large-scale adolescent survey), sexual socialization is not concerned with managing a pre-existing sexual structure, but rather with defining oneself as sexual and the subsequent management of such definitions. This means an analysis of the parts played by all those agents of socialization – including self-initiation – which influence learning experiences over the life span, looking not just at the important role of the family in childhood, but also at the role of peers (especially in adolescence), other significant role partners (especially spouses) and the impact throughout life of access to differential opportunity structures.[26] There is no argument here that sexual meanings have to be negotiated all the time; rather, as previously suggested, it is likely that individuals become 'committed' to a particular kind of sexual life and stabilize their self-conceptions in a particular kind of sexual way.

But how then are sexual meanings built up in the first place? In the family context, Gagnon suggests two processes of particular importance: negative labelling and non-labelling. The first process involves parents responding to the child's imputed sexual activity with negative injunctions, and the second involves responses that are ambiguous and ill-defined. The child's world is thus built up to contain a series of unexplained, ambiguous areas that are likely to evoke negative reactions from parents. Whereas in most areas of life the child is provided with help in the 'naming of parts' and the clarification of boundaries of reality, in the sexual sphere little such help is provided.[27]

The privatization of sexuality only helps to exacerbate the situation. One important consequence of this is the 'spillover effect', by which one training experience becomes confused with another. Thus a child who learns to identify 'genital play' as 'naughty' and 'sexual' may subsequently transfer ill-formed notions of sexuality to other aspects of its genitals (e.g. elimination) and to other non-genital areas of life (e.g. being aggressive) which are labelled 'naughty'. This confusion in naming may give rise to all manner of 'objects' being labelled 'sexual'. Earlier, in chapter 2, the range of sexual meanings was briefly raised; here the ways in which from the earliest days the child may begin to develop confused, ambiguous and often contradictory sexual meanings can be seen. In particular, in our culture, it is likely that many of these ambiguous meanings will become imbued with notions of guilt. As Simon and Gagnon (1969: 11) comment: 'Although we talk a lot about sexuality, as though trying to exorcise the demon of shame, learning about sex in our culture is in large part learning about guilt; and learning how to manage sexuality commonly involves learning how to manage guilt.'

For many groups, the most important stage in building up sexual meanings will be that of adolescence – a time when past unnamed 'sexual' encounters may be retrospectively interpreted, and a stable sexual world view allowed to emerge. A number of significant others will influence what takes place at this stage – isolated self-interaction, concrete peer interaction and generalized media interaction are three crucially important ones.

Isolated self-interaction is important because of the role that masturbation plays in adolescent sexuality – especially for boys.[28] Masturbation is essentially a solitary experience which most adolescent boys confront: it is also an experience which allows for a considerable degree of imaginary role-playing and the development of sexual meanings concomitantly. Boys don't masturbate purely mechanically: they 'conjure up' images of sexual things – 'things' being done to them, 'things' they just observe, 'things' they do. Such 'things', whatever they may be, are extremely important in understanding much of the sexual development of the adolescent, although I am not going as far here as some psychiatrists who suggest that the nature of the first masturbatory fantasy predetermines one's subsequent sexual life (cf. Ollendorf, 1966). I do not think it likely that the first masturbatory fantasy is well formed or even necessarily intelligible to the boy. But over time, a stock repertoire of masturbatory fantasies and meanings begin to emerge, and this may be very important in effecting a commitment to certain forms of sexual experience.

Masturbation is a physiologically pleasurable experience, which may initially be almost 'stumbled' into without any well-formed fantasies. However, as it becomes a routine experience, stable or recurrent fantasies interpreted as 'sexual' become important aids for masturbation. Many of these fantasies may either be viewed as anticipatory socialization, where sexual acts to be performed later in life are imagined, or fantastic socialization, where sexual acts are imagined which are seldom, if ever, likely to be encountered in later life (Stone, 1962: 109). Masturbation allows for enormous flexibility in sexual meanings, a flexibility which may be one of the main contributors to later-life sexual variation. A salient point here may be the differing importance of masturbation between boys and girls, and between class groups. Girls appear to masturbate less (Kinsey *et al.*, 1953), and working-class groups appear to have less sophisticated symbolic machineries (Bernstein, 1971; Ford *et al.*, 1967), so the variation of sexual experiences in later life *may* not be so great for these groups. There is of course a *little* empirical evidence for such an hypothesis (Kinsey *et al.*, 1948; 1953; Gebhard, 1965: 67).

Masturbation is perhaps the clearest example of self-initiated socialization experiences in adolescence. If a boy comes to use it exclusively for a long period, it may lead him to develop a commitment to non-sociable sexuality, and in some ways serve to hinder subsequent sociable sexual interaction. Important in the development of sociable sexuality, then, is social interaction with others, especially the peers. As Reiss (1960) notes: 'the sexual behaviour of adolescents is primarily peer-organized and peer-controlled'.

Now the peer group may be important not only in stimulating and encouraging the growth of particular sexual meanings, but also in providing support and reinterpretive, integrating mechanisms for potential sexual meanings developed earlier. Thus there is some evidence that males who state that they are likely to remain virgin until marriage have more male associates with comparable values, and that those who are highly sexually active function within reference groups that both encourage high sexuality and provide vocabularies of adjustment which function to legitimate and structure the sexual experience (Kanin, 1967). The weakness of the reference group variable here rests in the ambiguity as to whether it can be seen as a causal variable (exposure to aggressive male peer groups leads one to adopt aggressive sexuality), or whether it is itself a consequence of causation processes (prior sexual interest leads to participation in groups that are sexually interested and involved).

Much work again needs to be conducted of an empirical kind that will show the shifting identifications of adolescents over time, and the way consequently they make sexual sense of the world.

Yet this process of 'becoming sexual' does not end with families and peers at adolescence: as I stressed in chapter 2, socialization experiences must be seen as constantly emerging in all day to day encounters across the life span. While sexual commitments may be built up in the early years, they remain capable of great modification – of being heightened or minimized, broadened or narrowed – throughout life. Through interaction with many significant others, both in personal encounters (spouse, workmates, teachers, propagandists, etc.) and in impersonal ones (especially the mass media and its sexual imagery), sexual meanings constantly remain negotiable.[29]

While the above discussion has highlighted some substantive areas for detailed research, its main function has been to stress the importance of seeing sexual meanings as socially constructed, emergent and problematic categories that are learnt over the life span in interaction with a range of significant others, categories which may – but do not have to – become stabilized. This leads one to suspect that there may be an enormous degree of sexual differentiation with regard to sexual meanings.

Sexual differentiation as a consequence of sexual socialization

One key consequence of the way in which sexual socialization functions in this society is the likelihood of considerable sexual differentiation on a personal level.[30] By differentiation, I mean all combinations and extremes of imaginable sexual experience – and this includes on the one hand the 'wildest' experiences of highly active prostitutes, and on the other the experiences of an individual who is able to eliminate all sexual behaviour and fantasy from his life. By saying that there is widespread sexual differentiation, I acknowledge the probable existence of large numbers of people who have no sexual experiences and no interest in such matters. It is important to note that I am also referring to the privatized world of sexual experience and not the public one, where, as I hope to have shown earlier, there may well be shared rules publicly acknowledged and which serve as the basis for pluralistic ignorance. Individual actors may thus publicly acknowledge a fairly uniform series of standards, while privately experiencing massive differentiation. Let me briefly repeat some of the reasons for this differentiation before considering the evidence for such an assertion:

1 Sexual meanings are social constructs not intrinsic absolutes. Consequently they do not have to be 'tied' to some inevitable end-

product, but, according to the various definitional processes of men, may be tied to various objects and activities.

2 The social world into which man is born is one where values and norms do not constitute a unified, systematic, cohesive, coherent, logical whole. There may be large areas of consensus, but there are also contradictions, ambiguous categories, and groups which, through their occupancy of different positions in the social structure, come to develop different meanings. This society is culturally pluralistic (Douglas, 1971b; Berger and Luckmann, 1967: 142).

3 The learning process by which these meanings are built are complex and dimly understood. Different learning mechanisms are involved, but from an interactionist standpoint great emphasis must be placed upon the role of significant others and areas of self-initiation. The bestowal of meaning by others on sexuality is a privatized act; and privatization creates a potential for diversity.

4 Man's socialization experience cannot be likened to a simple 'printed circuit' in which he blanketly absorbs the sexual world outside upon his *tabula rasa* – rather he selects and interacts with his environment.

There seem good grounds, then, for arguing that there is considerable variation of sexual experience. But what of the empirical evidence here?

'Official evidence' about the widespread incidence of sexual differentiation can be gleaned from 'official reports'. The Registrar-General provides details of illegitimate births, the Medical Council provides details of venereal diseases, and the criminal statistics provide analysis of sex offenders. But it has recently been argued that such statistics are better at showing the routine work of statistic making and keeping organizations than at measuring the actual rates of the phenomena in society (Douglas, 1971b; Cicourel, 1968), and that there is considerable evidence of much unrecorded, undetected, unnoticed 'deviancy'. Criminologists are very much aware of the large amounts of unrecorded crime and delinquency, health officials note the degree of unrecorded handicap and mental-health experts suggest that there is a considerable amount of 'objective behaviour disorder' in the community that never comes before psychiatrists. Some put all these figures at a very high proportion (Hood and Sparks, 1970: ch. 1; Scheff, 1966: 47–50). Now given the previous discussion on the likelihood of widespread sexual differentiation in complex society, it becomes possible that *sexual behaviour in a heterogeneous complex society becomes widely differentiated and, while much of it has the potentiality for being publicly labelled deviant, only a minimal amount is*. This is an hypothesis which raises serious difficulties of falsification. Given the privatized and taboo nature of sexual experiences in society, measurement of the incidence of sexual activities is a precarious task. Apart from official statistics, however, this problem may be tentatively approached through: (a) self-report studies; (b) depth studies of specialized areas; (c) casual observation. I wish to look briefly at each of these methods and their findings in turn.

a   *Self-report studies:* In delinquency research, one technique employed to overcome problems of recording undetected delinquency is self-reporting, where random samples of the population (usually school children) are questioned about their delinquent activities (under a guarantee of anonymity) – often being asked to simply tick on checklists whether they have ever committed certain delinquencies. The researcher does not go to a sample of those already 'caught', but rather to the population at large to see if those who have not been caught display delinquent traits.

In sex research, the task is to go to a wide population sample and to question them about the nature of their sexual activity – allowing them to 'volunteer' the fullest information about their sexual lives. Clearly, this is a risky research task requiring great skill: some people are loath to talk about their sex lives in a simple way, let alone reveal the vagaries of their differentiations. Many researchers, such as Schofield, perceive this as an almost impossible task right at the outset of their researches and do not include questions on any items other than the most elementary sexual activities; nor do they suggest that their interviewers should 'probe' into such areas. In particular, there is a fear that such 'explosive' questions could put the respondent ill at ease and invalidate the rest of the research.

Possibly the only detailed work on sexual behaviour that has utilized a self-report technique is that of Kinsey *et al.* (1948, 1953). Their research used sophisticated, systematic interview techniques, which probed on a diverse and full range of items, including erotic imagery, prostitution, zoophilia, homosexuality, sado-masochism, scatology, fetishism, anilingus, cunnilingus and pornography (Kinsey *et al.*, 1948: 63–70). Given such an analysis – more detailed than any before or since – Kinsey's findings, while far from being truly reliable (Cochran *et al.*, 1954), provide considerable evidence about sexual differentiation. Indeed, the outcry that resonated around Kinsey's ears on publication of the male volume seems to have been an outcry at making public what individuals must have been personally aware of – at the breakdown of 'pluralistic ignorance' (Pomeroy, 1972). Kinsey's study highlights variations in both *extent* of sexual outlet, and *type* of sexual outlet. On the *extent* of sexual outlet, for example, Kinsey *et al.* (1948: 195) have this to say:

There are a few males who have gone through long periods of years without ejaculating: there is one male who, although apparently sound physically, has ejaculated only once in thirty years. There are others who have maintained average frequencies of 10, 20 or more for long periods of time: one male (a scholarly and skilled lawyer) has averaged over 30 per week for thirty years. This is a difference of several thousand times.

This discussion highlights the immense range of sexual outlet to be found among American men, suggesting that extreme differences are not found in extreme situations, but in everyday situations.

The second source of variation comes, not in outlet, but in *content*. Table 1 shows Kinsey's findings on the degree of sexual differentiation in American society.

TABLE 1   *Collated findings of Kinsey: Accumulative incidences of various sexual behaviour*

Type of behaviour	Male (%)	Female (%)
1 Masturbation—to orgasm by 45	92	58
2 Nocturnal sex dreams—to orgasm by 45	83	37
3 Premarital heterosexual petting—by 18	84	81
4 Premarital intercourse ⎱ 8	98	50
Educ. ⎰ 9–12	85	(40 to
grade ⎱ 13	63	orgasm)
5 Marital intercourse	100	100
– to orgasm in 1st year of marriage	100	75
– to orgasm in 20th year of marriage	100	90
6 Extramarital intercourse about	50	26
7 Intercourse with prostitute	69	–
8 Homosexual relations—to orgasm by 45	37	13
9 Animal relations	8	3·6

Such figures as shown here give a little indication of the variation in sexual experiences that may be found when self-reporting techniques are used. No more detailed work than Kinsey's exists, yet it relates to a sample of experiences now at least forty years out of date! Once again, a research task of considerable magnitude emerges.

b   *Depth studies of specialized areas:*   A second approach in assessing sexual variation is that of depth studies of limited fields. At present, there are very few of these, but their evidence suggests that whenever a researcher moves carefully into a taboo field of sexual behaviour, he is likely to discover much concealed activity beneath the visible surface structures. Bartell (1971: 20), one of several researchers who have conducted research in America into 'swinging' (wife-swapping or group sex), writes:

> We estimate that approximately eight thousand couples are involved in *organised* swinging within a two-hundred mile area around Chicago. Adam Fredericks, the editor of Kindred Spirits, a Chicago based swingers' magazine said that his estimate agreed with ours. We would venture an educated guess that in late 1970 half a million to a million people, less than one half of one per cent of the total population, may be involved in organised swinging. At most one per cent of the population are swingers.

Such a figure may not be high, but it is probably higher than is commonly supposed. Likewise, studies by North (1970: ch. 4) on rubber fetishism; by Gagnon (1965b) on child-molesters; by Henslin (1971b) on taxi-cab drivers; or by the President's Commission on Obscenity (1971), provide data which indicate that many more people may be involved in rubber fetishism, child-molestation, pornography and other activities than previously thought. As examples of these types of studies, I propose to look briefly at two.

The first such study was conducted by Lee (1969) into abortion in America. While abortion cannot itself be called a sexual deviation, it is often seen as deviance, and it is clearly related to sexuality. Her study was primarily concerned with the channels used by abortion seekers in locating an abortionist – the 'acquaintance networks' as she calls them. Abortion is a very time-limited operation – effectively limited to six weeks in which the decision to have an abortion must be taken, an abortionist located, the necessary money raised, and the abortion carried out. Such a task would not be difficult if abortions were legal and acceptable – they could be advertised in the market where normal supply and demand mechanisms would be operative. But such of course is not the case: the entire operation becomes complex through its secrecy. Informal, rather than formal, channels have to be used. When one considers that possibly a million illegal abortions are conducted in America each year, 'One would think that the sheer level of activity generated by so many people carrying out such a demanding task would make abortions a highly visible activity in the society.' 'Yet', continues Lee, 'outside certain small circles, abortion is carried on almost invisibly. . . . But it is still true to say that a very small amount of public notice is generated by what must be a great deal of activity.' Elsewhere she comments that 'abortions must involve millions of Americans each year, both in direct participation . . . and in supplying information to those seeking' (Lee, 1969: 7–8).[31]

At least two lessons may be drawn from this study and inferred to other fields of deviancy. First, a massive informal structure exists out of sight – away from the surface of society – which can be located by any individual actively seeking it. Homosexual bars and wife-swapping are two fields on which there is data confirming this informal structure, but if, for example, a researcher were to look a little closer at funeral parlours and cemetery work, he might discover an informal structure – much smaller in size – that focuses on necrophilia.

A second lesson suggests that not only are there many people who are *directly* involved in deviation, there are also many who are *indirectly* related to it. She shows how many more people other than pregnant women become involved in the informal structure (information network), and particularly how friends and family members become implicated. In her study this is a witting involvement, but it could be suggested that for some other deviations such as homosexuality many people may become involved in the problems of variance without direct knowledge. For example, if it is true that there are some two million exclusively homosexual men and women in England, then every *extended* family in the land must have access, knowing or unknowing, to at least one homosexual within their own family and probably several.

Another study that throws light upon the extent of concealed deviancy is Humphreys's ingenious research into sexual activity between men in public conveniences ('cottages'). While many toilets are rarely used for such purposes, Humphreys (1970: 10) found a considerable number where such activities were widespread:

> I have seen some [men] waiting in turn for this type of service. Leaving one such scene on a warm September Saturday, I remarked to a man who left close behind me: 'Kind of crowded in there, isn't it?' 'Hell, yes,' he answered, 'It's getting so you have to take a number and wait in line in these places'.

In a footnote, the author provides a very sketchy 'guestimate' that possibly '5% of the adult male population of the metropolitan area are involved in these encounters over a year's time'. Even if his figure is a gross exaggeration, there is certainly much more of this activity in American society than is popularly supposed.

Perhaps a more significant feature of this study however is the data that it provided about the backgrounds of participants in public sex. Humphreys interviewed fifty men, and demonstrates that not only were over half of these men married, but that many adopted an ultra-respectable public image, appearing to all outward appearances as 'very good neighbours' and 'decent folk'. Some even appeared morally indignant – the archetypes of moral reformers. Now if this study was replicated in other fields – say, prostitution, pornography, and fetishism – and the participants' backgrounds ascertained, similar findings may be arrived at. Such studies hint directly at the existence of massive informal structures of sexual differentiation.

c *Casual observation:* A third possible technique for studying the degree of sexual variation is also the least reliable. Once involved in the field of sexual research, the researcher is likely to be constantly confronted with 'evidence' of sexual variation all around him. He becomes 'involved' in 'worlds' where sexual 'deviation' is common and where 'deviants' appear everywhere. No wonder is it that Becker (1963: 20–1) could write in his discussion of 'secret deviants':

> I am convinced that the amount [of secret, sexual deviance] is very sizeable, much more than we are apt to think. One brief observation convinces me this is the case. Most people probably think of fetishism as a rare and exotic perversion. I had occasion several years ago, however, to examine the catalog of a dealer in pornography pictures designed exclusively for devotees of this speciality. The catalog contained no pictures of nudes, no pictures of any version of the sex act. Instead, it contained page after page of pictures of girls in strait-jackets, girls wearing boots with six inch heels, girls holding whips, girls in handcuffs, and girls spanking one another. Each page served as a sample of as many as 120 pictures stocked by the dealer. A quick calculation revealed that the catalog advertised for immediate sale somewhere between fifteen and twenty thousand different photographs. The catalog itself was expensively printed and this fact, taken together with the number of photographs for sale, indicated clearly that the dealer did a land-office business and had a very sizeable clientele. Yet one does not run across sado-masochistic fetishists every day. Obviously they are able to keep the fact of their perversion secret. 'All orders mailed in a plain envelope.'

Certainly Becker is drawing our attention to a phenomenon that is more widespread than popularly thought, but chance observations of this kind are likely to have a 'blinding effect': contact with 'conventional day-to-day reality' is lost. Thus, for example, 'fifteen to twenty thousand' photos may well indicate no more than a few hundred customers, and the 'expensively printed catalogue' may well be possible because the few hundred customers have to pay very high prices. Further, Becker ignores the many catalogues – expensively printed and listing many items – that department stores and mail-order firms produce free of charge for their market, which do not necessarily indicate a very wide level of demand. Such observations need to be subjected to critical scrutiny, then, if much sense is going to be made of them.

Nevertheless, casual studies do seem to accumulate which lend support to the general argument. Thus, for example, *case histories* bring to light a considerable amount of concealed sexual variation which takes place without notice – as illustrated by the case discussed by Allen in his textbook, or the stories produced by Tony Parker (Allen, 1969; Parker, 1969). *Casual observation* may also bring to light a marked degree of organizational competence for certain commodities or sexual interests which must indicate a minimal level of organized demand – organizations for transvestites, strip-tease clubs in the centres of many large towns, model and 'pen-pal' books, rubber-wear magazines, nudist colonies and so on. Finally, some small-scale *empirical studies* point out that many acts of 'deviance' pass undetected: Dunham in a study of Michigan and New Jersey suggested that public acts of deviance like exhibitionism and rape have at least as many acts passing unreported as those that are reported, and Coleman (1964: 402) notes in a study of cinema exposures that out of twenty-five to thirty incidents only three were reported to the police. Now individually these studies and observations do not really mean very much; their impact is perhaps a cumulative one. At the same time such casual remarks are really no substitute for the rigorous study that is implied in both self-reporting techniques and depth studies.[32]

In sum, not only are there good theoretical reasons for suspecting widespread sexual variation; there is also some empirical support for this.[33] This position leads me to agree with Becker that 'We ought not to view [deviance] as something special, as depraved or in some magical way better than other kinds of behaviour' (Becker, 1963: 176). It is continuous with and contingent upon 'normal' sexuality. With this in mind, the problem of sexual deviation can now be raised.

4 The emergence of sexually deviant conduct

Most studies of sexual deviance fail to take the categorization of deviance as a problem in itself: perversion is an entity that possesses certain characteristics that exist 'objectively', and the task of the student therefore is merely to describe and explain 'it'. But what 'it' is, is not a problem. In sharp contrast with this predominantly clinical approach, interactionist study must unveil the phenomenon as constituted in the everyday world, and look beyond the 'obvious'. 'Sexual deviance' is then seen not as an absolute, objective phenomenon, but rather as a social construction. In this chapter, I will examine some of the definitions and characterizations of deviance as conventionally held, suggest their socially constructed nature, and present an interactionist alternative.

The nature of sexual deviance

In the past, definitions of sexual deviancy have been provided in two ways. For the anthropologist and sociologist, strong awareness of the cultural relativity of sexual norms has led them to define deviance absolutely only within the confines of a given society: thus in the work of Oliver, sexual deviance is 'Sexual behaviour that offends a particular society' (Oliver, 1967: 15). The tendency here is to reify society and render it consensual, so that some conduct clearly offends society and some clearly does not. Such definitions are absolutist within a specific society.

A second type of definition – provided particularly by clinicians – views sexual deviance as universally and intrinsically deviant. Sexual deviance is here defined as a sickness,[1] a form of immaturity[2] and a deflection from the 'normal sexual aim'.[3] It is characterized usually as compulsively exclusive, pathological, and ridden with guilt.[4] Such attributes *may*, by definition, be central aspects of sexual

68

deviance as it is socially constructed in this society – prostitutes, paedophiliacs and panty-fetishists *may* well be sick, compulsive, immature, guilt ridden and pathological. But the interactionist's problem is concerned with how that reality was built, how these attributes came to be important, and how such meanings come to be bestowed. And when this task is performed, it becomes increasingly easy to see that while much sexual experience may be similar to the characterizations above, it certainly does not *have* to be like that. Sexual deviance becomes relativized.

I wish to comment briefly upon these attributes and locate them socially. The first, and paramount, thing to notice is that most of these attributes bypass the problem of values, and assume that their account of the world corresponds to a scientifically objective one.[5] Yet it should be clear that words like immature and abnormal only make sense by reference to evaluative standards of maturity and normality. Such standards are assumed in most studies of sexual deviance. Deviance is enacted against a vast consensual backdrop, characterized largely by a linear sequence of 'normal sexual development' (derived from Freud), 'natural goal' of heterosexual intercourse (derived from Nature), and a divinely inspired situation of marriage (derived from God or St Paul).[6] Sickness, initially conceived as a construction to characterize organic disorders, becomes a label applied to behaviour variations, and an array of techniques are employed which serve to maintain the probably fictional picture of a unanimity of values (Young, 1971: ch. 3). In sum, what passes for objectivity is pervaded by values from top to bottom (Goode, 1969).

I am not saying that there are no such things as biological norms or organic pathologies which inhibit sexual functioning; there may well be. But I am saying that one cannot move from a possible biological fact to a social one without seeing meaning as an intervening variable. Even if there exists a biological norm of heterosexual reproduction, as Bieber and Gadpaille among others have suggested, such a norm has no necessary linkages to social norms (Bieber *et al.*, 1962: 319; Gadpaille, 1972; Marmor, 1971). Man constantly transcends the level of biology and 'nature'. And even where sexual functioning is severely restricted by organic error, such errors still have to be mediated at the symbolic level. Man does not inhabit an automatic world of meanings, and the meanings attributed to 'sexual deviance' by many scientists cannot thus be seen as invariant properties of those acts. With this clear, the value designations of most scientists towards the sexually different become a problem in themselves.

Traditional deviancy definitions, however, do not only ignore the world of tacit evaluations that surround their work, they also assume properties like 'exclusiveness' and 'guilt' to be the essence of such deviation without seriously unravelling (a) whether such properties are accurate, and (b) whether – if accurate – they are a consequence of the experience itself, or whether they are a consequence of the fashion in which sexuality is socially organized. Although I do think that these assumptions are often inaccurate,[7] I will ignore this and explore the second problem more fully.

Are masturbation, paedophilia, premarital intercourse and homosexuality (to name four areas that have been conceptualized as deviancy in our society) characterized by guilt, compulsion and pathology in themselves, or are these attributes largely emergent from social organization? Put in such a blunt form, an answer is not difficult: the anthropological literature clearly demonstrates that all these experiences may occur in other societies without displaying the defining attributes. For example, anthropological studies suggest that forms of sexual variation associated with 'guilt' features in our culture do not manifest such features in other cultures where sexuality is managed in a more open manner. Malinowski's description of Melanesian children shows how masturbation and childhood intercourse ('copulation amusement') may be enjoyable, and not linked with guilt, inadequacy or compulsion. Thus the argument that masturbation leads to 'self-reproach, shame and fear'[8] is one based upon a cultural specification in which the socially constructed sexual meanings that surround certain acts are confused with the intrinsic nature of the acts themselves. Indeed, many of the 'symptoms' which are commonly associated with sexual deviance in this culture may well become associated with other phenomena in other cultures – Suggs cites the Marquesans as being very casual in their sexual behaviour, but exhibiting the kind of neurotic symptoms we normally ascribe to sex in all matters pertaining to food.

Thus, taken-for-granted characteristics of sexual deviance need to be seriously questioned with regard to their sources. It is hardly appropriate to characterize sexual deviance as 'guilt-ridden', when – as Simon and Gagnon (1969) have noted – contemporary sexual meanings are permeated throughout by notions of guilt.[9] And it is likewise highly inappropriate to see sexual deviance as compulsively restrictive and exclusive, when this is probably the major manner in which most people organize their sexuality: if the 'ideal' of restricting sexuality to heterosexual coitus is an actuality, it is a highly compulsive, exclusive and restricting one!

The more general question of pathology may be linked to the fact that sexual deviance is norm-violating behaviour, and that consequences flow from this. In a study of drinking and norm violation, Mizruchi and Perucci (1962: 398) have suggested how 'proscriptive norms are more likely to lead to extreme degrees of pathological reactions when deviance occurs than predominantly prescriptive norms'. They suggest that those groups (such as the Jews) who have developed a code of drinking norms that tell them when to drink and when not to drink, produce 'social drinkers', while those groups such as Mormons and Methodists, who have no directives for the use of alcohol and simply prohibit it, are more likely to produce 'alcoholics'. On a broader scale, Jellinek (1960) has demonstrated how widespread organic alcoholism exists in France, but how, because social drinking is so widely prescribed there, there exists no pathological role compounded with psychological misery. These examples suggest that even experiences that may be organically damaging do not necessarily produce personal pathology, and that where there exist supportive norms such pathology is much less likely to occur.

Now applied to the sphere of sexual deviance, pathology is likely to be exhibited among deviants to the extent that they function within proscriptive norms and gain no access to supportive norms. Personal pathology is thus predictable among isolated sexual deviants who function in extremely repressive environments. But such pathology will not be demonstrated when the 'deviant' functions in tolerant groups such as a tolerant society or a supportive subculture. The homosexual who feels thwarted, repressed, devalued in his community could well develop pathological symptoms; the homosexual who functions in a tolerant society or who gains access to a subculture in which he finds supportive norms may be much less likely to develop pathological symptoms.

One study which supports this general thesis is Christensen's comparison of premarital attitudes and behaviour in three cultures: Mormon Utah, Indiana Mid-west, and Scandinavian Denmark. Predictably, he discovered that permissive attitudes increased from the former to the latter. Of greater interest here were the attendant behavioural consequences of such attitudes in the three cultures. Predictably again, Christensen found the most deleterious consequences in Utah and the least in Denmark. Both subjectively in terms of guilt feelings and objectively in terms of hurried marriages and divorce rates, Utah was found to suffer most. Problems do not arise through the 'deviations' themselves, but through the social context in which they are enmeshed (Christensen, 1960: 1966; Christensen and Carpenter, 1962; Christensen and Gregg, 1970).

Who are the 'perverts'?

While the inspection of social contexts will tell a great deal about the characteristics of sexual deviants, the problem still remains as to what the phenomenon actually is. The clinical literature in general does not regard this as a problem – who the perverts are is known un-problematically. But for the interactionist, committed to a brand of relativism, this can become a very troublesome matter. If, for example, sexual deviance is truly relative, why should he study homosexuality as deviance and heterosexuality as normality? Indeed, to study homosexuality as deviance may be to reinforce the societal conception that it is deviance. The control function of the sociologist becomes explicit.

I have already referred to this problem more generally in chapter 2, where I made a distinction between societal and situational deviance. In studying the world as it exists, therefore, the sociologist has to take into cognizance the existence of broad societal values which do publicly designate certain conduct as perversion, while at the same time recognizing that on a situational level any kind of conduct may have the potentiality for being normalized or rendered deviant. All that is required for situational deviance to occur is the presence of two factors: norm-violation and stigmatizing responses. And since both norms and responses (societal and self) may clearly differ from context to context, while being constrained by broader abstract norms, the concept of sexual deviance must inherently be an ambiguous concept (Schur, 1971: 26) with outer limits set by any given society. Who or what is deviant can only be determined by analysing the situation at hand. It is not possible, as most clinicians and some sociologists would like, to order the world neatly into a series of types: 'normals' and 'perverts', the 'perverts displaying distinctive differences from the 'normals'. The interactionist must locate deviancy in situations and not some abstract society, though he must remain sensitive to the latter.

Within such a broad statement, certain systematic variations need to be noted. There is a world of difference between casual norm violation in bed between husband and wife consensually, and a necrophiliac driven day after day to seek corpses, real or imaginary, and organizing his life around this pursuit. Indeed much of the previous chapter was concerned with depicting widespread differentiation, presumably much of it norm-violating, with the implication that perhaps it was not after all really deviance. Much of this differentiation could be called deviance in the sense of Lemert's primary deviance, remaining insignificant at the level of self-regarding attitude. But some of it goes on to become Lemert's secondary deviance – where the life of the individual is organized around the fact of his deviance. The crucial variable in this movement from primary to secondary deviance – from sexual differentiation to sexual deviance – is that of the societal reaction and/or the self-reaction flowing from the societal reaction. (It should be stressed, for it is the cause of much confusion, that the reaction towards deviance need not always be real but only implied. It is often sufficient for a sexually different person simply to reconstruct in his imagination what the consequences of a perceived reaction might be for it to have sufficient impact upon him to come to see himself as deviant.)

It is thus with this movement from transitory, causal, widespread sexual differentiation in society towards a more stable, highly signified experience of sexual deviance that a theory of sexual deviance has to address itself. The most appropriate starting-point to such an inquiry rests with studying those factors used in identifying – by self or others – sexual differentiation as sexual deviance. From there, one can study the consequences of such identification.

Identifying sexual deviants[10]

Deviance does not arrive unannounced. Rather, it has to be identified, interpreted and subsequently fashioned and structured. Such processes – neither linear, monolithic nor automatic – involve a range of 'identifiers', from the public and formal to the private and informal. While the former – such as the police – are usually seen as central in this process, it is more likely that the key role is played by the latter. Out of a vast pool of sexual differentiation, only a little may be identified by official control agents as deviance, while much more may be so recognized by the deviants themselves. Self-labelling is more pervasive and more powerful than formal labelling.

Two contrasting accounts exist of the process of identification. One – the *just* account – assumes that it is the 'most dangerous' or the 'most disturbed' who are most likely to be identified as deviant: identification depends upon relevant factors within the individual. A second – the *unjust* account – assumes that identification occurs through contingencies extraneous to the deviant action (powerlessness, visibility, the tolerance of surrounding groups): identification depends upon contingencies in the social system. While clinicians have overemphasized the former, some interactionists have over-emphasized the latter. Both accounts need to be considered: while a great deal of inappropriate labelling may occur, at the margins of extreme pathology identification processes are more likely to be just and appropriate. In what follows I wish to suggest a few of the contingencies that may result in the identification of deviance, while simultaneously stressing the role of the deviant in contributing to his own labelling. Three broad sets of contingencies may be distinguished: (1) the societal reaction, (2) the visibility of the sexual act and (3) the problematics of the sexual act. I will discuss each briefly in turn.

1 The societal reaction

From the viewpoint of reactors to deviance, identification is closely linked to (a) their tolerance levels (Lemert, 1951: 57), and (b) the nature of their beliefs about deviancy.

a *Tolerance levels* vary greatly between societies, communities, groups and individuals.

1 The existence of varying tolerance towards sexual variation *across cultures* has been well documented (e.g. Ford and Beach, 1952; Marshall and Suggs, 1971), and it is frequently suggested that the tolerance level has a direct effect upon a society's rate of sexual deviation. Other things being equal, a society that is generally more tolerant towards sexual differentiation (sex-positive)[11] is likely to have less systematically organized sexual deviance than a society that constantly displays hostility to such conduct (sex-negative). I think this is generally so, but not for the usual reason.

The usual reason given by scientists and 'radical' laymen alike is that of the 'blocked-conduit' theory: it assumes an image of sexuality as an instinctual reservoir and a definition of deviancy as absolute. In a sex-negative society 'normal' sexuality becomes dammed up in this reservoir, and 'breaks out' in perverted forms. What is normal and what is perverted may be taken for granted. On the other hand, in a sex-positive society, 'normal sexuality' is possible, there is no 'damming up', and consequently fewer people need to resort to perversions. Again what is normal, and what is not, may be taken for granted. More specifically, Ollendorf (1966) has suggested that homosexuality is only to be found in sex-negative societies where 'normal' outlets are limited; it is not to be found in sex-positive societies.

Now interactionism is unhappy with both 'absolutism' and 'instincts', but still sees tolerance as important in understanding the prevalence of sexual deviation. For two basic tenets of labelling theory are that the more things that are defined in a society as deviant, the more deviance that society will have, and when a given experience is defined as deviant, it develops the consequences of deviancy. Thus, in a society that is riddled with deviancy definitions and intolerance, much sexual deviance will emerge. In a society that is riddled with a diverse range of sexual meanings but few deviancy definitions, sexual differentiation will be widespread but sexual deviancy minimal. In a society that has few sexual meanings available, and therefore could have few definitions of deviancy since such definitions would be outside the meaning structure of that society, then again deviancy may be minimal (Messenger, 1971). It is, then, the combined situation of multiple sexual meanings *and* deviancy definitions that is most likely to produce 'sexual deviance'. Such, of course, is the nature of this society.

2 *Within any one society*, different communities may have different tolerance of deviation – larger urban centres creating conditions of impersonality where tolerance of variation is greater, and smaller communities possessing omniscient, close-knit, networks where 'deviants' become outlawed.[12]

3 *Within groups*, a number of studies have suggested how tolerance rates vary from one context to another. Girls entering striptease may never have intended to do so, but when placed in 'stripping contexts' providing release from the wider normative constraints condemning stripping, may find themselves involved with few feelings of shame (Skipper and McCaghy, 1970). Likewise, there are data on adolescent groups suggesting that they develop organized norms to support such activities as visiting prostitutes (Kirkendall, 1960), becoming prostitutes (Reiss, 1961), premarital sexual behaviour (Reiss, 1967), and aggressive sexuality (Kanin, 1967). Through the potential contradictions, conflict and dissensus in contemporary society, scope is created for different groups to provide support, legitimation for their members, and protection from other competing groups. Tolerance of 'homosexuals', 'swingers' and 'strippers', etc., seems to increase as one gains contact with members of such groups. The tolerance rates of groups well versed in variation then are likely to be higher than those not so well versed.

4 Finally, tolerance levels take on the greatest personal significance at the *level of individual action*. When sexual partners meet, there is not always a consensus as to who does what to whom, where and when. The boy who expects sexual favours from his girlfriend and gets them remains simply another case of premarital intercourse undetected; but the boy who does not get them may well find himself accused of rape. The married husband who attempts cunnilingus may meet the wife's approval; or may find himself with a visit arranged to the marriage-guidance counsellor. The child-molester who finds children are willing to be fondled, especially if given money, may proceed safely until the girl or boy is confronted who objects loudly or publicly.[13] In each case, tolerant partners may be found who will consent with very little difficulty ensuing; but the choice of an intolerant partner is likely to raise problems.

Not only do the tolerance rates vary between groups in society, so too do the nature of rules. Frequently, there is a wide discrepancy between the official rules governing a society (the legal order) and the rules governing relationships (the relational rules). Behaviour may be tolerated between two individuals in a personal relationship that would never be tolerated in impersonal relationships in a wider community. Indeed, personal relationships may often be used to protect and insulate deviance from the wider community – as in the case of wives who protect their 'mentally ill' husbands from institutionalization. For 'sexual deviants' it seems likely that if relationships can be established where 'perversions' are accepted by both partners – their 'problematic' nature decreases. If the wife willingly dresses in rubber wear for her husband (North, 1970: 17); if the friend willingly lends her underwear to an acquaintance; if the child willingly exposes itself to another – if these acts are built into the situated rules governing their relationships, then there may be little reason for deviance to become public or significant.

On the other hand, when the relationship breaks down, or when the deviant is only minimally involved in a relational social network – the charge of public recognition becomes correspondingly greater. An intolerant friend or a solitary existence may be more important in understanding how sexual deviance comes to the surface of society than psychodynamics. Denzin (1970) has suggested the importance of the study of relational rules, and personal sexual rules would seem to be an important subcategory of this analysis about which at present we know little.

b   *The nature* of the reaction may primarily be expressed in terms of the mythology, stereotypes and folklore that surround the deviance, and which serve to sentitize members of the community or officials to certain traits. While some of these traits may have their basis in the objective behaviour patterns of those deviants, much of it may have little such foundation. Thus, for example, rape is often seen as an explosive and violent act that takes place between two strangers (often a Negro man and a white woman) in a dead-end street or a dark alley, under the influence of alcohol (Amir, 1971: 336); sexual offenders are seen as oversexed men who suffer from a glandular imbalance who are prone to physical violence and recidivism (Coleman, 1964: 381) and homosexuals are effeminate, promiscuous, sex-hungry perverts prone to certain kinds of more artistic professions (Kimball-Jones, 1967: 27–34). All of these observations are in fact demonstrated by the researchers to be largely or wholly untrue; but they may well still be used as a basis for imputing deviation in daily life.

Such stereotypes may also serve as the basis for action by official control agents. To date, there have been no full studies of the 'typifications' employed in 'processing' sexual deviants – but that they are used is hinted at strongly in Sudnow's comments on child-molesters and the courts, Rains's comments on unmarried mothers in maternity homes, and Skolnick's observations on the police and prostitutes (Sudnow, 1965; Rains, 1971; Skolnick, 1966).

In sum, it seems plausible that the more hostile the reaction, and the more rigid the stereotypes of the deviant, the greater the potential for labelling.

2 The visibility of the sexual act

Most sexual behaviour has a very low visibility. It typically takes place away from public view, in those back regions of life where it may pass unnoticed, and is immune from public labelling. Yet there are many factors which may disturb the smooth flow of concealed sexuality and render the invisible visible.

One apparent factor which affects visibility is its incidence: the greater the number of times a deviant activity takes place, the greater the chance of it being seen by somebody. Unfortunately, this hypothesis by itself is unhelpful for some of the most widespread differential sexual activity (e.g. masturbation and premarital intercourse) typically does not manifest very strong secondary deviance and can generally remain concealed. Further, if a sexual activity becomes widespread in its occurrence and 'known-aboutness', then it will have an increasing tendency to become normalized. Thus, incidence on its own will not be of much help.

Far more important is the degree to which the sexual activity disturbs the equilibrium of the community or family. Much sexuality flows privately between one, two, or more individuals; but as soon as the smooth flow of sexuality is interrupted – someone is called in from outside, or a fuss is made from within the situation by some-body – then the situation becomes potentially very visible. It is thus the consequences of illicit sex and not the sexuality itself that typically creates visibility. For example, premarital intercourse does not disturb the community until something 'goes wrong' and pregnancy ensues. Then it has disturbed the principle of legitimacy and has brought manifestly visible signs of 'sin', with inevitable stigma.[14] Another example emerges in fetishism, where the desire for fetishistic objects results in theft. Many fetishistic objects may be borrowed and returned privately from friends and lovers; it is only when one goes outside into the community and 'steals' that the fetishist and his work becomes visible.[15]

A further factor which influences visibility is the actor's sensitivity which changes over time. What is well concealed today may become public knowledge tomorrow if the public starts earnestly to look for it. Two powerful forces play their roles here: the media, which can generate a 'moral panic', and the agents of control, who may exert effort towards certain forms of deviancy in 'crime drives'. In both cases a previously concealed sexual activity is brought sharply into focus and public consciousness – sometimes with hysterical effect. The police, for example, may make an all-out effort to eliminate pornography from the shop windows, or the prostitutes from the street; and the media may 'discover' sexual perversions that create an oversensitive awareness in the community. After the New York City Child Murders of 1937, in which four girls were killed and sexually assaulted, one observer (Sutherland, 1950a: 143) wrote:

> For a while it was utterly unsafe to speak to a child on the street unless one was well dressed and well known in the neighbourhood. To try to help a lost child, with tears streaming down its face, to find its way home would in some neighbourhoods cause a mob to form and violence threatened.

Another factor related to visibility is the degree of congruence between the actor and the stereotypes of sexual deviance discussed earlier. In this case, it does not matter whether one is behaving sexually differently or not: the point is that one looks as though one is. It is here that the greatest irony of this perspective on sexual deviance can be found: namely, that while some people may be behaving in a sexually different fashion and pass unnoticed, others who are behaving 'normally' may be caught up in the labelling machine. Thus the effeminate-looking man may be recognized as a homosexual, the ageing man as impotent, and the 'tartily' dressed girl as a 'good screw'. In these cases, it does not matter what one is but rather what one looks like, since it is the impressions that serve as the basis for action, not the 'actuality'.

Some variations by their very nature are likely to be highly visible. Exhibitionism is an obvious example, but also included would be those deviations where partners or audiences are required: striptease artistes, models, and drag artistes, for example, render themselves visible in order to sell their wares. Prostitutes likewise become visible by being located in known quarters and wearing conspicuous dress (Lemert, 1951: 253).

While prostitutes and strippers must render themselves partially visible, they do so in a restricted manner: not all members of society have an equal chance of seeing them. This leads to a final important factor in briefly considering identification factors – the social visibility of the sexual setting. A setting is socially visible when it precludes the initial consent to copresence of those who may be involved as witnesses or participants in the acts occurring there. There is involuntary accessibility. Given this, Humphreys (1970: 162) has constructed a continuum of the social visibility of sexual settings and suggested that the more public a sexual act becomes, the greater the severity of public reaction. He outlines six stages on his continuum, and the five most significant may be tabulated as in Table 2.

Thus, only the brave and the foolhardy are likely to have sexual

TABLE 2 *Social settings and the 'visibility' of sexual activity*

Type of sexual setting	Consent to copresence	Nature of sexual activity	Examples
1 Highest visibility	Lowest level of consent to copresence	No sexual activity, except by most daring	Church service; busy shopping street
2 High visibility	Little consent to copresence	Sexual activity by a few, but many attempts to control	Public conveniences; public beaches; public parks
3 Marginal visibility	Marginal consent	Sexual activity is easy but risks still attached	Private car parked on lonely lane
4 Low visibility	Consent to be granted entrance is high	Sexual activity is relatively safe	A brothel; a 'gay' sauna bath
5 Invisible	Consent to enter totally controlled	Sexual activity easy, safe and widespread	Bedrooms at home

activities in the first kind of setting where public surveillance is wide; most sexual experience will take place in the more private realms, relatively immune from public recognition. To the extent that sexual variations take place here – and most of the variant activities probably do – one is at least safe from public detection. Such immunity may not however be equally available to all groups – young people, for example, are more restricted in their access to private places (Gagnon and Simon, 1973; Cummins, 1971). Likewise, the working class are more vulnerable to public visibility by agencies of law enforcement (Chapman, 1968). Not only do such groups not have the means to readily 'cover up' their deviance, they also generally live in areas that are more likely to be heavily policed by control agents. Thus, for example, Skolnick and Woodworth found that the detection of statutory rape cases by the police largely depended on referrals from public welfare agencies: 'Statutory rape is punished mainly among the poor who become visible by applying for maternity aid from welfare authorities' (Skolnick and Woodworth, 1967: 109).

3 The problematics of the sexual act

A false picture may so far have been created of an enormous impersonal labelling machine judiciously 'slapping' sex-pervert labels on those it cannot tolerate and those it can see. Such a picture is as absurd as it is false: individuals not only receive labels, but often create them for themselves with little help from outside agencies directly. The presence of an external 'force' is always essential – because it provides the definitions and stereotypes which the actor can use as 'signals' to fashion and interpret his sexual experiences. But it does not necessarily have to do the labelling itself. Once it has provided models of stigma, individuals may often use them as a basis for assessing their acts.

Such self-labelling has its origins in *practical* and *internal* problems which highlight the way deviance is rendered 'a problem' through a hostile societal reaction. *The stronger the awareness of these problems, the greater the likelihood for self-labelling.*

A key *practical* problem is that of access: the easier it is to practically carry out the desired sexual activity *in the first instance*, the less chance of it 'becoming deviant'. It is not typically very difficult for a boy to find a girl who is willing to have sexual intercourse with him; it is however harder to find a boy. It is not too difficult for a boy to masturbate with fantasies; it is harder if he needs stimulation in the form of pornography or a fetish.

A key *internal* problem is that of identity management and guilt negation. If an individual toys with a desired act which he perceives others around him will devalue or condemn, he has a great potentiality for feeling guilty. He may thus find the experience is given a significance in his life which it would not normally have in conditions where it was seen as an acceptable activity. This is a serious problem indeed, and contains a great potentiality for self-definition as a sexual deviant. If he remains alone with his problem, it is possible that feelings of guilt will spiral and become unmanageable; if he gains access to a supportive deviant group, it is possible that, while neutralizing his guilt, they will help to stabilize him within a deviant role.

In summary, there seem to be three crucial areas for understanding why people come to adopt deviant labels, or come very near to adopting them: the nature and the strength of the societal reaction, the visibility of the act, and the problematics of the act. Above, I have briefly considered some of these factors – although the precise causal nexus is a task for research. It is important to stress however that while the approach above, following Goffman, highlights 'contingencies' rather than individual pathology as precipitating factors in the creation of deviancy, it does not suggest that the individual deviant has nothing to do with this labelling process. On the contrary, the societal reaction and the individual deviant must constantly be seen together—the deviant may well contribute to his own visibility, or render himself a carbon copy of official stereotypes. Indeed, a study of the labelling of homosexuals in the military concluded that 'the examination of the deviant himself is as important as the social control system that he offends' (Williams and Weinberg, 1971: 179). These authors found that homosexuals who received 'less than honourable discharge' for homosexual activities in the military differed in several significant ways from those who were also homosexual in the military but who received no discharges. The discharged group were more likely to have had a greater degree of sexual experience than the others, were more likely to have had sexual experience in the military, and were more likely to have been involved in the 'gay world' before entering the military. Thus, while the societal reaction may be a central determinant of sexual deviation, it cannot be seen in isolation from the individual actor.

Denial, diffusion and deference

So far I have suggested that only some individuals whose sexual experience varies will come to be seen or come to see themselves as 'deviant'. But not even these 'selected' individuals are inevitably going to accept or remain in the position of being sexually deviant. Put at its simplest, the individual potentially identified as being sexually deviant has three broad choices: denial, where he refuses to see himself as deviant or let others see him in this light; diffusion, where he becomes conscious of his potential deviance but finds much anxiety in such consciousness; deference, where he ultimately comes to accept his deviancy. I will illustrate each of these briefly:

a *Denial:* The actor disavows he is deviant publicly or to himself with such force that he, society and preferably both accepts an identity as 'normal'. Three strategies of disavowal may be mentioned.

First, the actor may provide 'accounts' – either before or after the acts – which rationalize his behaviour as 'normal' and insulate him from deviant self-conceptions (Mills, 1940; Sykes and Matza, 1957; Lofland, 1969; Lyman and Scott, 1970). Rains, for example, in her discussion of the processes of becoming an unwed mother, explicitly notes the neutralizing techniques employed by girls before premarital intercourse which serve to 'maintain their reputations as essentially non-promiscuous in their own and others' eyes' (Rains, 1971: 15). Thus the convention of love, the patterns of ritual courtship, the maintenance of technical virginity, and the structured use or non-use of contraceptive methods may all help to prevent 'good girls' from seeing themselves as 'bad girls' even when involved in 'bad behaviour'. Likewise, McCaghy (1968b: 48) discusses the 'accounts' provided by child-molesters for the courts – this time after the act – and shows how they attempt to excuse their behaviour by blaming it upon drinking: 'Drinking is the reason. I could always get a woman. I can't figure it out. A man's mind doesn't function right when he's got liquor in it'; 'If I were sober, it never would have happened'; 'I have an alcoholic drinking problem, not a sex problem'. A number of other recent studies have dealt with this process of neutralizing through accounts.[16]

A second denial technique is a counter-reaction, where the 'deviant' reacts against the threat of his 'deviancy' by joining the 'other side', moral crusaders. Humphreys's respondents in *Tea-room Trade* (1970: 141) were later interviewed (although the fact that the researcher knew of their sexual proclivities was never revealed), and their comments were reminiscent of those traditionally associated with moral entrepreneurs:

> So consistent were the replies of 'trade' and 'closet queens' (the participants most likely to be arrested in tea-rooms) in encouraging more vice squad activity that a portrait emerges of these men as moral crusaders. This at least suggests the ironic possibility of a type of moral entrepreneur who contributes to his own stigmatisation. Homosexual folklore insists that 'there is a witch behind every witch hunt'. These data suggest not only the truth underlying that perception, but that deviant behaviour may be plagued by a sort of moral arms race in which the deviant is caught in the cycle of establishing new strategic defences to protect himself from the fall out of his own defensive weapons.

A third denial technique resides less in the deviant and more in the reactor. Lofland (1969: 209–95), in his discussion of the ways in which deviants can be led to resume 'normal' identities, specifies the role of 'normal-smiths' as being particularly important. 'Normal-smiths' are 'promiscuous imputors of pivotal normality', people who through craftsmanlike skills help to restore and maintain identities of normality in so-called deviants. They constantly deny in the face of sometimes 'obvious' evidence that the individuals are, or can be, deviant. Priests who discover that one of their most loyal church members has been arrested on a morals charge are willing to testify that he is a man of upright character incapable of doing such a thing; and parents confronted with a son who declares his homosexuality, may spend much time assuring him that 'he will grow out of it', 'that he is mistaken'. Such definitions of 'normality' by others may at times result in insulation from a deviant role.

b *Diffusion:* When deviancy denial does not work or is not attempted, the deviant may be left with an identity diffusion. This is a highly critical point – a moratorium, which may last for but a moment, for week upon week, or even for a lifetime. It is the state of not knowing who one is – of thinking one is a sexual deviant, but hoping not – and is often associated with a great deal of self-hate and despair. It is the stage that a sexual deviant reaches when he arrives at the door of some social workers and psychiatrists. His problem, however, is not his deviance *per se*, but rather his inability to accept or reject it. Because it figures so highly in his consciousness, this phase can also be seen as 'secondary deviance' but is considerably removed from the career deviance often described in the literature.

c *Deference:* A third alternative response involves the final stabilization into the deviant role, the acceptance that one is after all a 'sexual deviant' (by whatever name that it is identified). This can be seen as a series of moves by which *it becomes increasingly hard to leave that 'status' and increasingly easy to stay in it.* 'Role imprisonment' begins to take place – although it should never be seen as an absolutely irretrievable imprisonment. The question that needs answering here is simply: what factors work to stabilize the secondary deviance?

Two may be suggested – the 'inner' and the 'outer'. The inner factors refer to those that arise because of the nature of the 'deviancy' itself – 'stripping is fun', 'prostitution brings in the "bread"', 'nudism is friendly, free and healthy', and 'homosexual sex is the "fantastic sex" '; while the outer factors refer to the group influences both favourable and unfavourable to the deviancy – the favourable sources providing supportive beliefs which may eliminate guilt and provide alternatives, and the unfavourable providing restrictive and punitive stereotypes of sexual deviance that make it hard for the 'deviant' to leave that role.

It is important to stress the 'inner factors' that help to sustain sexual deviance, since many labelling studies in the past place all the emphasis upon external contingencies over which the individual has little control. Scheff and Goffman's discussions of mental illness suggest that most of the mentally ill are unfortunate victims of 'asylum custodians' and 'stereotypes of insanity'. While it may be true that there is little 'intrinsically pleasurable' (apart from the abdication of responsibility) about mental illness,[17] this is not so for sexual deviance: much of its permanency over time in any one individual can be seen to flow from this simple fact. Because sexual deviations are usually pleasurable, individuals become attached to them.

'Outer' supports also help stabilize the deviation. Some of the earlier problems – of guilt, of access, of technique – may become resolved. Consider, for example, the fears felt by a 'pornophile' at the outset of buying his first pornographic book: he has to locate shops that are able to 'sell' him the desired commodity; he has to work up courage to enter; he does not want to be seen going in; he worries about what the people in the shop will think of him; he does not know how much to pay; he may not find the 'right' type of books; he has to plan where to 'hide' the books once bought; and he has to cope with all the incipient guilt. These are all very real problems for the neophyte buyer of pornography, but they soon begin to disappear once he establishes his interests. He gets to know where the 'good' shops are, and 'knows' the shopkeeper; he sees that there are many people buying such books and many such books available; he realizes that the chance of meeting an 'acquaintance' on the way out of the shop with a book in his hand is very slim, and besides he soon learns that the owner will put it in a 'brown paper bag' – and besides again, 'what's wrong with it anyway?' From a very difficult and worrying task, the 'pornophile's' task becomes no harder and no more worrying than any shopping task. A growing body of research on the socialization of 'sexual deviants' into their deviant roles has documented the construction of facilitating belief systems and supports for regular sexual deviance.[18]

To focus upon the pleasure and the ease of becoming a sexual deviant may do an injustice to the misery and pathos that is sometimes to be found in sexual deviation (cf. Matza, 1969). As there are many studies that deal with this aspect of deviance, I have chosen to emphasize the positive side here. Most of the people who experience misery as a result of their deviation do so because of a failure in the role itself, falling into the identity diffusion stage of the erotic career rather than the identity deference phase. It is not the sexual deviance *per se* that brings them misery but the inability to find a solution to the problems raised by that deviance. Some people, of course, may actually need to have 'sexual deviance' problems in order to solve other personal problems not actually related to the sexual area.

A further factor which aids the stabilization of secondary deviance, is the existence of sexual stereotypes which provide cues for an individual to 'recognize' his own deviation, and a concomitant imagery of exclusiveness in sexual roles. Thus, in a complex society, individuals function with a series of conceptual stereotypes more frequently than they do with a series of primary (face to face) experiences. In an authoritarian, restrictive society stereotypes tend to be more rigidly drawn. Taking these two statements together, it is possible that in a restrictive complex society individuals learn sexual stereotypes which have a tendency towards simplification – which are rigid and well cut. This applies as much to heterosexuality as the 'sexual deviations' but the concern here lies with the latter. For here one is told that homosexual men cannot like women; a paedophile cannot have sexual relationships with an adult; and a prostitute cannot have stable relationships. Further, the number of public stereotypes will be limited, more 'unusual' variations will remain unstereotyped, and the individual may consequently have to force himself into the wrong category. Because the stereotypical conceptions of sexuality in our culture are narrow, any early sexual cues become translated in a distorted and restrictive way. This account of the restrictive and limited nature of many sexual deviants locates explanations in the wider culture that promulgates restrictive notions of sexuality, and not in the deviance *per se* or the pathology of the individual.

Social organization of sexual deviance

All sexual experiences become socially organized. No matter what form sexuality takes – from marital copulation through to necrophiliac murder[19] – a social pattern is assumed: a chaotic multipotential of sexual capacities is constantly reduced to some level of predictable, if not acceptable, order. Sexual experiences of all kinds become enmeshed in a finely woven web of norms and tacit rules which serve to regulate and structure those experiences.

While all sexual experience becomes socially organized in this sense, a much more limited amount becomes group organized. Thus the masturbator, the necrophile and the frotteurist will organize their sexual experiences, in the main, without any kind of collective support, while 'swingers', homosexuals and premarital lovers are more likely to organize their experiences in group situations with others. Both kinds of sexual experience become socially organized, but only the latter becomes enmeshed in collectively evolved norms.

As I have suggested earlier, when actors gain access to supportive norms, it is likely that less pathology will arise than when individuals gain no such access and feel their behaviour to be 'wrong'. If this is so, then it is probable that when sexual deviants gain access to group forms their experiences become more stable and orderly than when they do not. As long as sexual deviance remains an individual experience, it will remain problematic and unstable: once it becomes collectively organized, it becomes less problematic and more stable.

Sexual subcultures

An important area of collective organization is that of subcultures, in which individuals facing common 'sexual' problems come to evolve shared solutions (through mutual interaction with each other). Norms are generated which structure sexuality and which give support to its participants. Not all sexual experiences become enveloped by subcultural formations, and so a first question to be raised here concerns the conditions under which such subcultures emerge; after this, I will turn to some of the consequences of these deviant subcultures.

Subcultural emergence: Six factors contribute to the emergence of subcultures. First, since a subculture typically implies a group solution to a problem, the problem must be sufficiently widespread for the interactors to encounter each other. Not all sexual differentiation exhibits the same rate in a society – masturbation is usually common, zoophilia much less common[20] – and only when a problem is common can subcultures arise. But, clearly, frequency is not enough – for if that was the case, there would be a well-developed subculture of masturbation, and I suspect that there is not!

Second, then, even when a problem is widespread it may not require collective resolution. There are two aspects to this. First, there are many kinds of sexual experience which do not really require contact with 'like-minded individuals': masturbators do not need contact with other masturbators, child-molesters do not need contact with other child-molesters[21] and pornophiles do not need contact with other pornophiles. Thus, there is no endemic reason why such groups should meet. But, second, such groups may well have other reasons for meeting – for example, the exchange of views and the neutralization of guilt. It is unlikely however that such groups would in fact meet. For a third condition for subcultural emergence is the existence of effective communication between actors, and it is clear that because of the privatized and stigmatizing nature of sexual deviance many actors will remain concealed from each other. As Cohen says (1955: 71):

> Where the problems themselves are of a peculiarly delicate,
> guilt laden nature, like many problems arising in the area of sex,
> inhibitions on communication may be so powerful that persons
> with like problems may never reveal themselves to one another,
> although circumstances are otherwise favourable for mutual
> exploration.

Players of the same deviant role may thus maintain pluralistic ignorance by stigmatizing other players, effectively insulating themselves from involvement in subcultures.

Fourth, if the *supply* of any particular form of sexual activity is restricted, it becomes difficult for large groups to develop around it. Rubber fetishism undoubtedly does have group forms (as exemplified in magazines like *Gayetime Mackintoshes Magazine* and *Mackintosh Monthly*), but in general 'it does not seem to create anything that could be described as a subculture – in part at least due to the scarcity of female partners' (North, 1970: 57). It may be that when the supply of a deviant form is scarce, prostitution may be the only organized form available to supply it.

Fifth, subcultures can only emerge when the problem around the deviation is a recurrent one – illegitimacy, for example, is usually a 'once-and-for-all' occurrence and girls do not usually join a subculture of unmarried mothers. Likewise, Schur has observed the way in which abortion clients do not create an abortion subculture, and suggests this may in part be due to the non-continuing nature of the deviant behaviour (Schur, 1965: 172). None the less, both abortion and illegitimacy can become socially organized on the supply side, where agencies come to deal with the unmarried mother, and abortion clinics are set up (Rains, 1971; Ball, 1966).

Finally, a subculture is unlikely to emerge if the deviation can be readily incorporated into the orthodox pattern of sexuality. Thus most activities which may fairly readily take place between a heterosexual couple in courtship or marriage (e.g. cunnilingus fellatio, mild fetishism), even if popularly seen as 'deviant', will not develop subcultural forms since they can be readily incorporated into the dominant sexual institutions.

Subcultural functions: Subcultures develop around only some forms of sexual deviation. Once established, they perform a number of important functions – both for the deviant and the wider society – which may well have a stabilizing effect. Indeed, once a subculture emerges and an individual enters that subculture, his deviance is likely to take on a form that is systematic and stable. Clearly, I have moved a long way from the earlier stages of the theoretical model when 'deviance' was merely casual and randomly differentiated.

Among the more important functions served by the subculture *for the deviant* are those of providing a regular access to the sexual (or social) commodity required, and an access to a whole machinery for legitimation. Strippers, for example, may be very worried about their striptease acts at the outset, but over time become not only skilled at it, but also provided with a vocabulary of legitimations; while prostitutes may also become very adept at presenting audiences with 'sad tales'.

But functions are also provided *for the wider society* – the subculture may serve to segregate the deviant from the wider population, and may also thus contain and control it. When Weinberg compared the degree of involvement of a sample of nudists in the community at large with the involvement of a non-nudist control, he found that the former were significantly more isolated (Weinberg, 1965). More specifically, the police and other control agents may be aware of subcultures and opt to let them continue relatively undisturbed, in order to facilitate the containment of the problem. As one police chief commented about the homosexual subculture: 'This way we know where the perverts are and we can keep an eye on them. Otherwise, we would constantly be bothered by their causing trouble in the wrong places' (Chambliss, 1966: 95).

Varieties of sexual experience

With the stabilization of the erotic career in a deviant pattern, these comments can end.[22] One cautionary word is in order, however, and this concerns the range of experience that I have subsumed under the heading of sexual deviation. My discussion has drawn from a scattering of variant sexual experiences, some of which the reader may not feel to be 'really deviant'. Further, the theory has not differentiated between kinds of deviance as traditionally conceived: a leg-fetishist may be seen simply as sexual differentiation or as pivotal deviance – it may be transitory and insignificant, or it may result in the individual shaping his life by that experience (taking up a job in a hosiery-modelling firm for example).[23] It may thus be anticipated that the theory outlined may be criticized because (a) it takes in too much sexual experience, and (b) it does not differentiate adequately between established patterns of deviance.

Clearly, an elementary interactionist classification of patterns of sexual deviation is required. And to remain loyal to the theory outlined above, two criteria need to be met by such a typology – both criteria refuting the criticisms made above. First, the typology should not provide rigid, absolutist categories by which some kinds of sexual experience are inviolably seen as deviant. For clearly, it has been central to my argument that any sexual experience may be deviant and no experience has to be. Yet most studies do in fact provide 'lists' of those experiences known to be deviant (e.g. Freud, 1962; Scott, 1964; Coleman, 1964; Allen, 1969). Second, the typology should be consistent with interactionism, and not with the theoretical dictates of alternative stances. As most theories of sexual deviation tend to work from individualistic theories, so most typologies tend to work from the characteristics of individuals: deviations are classified as disorders of the sexual expression, the instinctual object, the sexual stimulus and the instinctual strength (Allen, 1969). Clearly, such a typology may be highly useful for certain theoretical purposes, though dubiously so for interactionists.

A central theoretical distinction being made is that between primary and secondary deviance (or sexual differentiation and sexual deviance). I have suggested that while members of a society may come to experience a wide range of sexual meanings in their day to day life, it is only when public or self-labelling as deviant arises that damaging consequences may ensue. By this kind of argument, the wife who experiences strong guilt feelings about sexuality may come to see herself as significantly different from other women when she refuses to co-operate with her husband's desires in the marital bed. From this may flow a full-bodied deviant identity, consequential avoidance of the marital bed, and the possible breakdown of the marriage. The deviant is someone whose life is organized around the fact of her deviance. And, in this example, deviant sexuality is located in heterosexual marriage.

A second, but lesser, theoretical distinction made by the interactionist is that between sexual variations that remain on the level of individuals or dyads, and those which become socially organized on a group or institutional level. All sexual experience is socially organized and patterned, even the most individual acts of masturbation; but clearly some are supported by group structures (wife-swapping, gay bars) and others are not.

Taking these two sets of variables relevant to interactionism, an ideal theoretic typology may be constructed that cuts across conventional boundaries.[24] This is illustrated in Table 3. Such a typology transcends the conventional clinical boundaries. Some traditionally conceived deviant groups may fit into each of the categories

TABLE 3   *An interactionist classification of the forms of sexual variant experiences*

Nature of deviance	Primary deviance	Secondary deviance
Attendant structure:		
Individual/Dyad	(1) Individual sexual differentiation	(2) Individual sexual deviance
Group Institution	Subcultural sexual differentiation (3)	Subcultural sexual deviance (4)

at various stages of their emergence. Thus as a child, a boy may masturbate by fantasizing a schoolgirl's underwear (or by actually possessing them), but the incident remains trivial and casual (type 1). A little later, as an adolescent he may become involved with other boys at his college in 'panty raids' on the schoolgirls' dormitory, again in a fairly casual and insignificant manner (type 3). Later in marriage, he may find the kind of underwear that his wife wears to be increasingly important, worry about it, label himself perverted or be discovered by his wife fondling her underwear in solitude, and consequently find his whole sexuality (and possibly life) to be permeated by this fact (type 2). Finally, he could, through the pages of a sex magazine, locate the existence of a group of people involved in the fetishistic exchange of underwear – a subculture of panty-fetishists (type 4). Underwear fetishism is usually seen as a disorder of the sexual stimulus, but clearly it is possible to conceptualize it theoretically in a very different fashion. The important theoretical questions here do not concern the initial disposition towards underwear, but rather the conditions under which this may take on a group form and the conditions under which it comes to be seen as deviant and take on a pivotal significance.

Finally, while it is beyond the scope of this book, it might ultimately be possible to attempt some kind of synthesis between traditional classifications of deviants in terms of goals, etc., and interactionist classifications in terms of attendant structures and primary and secondary deviance. Such a task would be clearly a very complex business.[25]

Conclusion: in search of a theory of sexual deviance

There is little research and theorizing about sexual deviance in general, and practically none from a sociological stance. In this chapter, I have tried to raise problems, assemble materials and construct preliminary frameworks which hopefully may further such research and theory work by giving a coherence to the field. This 'ordering process' has been criticized by some sociologists (Gouldner, 1971: 84), but I believe it to be a necessary feature of inquiry. While the world itself may not possess logic and order, the social scientist must approach it in such a way if he is ever to comprehend it.[26]

Thus, while this section has travelled through largely unexplored regions, it has hopefully done so systematically in a way that will further research inquiry and theory construction. It has asked questions that have been relatively ignored in other theoretical approaches to sexual deviance, and herein lies its justification. But it is not itself a theory, and makes no claims to be. For as I have suggested elsewhere (Plummer, 1973a), an interactionist approach to theory stresses grounding theory in the everyday world and not in the armchair. The world can only be understood through a detailed inspection of that world. Yet grounded theory should not be seen as a plea for a naïve inductivism, for a return to Popper's 'bucket theory of the mind'. All research must be guided by broad theoretical perspectives – tacit or public – and broad problem areas, and grounded theory is no exception to this. (Glaser and Strauss were interactionists interested in the area of dying, after all!) Thus, I see the previous discussion as a preliminary task in theory building.[27]

part three

The case of male homosexuality

One of the factors that materially contributes to the development
of exclusively homosexual histories is the ostracism which
society imposes upon one who is discovered to have had
perhaps no more than a lone experience.

(Kinsey *et al.*, 1948: 663)

I would *very tentatively* suggest the following: . . . Homosexuality
as a clinical entity does not exist. Its forms are as varied as
heterosexuality.

(Hooker, 1957: 31)

Even if the exact nature and extent of its influence are not
known, there is little doubt that society's reaction (both informal
and formal) significantly shapes the problem of homosexuality.

(Schur, 1963: 113)

Homosexuality . . . in itself has only minor effects upon the
development of the personality. But the attitudes, not of the
homosexual, but of other people towards him, create a stress
situation which can have a profound effect upon personality
development and can lead to character deterioration of a kind
which prohibits effective integration with the community.

(Schofield, 1965: 203)

It is necessary to move away from an obsessive concern with the
sexuality of the individual, and attempt to see the homosexual in
terms of the broader attachments that he must make to live in the
world around him.

(Simon and Gagnon, 1967a: 181)

5   Introductory: interactionism and the forms of homosexuality

Part 2 of this book has presented a framework and perspective on sexual deviance derived from interactionism. Such a statement now requires detailed critical elaboration and empirical research over a range of sexual experiences, and the remainder of the book serves as an example of how such work may move. I have had to greatly restrict my concerns, however, to only one variety of sexual experience: that of male homosexuality in contemporary England and America.

Continuous with earlier arguments, I will focus upon three interrelated areas: reaction, action and interaction. Chapter 6 examines societal *reactions* towards homosexuality – looking both at some of its characteristics, and reviewing theories evolved to explain its existence. The subsequent two chapters examine the forms and evolution of the homosexual *act* – both as an individual experience and as a collective one. Finally, chapter 9 looks specifically at some of the *interaction* problems encountered by the homosexual. While, for analysis, these three elements may be isolated, they are interconnected: sexual deviance is an interactive phenomenon, and this means that both societal reaction *and* action are constantly in a process of mutual interaction, modifying and altering each other.

To set the stage for the analysis that follows, and as a partial résumé of ideas developed in parts one and two, this chapter deals with some of the assumptions that an interactionist theory holds about homosexuality, contrasting them with the assumptions of other perspectives.

Homosexuality and the assumptions of interactionism

One prevalent way of looking at homosexuality is to view it as an abnormality of the personality.[1] At the very least it is seen as a 'condition'[2], but in its more extreme forms it is seen as a sickness, a neurosis or even a psychosis.[3] Accompanying such notions frequently are assumptions about the nature of science: that it is possible to apply the methods of the physical sciences to social phenomena. At the very least it is possible to divorce the researched homosexual from the researcher; it is possible to exclude 'values' from the research; it is possible to isolate the deviant from the meaningful world in which he is enmeshed. Homosexuality, in sum, is a condition of individuals which can be studied objectively. Such a position is not objectivity: rather it is objectivation. In other words, through the procedures of positivistic science, homosexuality is simultaneously explained as and rendered as a condition; it is simultaneoulsy explained as and rendered as a sickness. Clearly, homosexuality may be constituted as both a condition and a sickness in this society; but the point remains that it need not be.

I have expressed in a few words a complex argument that has been developed earlier and elsewhere (cf. Filmer *et al.*, 1972). Three general observations need adding here.

First, I am *not* denying that homosexuality is either a condition or a sickness in *this* society. Clearly, in a society where homosexuals go to psychiatrists for cures and treatments, and where many people see it as a sickness, it is effectively constituted as a sickness. It serves as the 'objectified reality' which is regarded as natural.

Second, however, I am suggesting that the meanings of homosexuality need to be seen in the context of the preconstituted social world, and that things need not be the way they are currently constituted. Clearly, and importantly, the homosexual experience has been organized socially in many ways other than that of the medical model (Eglinton, 1971; Devereux, 1937; Taylor, 1965b). Thus, though much of the homosexual experience may be a 'sickness' now, it was not in the past and need not be in the future. Indeed, the ongoing debate between various schools of scientific thought (Crompton, 1969; Green, 1972), and between the homophile movements and the public concerning the nature of homosexuality suggests that it might be reconceptualized in the immediate future as either a relationship or a political phenomenon.

Third, and as I have commented throughout, the debate as to the ultimate validity of these conceptualizations is not part of this book.

The interactionist, then, in trying to remain sensitive to the preconstituted and emergent meanings of the social world, works from a different series of underlying assumptions about the nature of homosexuality. Homosexuality may ultimately become solidified into a 'sick condition' of individuals in this culture: but the interactional concern is with viewing homosexuality as a process emerging through interactive encounters (part of which will include a potentially hostile reaction) in an intersubjective world. His concern, as discussed in chapter 2, rests with processes, reactions and subjective realities. I will look at each briefly in turn.

a *Reactions:* A key assumption of the interactionist approach is that homosexuality cannot be understood in isolation from the reactions of a society which potentially stigmatizes it. It is true that if homosexuality were commonplace, accepted everyday behaviour in society, the major area of analysis could perhaps be satisfactorily confined to the isolated actor. But much of what is distinctive about homosexuality as it exists in England is a direct consequence of the fact that it has been bedevilled by ban, has been rendered deviant (Matza, 1969: 146). The features of homosexuality as it is found in this society do not simply emerge from same-sex experiences: rather they flow from the social contexts in which they are located. Thus, it may be true that homosexuals exhibit pathology, are promiscuous, are exaggeratedly effeminate and so forth. But if this is the case (and I suspect that it is not generally true), the explanation for this may not reside in the homosexual experience *per se*, but rather in the hostile reactions surrounding it – which lead for example to self-devaluation and despair, and inhibit stable relationships.[4] Homosexuality cannot be understood as an individualistic phenomenon: rather it needs to be seen as an interactive phenomenon, and constantly linked to the reactions of society's members. As Schur (1969a) comments:

> In the broadest sense, then, the main 'cause' of deviance is the societal reaction to it. This does not primarily mean, of course, that the *behaviour* itself is *created* by the reaction to it (although there is some element of truth in that too . . .) but rather that the *meaning* of the behaviour (including its characterisation as deviance) and its place in the social order is produced through this process of reaction.

In each of the chapters that follow, while the emphases may differ, the homosexual experience and the reaction towards it will be seen as constantly interrelated. One cannot be comprehended without the other.

b *Homosexuality as a process:* Most recent researchers depict homosexuality as a condition, which people either have or do not have. The world thus conceived is populated by two 'kinds' of people – homosexuals and heterosexuals, although to account for ambiguity in such a picture, a spectrum of subtypes may be introduced.[5] The portrait given tends to emphasize the fashion in which homosexuals differ from heterosexuals; and to provide static snapshots of the experience rather than ongoing sequences. The interactionist, while he would not deny that homosexuality becomes stabilized and polarized in this society, starts from an assumption that homosexuality is best viewed as a process. Thus in trying to comprehend homosexuality at a moment in time, he sees it as part of an ongoing accomplishment and not a finished product (as I demonstrate in chapter 9), and in trying to comprehend the causal factors involved in homosexuality, he sees it as part of a sequential process and not simply as an abrupt leap from one state to another (as I demonstrate in chapter 8).

A useful concept in this task is that of *role*,[6] which sensitizes the interactionist not only to the patterned expectations surrounding homosexuality (and which vary from culture to culture, as well as perhaps group to group), but also to the dynamics of taking and making roles in everyday situations (Turner, 1962; 1972). While a condition is something which one either has or does not have, a role is something which one can adopt and drop, embrace or become distant from (Goffman, 1961a), and as a metaphor it raises more subtle problems than that of a condition. Under what situations are homosexual roles adopted? How are they built up, modified, sustained? How might individuals become committed to them, and stabilized within them? How might homosexual roles be related to other roles an individual takes? These are some of the new questions that might be raised, and much of the analysis in chapters 7 to 9 will be concerned with such problems.

c *Homosexuality within a subjective reality:* The interactionist does not take the socially constructed world for granted but renders it problematic. Thus, while most researchers into homosexuality can assume that homosexuality constitutes some form of 'oddity' – an evil, a sin, a sickness, a miserable situation to be in – the interactionist throws such assumptions into disarray, showing their socially constructed nature and the processes by which they become objectified into the 'truth'. What was once part of an 'objective' truth becomes visible as a subjective value stance; what was once taken to be absolute becomes highly relativized. In chapter 6, my central concern will be with analysing the nature and emergence of this broader subjective reality.

In sum, in the pages that follow homosexuality will be conceptualized as a form of role-playing, juxtaposed constantly with the reactions of society's members, and located in a subjective world where meanings are problematic.

A note on the forms of homosexual experience

Homosexuality refers to sexual experience, actual or imagined, between members of the same sex, which may be accompanied by emotional involvements.[7] As such, it involves a wide range of individuals in numerous different contexts, and the search for a common pattern here is as doomed to failure as a similar search would be into heterosexuality. Adequate understanding thus requires the construction of useful typological groups from this broad categorization, in order that some generalizations about certain forms of homosexual experience may be made (cf. Churchill, 1967: 32; West, 1968: 157).

Most studies recognize the diversity of the homosexual experience, and go on to classify such variance in individualistic terms, as properties of people. Freud, for example, provides a basic distinction between the absolute invert (who is only interested in the same sex and is indifferent or repulsed by the opposite sex), the amphigenic invert (the bisexual) and the contingent invert (who behaves homosexually under certain conditions), and such a distinction is one widely made in the literature (though often in different terminology) (Freud, 1962). From this typology, the homosexual condition may be further subdivided in a number of ways – Allen, for example, presents a somewhat arbitrary clinical typology of twelve types, including the compulsive homosexual, the nervous homosexual, the neurotic and psychotic varieties, the psychopathic homosexual and the alcoholic homosexual (Allen, 1969: 218).[8] Non-clinical approaches also tend to use the 'types of person' approach, as exemplified in the work of Richard Hauser, who identified no less than forty-six types including the 'demoralized young man', the 'religious homosexual', the 'body builder', the 'woman hater', the 'war queer', and the 'ship's queer' (Hauser, 1962: ch. 2).[9] Clearly, such *ad hoc* listing of types could be extended indefinitely – 'homosexuals' displaying as much variety as 'heterosexuals' – and hence is of dubious value.

Kinsey recognized this difficulty when he constructed his famous seven-point rating scale.[10] He wrote (Kinsey *et al.*, 1948: 617):

> It would encourage clearer thinking on these matters if persons were not characterised as heterosexual or homosexual, but as individuals who have had certain amounts of heterosexual experience and certain amounts of homosexual experience. Instead of using these terms as substantives which stand for persons, they may better be used to describe the nature of the overt sexual relations, or of the stimuli to which an individual erotically responds.

An attempt is made here to move away from defining homosexuality as a condition and people as homosexuals, but it still restricts analysis to individuals: those with more and those with less homosexual experience. Most of the research work, as with most of popular thinking, accounts for variations in homosexuality as variations in types of people.

This book suggests an alternative typology derived from interactionist principles, especially the insights of Lemert, Clinard and Gagnon and Simon (Lemert, 1951; Clinard, 1968: 361; Gagnon and Simon, 1968a). In looking at any homosexual experience it suggests two questions should be asked. First, does the homosexual experience arise in a highly socially structured context, or is it only marginally socially organized? Second, is it pivotally important for the individual experiencing it, bringing about self-conceptions of 'being a homosexual' and serving as a key factor in decisions made about the rest of his life, or does it have only marginal implications for the individual's self? The first question raises the variable of social organization, and the second raises the variable of primary and secondary deviation, both providing continuous rather than discrete categories.[11] Cross-tabulating the answers to these questions, four broad forms of homosexual experience are generated, as shown in Table 4.

TABLE 4 *An interactionist classification of the forms of homosexual experience*

Significance of homosexuality		Primary deviance	Secondary deviance
Social organization of homosexuality	Low	(1) Casual homosexuality	(2) Personalized homosexuality
	High	(3) Homosexuality as a situated activity	(4) Homosexuality as a way of life

These types merge into each other, and contain many possible variations within themselves. Thus what might begin as 'casual homosexual' encounters in the schoolboy lavatories may take on added significance later in life and become 'personalized homosexuality'. Further what is called 'homosexuality as a way of life' may have a number of varieties; from the individual who makes his money from it (the hustler), to the individual who spends most of his time championing it (the Gay Liberationist). Because of these variations and ambiguities, I wish to point to the boundaries of each type.

1 Casual homosexuality is a fleeting homosexual encounter (real or imaginary) which, while it may involve several people, remains only marginally socially structured and fails to have an overwhelming significance for the actors. Schoolboy masturbation, schoolboy crushes, and the casual sexual attraction of one man for another[12] are examples of this. There is probably a great deal of this kind of homosexuality, although little is known about it[13] and it remains insulated from becoming significant to the individuals who are involved in it.

2 *Personalized homosexuality* is the kind of homosexuality which has traditionally been the concern of clinicians. The homosexual experience becomes a pivotal point of an individual's life, but he remains isolated from any well-developed group structures that could organize and support his experience.

This form, like the others, has several variants within it – including both the group that researchers most frequently study and the group that researchers are least likely to study. The first group are those individuals most likely to find themselves upon the psychiatrist's couch or inside a prison cell with a highly personal homosexual problem, and these were for a long time the most popular collecting sources for data on 'homosexuals'. While one cannot be sure of anything statistically in this area, several recent studies have pointed to the possibility that psychiatric and imprisoned individuals are more likely to take homosexuality as a solitary experience, limiting themselves to chance encounters and impersonal contacts.[14] One respondent who finally found himself upon a psychiatric couch at the age of forty related how he had spent the previous sixteen years meeting homosexuals furtively, and infrequently, in public conveniences, but had never been able to sustain a relationship for more than one night: he had never met another 'homosexual' socially. This respondent was not socially isolated – he had contacts and knew about the 'cottaging' scene, and this fits more appropriately into the fourth category. At the same time most of his homosexual experiences seem to fit into cell two, since while he was constantly aware of his homosexuality, and had turned it into one of the dominating features of his life, he knew nothing of the gay world, and had only the most meagre experience of sociable homosexuality with other people. Most of the time it remained central to his consciousness while isolated from any form of group organization.

The second category comprises those individuals whose homosexual experiences are acute, but who are in such isolation from others that it is almost impossible to locate them. While the isolated homosexual is often talked about, very little is known about him – the Albany Survey[15] revealed that one-tenth of their sample, which numbered 2,600, had no friends or acquaintances that could be called 'homosexuals', and less than a half of the sample had more than a dozen 'homosexual' friends. Again, of course, even these figures tell us little about the group this subcategory really implies – for all of these had at least heard of the Albany Trust, and thus were not totally socially isolated. Indeed, this group becomes a research impossibility; I know of at least one researcher who set out with the task of locating some isolated homosexuals and gave up in mid-course. Their form of experience is at present uncharted.

3 Homosexuality as a situated activity: In a number of contexts, individuals may experience homosexuality within an organized group but not come to see themselves as homosexuals or to make it a central part of their life style. The most frequently cited base for this experience are same-sex residential settings – prisons, boarding schools, military camps[16] – where many members become involved in regular and socially organized homosexual activity without coming to see themselves as homosexuals. But there are probably a number of other such settings, such as those described by Humphreys among 'straight' married men in public conveniences and those described by Reiss among boy prostitutes (Humphreys, 1970; Reiss, 1961). In both these cases, there is direct and structured homosexual activity; but the participants (some of them at any rate) do not come to see themselves as homosexual. The boundaries of this category are likely to collapse into the fourth category, however, if the situated activity is recurrent without any mechanism for insulating oneself from a homosexual self-conception.

4 Homosexuality as a way of life: Some recent studies have commented that homosexuality is increasingly becoming a life style rather than an individual condition (Dank, 1971). Individuals experiencing this form of homosexuality have defined themselves as homosexuals; have made it a central part of their life style; have developed fairly stable patterns of interaction with other self-defined homosexuals; and have fostered their own series of beliefs, values, and perspectives on homosexuality. In many ways, this could be called a homosexual subculture.

The notion of 'way of life', however, conceals the many different forms of homosexuality encompassed by such a classification. On one level, there are a series of well-developed formal institutions – the homosexual bars and clubs, the homophile movements, the homosexual church – where, within an organized framework, homosexuality becomes the reason for the existence of the institution and provides meanings for homosexuals to develop as life styles. There can be little doubt that many of the people who frequent gay bars, belong to the nuclei of the homophile movements or who participate in the militant activities of the Gay Liberation Front have transformed their homosexual experiences into a dominating way of life. At another level, homosexuality emerges as a way of life around which friendship cliques are able to develop. Many homosexuals remain relatively unconnected with the more public and formally organized aspects of homosexual life, but through their friends are still able to develop informal but highly organized life styles, involving living together and meeting in each other's homes.

In the chapters to follow, I will primarily be considering this form of homosexuality – because it is the most amenable to sociological inquiry. I believe, however, that the other three types would make interesting and important studies.

6 Some issues in the societal reactions to homosexuality

The single most important factor about homosexuality as it exists in this culture is the perceived hostility of the societal reactions that surround it. From this one critical factor flow many of the features that are distinctive about homosexuality. It renders the business of becoming a homosexual a process that is characterized by problems of access, problems of guilt and problems of identity. It leads to the emergence of a subculture of homosexuality. It leads to a series of interaction problems involved with concealing the discreditable stigma. And it inhibits the development of stable relationships among homosexuals to a considerable degree (Plummer, 1974a). Homosexuality as a social experience simply cannot be understood without an analysis of the societal reactions towards it.

Given the importance of 'reactions' in shaping the nature of homosexual experiences, it is surprising that most studies of homosexuality perform what would have appeared to be the impossible: they divorce homosexuality from the societal context, take for granted the existence of 'reactions', and study homosexuality as an individualistic phenomenon. But I am arguing that the homosexual experience is very much a social product, variable between cultures and historical periods, and that it simply cannot be comprehended apart from the broader societal context in which it is enmeshed. If I labour this point, it is because I have been frequently challenged that 'when all is said and done, homosexuality is basically a psychological/personality problem – and the sociological contribution is really only minimal'. I do not deny the importance of the psychological approach, but I do deny the validity of those psychological approaches which fail to consider the location of the homosexual in a hostile society: in saying that, I reject much of the extant clinical literature as reductionist and erroneous.[1]

While subsequent chapters will examine the homosexual experience juxtaposing it with the societal reactions, this chapter will be concerned with some problems involved in the reactions themselves. There is very little known about these responses, and much that needs to be known: this chapter serves as little more than a prolegomenon for fuller research. After a brief look at cross-cultural reactions, I will consider the nature and origins of reactions in contemporary England and America.

Cross-cultural reactions

Homosexuality is not always condemned with the vitriol that it has been in those cultures directly influenced by the Judaeo-Christian tradition, as any brief review of the historical and anthropological literature reveals. Ford and Beach in the classic statement of sexual patterns in simpler societies found that in 64 per cent of the societies studied ($n = 76$), homosexuality was considered acceptable for some groups; while Gebhard reports on a survey of 193 world cultures where only 14 per cent rejected homosexuality (Ford and Beach, 1952: ch. 7; Weltge, 1969: 4). Similarly, Westermarck's historical survey in the earlier part of the twentieth century, along with other more recent reviews such as de Becker's, suggest strongly that in a number of cultures throughout history, homosexuality has been tolerated if not condoned (Westermarck, 1917; de Becker, 1967; Churchill, 1967; Karlen, 1971). There are controversies over all these findings, but at their most general they indicate that homosexuality is not always treated with extreme severity, and that on occasions it may be positively accepted.[2]

These studies are primarily concerned with simpler societies and societies of the past; there is little documentation of the reactions found in contemporary industrial and industrializing societies. Yet it is these societies where hostility towards homosexuality is generally quite pronounced.[3] In the Western world, 'the ethical position on homosexuality . . . is unequivocal. It is condemned as wrong; a sinful, moral disease' (Cappon, 1965: 159). More specifically, as Kinsey (1953: 47) notes: 'There are practically no other European groups, unless it be England, and few if any other cultures elsewhere in the world which have become as disturbed over male homosexuality as we have in the United States.'

In England and America the reaction towards homosexuals has been particularly hostile – indeed, for some authors such as Gorer, the reaction takes an extreme significance in understanding national character (Gorer, 1948). Other writers have recently begun to characterize this phenomenon with such names as 'dread of homosexuality' (Hoffman, 1968), 'homophobia' (Smith, 1971; Weinberg, 1973), 'homoerotophobia' (Churchill, 1967) and 'anti-homosexualism'

(Hacker, 1971). It is this phenomenon, as it exists in England and America, which will be the central concern in what follows.

The nature of the societal reactions towards homosexuals

Some researchers now pay homage to the great variety of homosexual experiences, to the sensitive process of building up homosexual meanings, to the elements of choice that confront the homosexual, and to the pluralistic ignorance that leads to individuals experiencing homosexuality privately, while publicly denying it. While such advances have been taking place in the study of homosexuality itself, little similar progress has been made in the study of societal reactions. When 'reactions' are mentioned, they are often assumed to be unanimous, well defined and stable; individuals are assumed to experience hostility in an automatic and invariant fashion; what they 'say' about homosexuals is supposed to mirror what they 'do' to homosexuals. While the sphere of studying deviant *actors* has become more sophisticated in recent years, the study of deviance *reactors* has remained generally meagre. In this section, therefore, I explore the extant studies of reactions towards homosexuality, before presenting some critical comments which lead to an alternative research path.

Reactions to homosexuals: the existing research

There are few studies that provide data on the reactions towards homosexuality, and most of these avoid situated analyses of the ways in which people actually respond to homosexuals in concrete situations, in preference for the 'easier to manage' standard questionnaire and interview on attitudes. Individuals – most typically students – are approached to express their views on moral issues in general, and homosexuality in particular. Such studies generally assume the existence of some preformed structure known as an 'attitude' which can be simply 'released' to the interviewer, and I will comment upon this more critically later. In addition, a congruence between 'words and deeds' is often unwarrantedly assumed: many individual actors may 'release' hostile attitudes in general about homosexuals, while simultaneously maintaining close relationships with specific homosexuals as 'honourable exceptions' (Deutscher, 1966).[4]

Such studies of attitudes to homosexuality cannot be taken as a very reliable guide to either what people actually believe or what they would do in a concrete situation. They may even become part of a global reified notion of 'societal reaction' which precipitates a self-fulfilling prophecy, an issue to be taken up more fully later.

Such studies which tap attitudes through questionnaire techniques fall into three main groups: (a) those whose *central* concern is with 'scientifically' tapping responses towards homosexuals (e.g. Kitsuse, 1962; Steffensmeier, 1970; Dunbar *et al.*, 1973); (b) those with a loose sociological orientation towards social problems, and which gather data on homosexuality as part of a broader project (e.g. Simmons, 1965; Rooney and Gibbons, 1966); (c) those conducted by market-research agencies, which simply 'poll' opinions (cf. Lofland, 1969: 20–1; Oberholtzer, 1971: 33). The latter are, of course, the most dubious.

Many of the earlier studies in groups (b) and (c) above were especially concerned with tapping the attitudes to legal changes, and thus much of the work on attitudes towards homosexuality is really about law reform. Other work has attempted to tap the general imagery or stereotypy held by the public about homosexuals. One or two have tried to study the actual response of society's members to homosexuals through interviews. I shall consider each of these in turn briefly.

(a) Legal changes: Most of the knowledge about attitudes towards legalizing homosexual activity has been provided periodically by market-research agencies but it remains unexciting, unconvincing and uninformative. For example, in 1960 Gallup showed that 47 per cent were against a change in the law, 38 per cent favoured a change, and 17 per cent were uncertain. In 1964, Gallup found only 26 per cent of the population thought that homosexuals should be punished by the law. In 1965, National Opinion Polls found that 36 per cent agreed with the statement that 'Homosexual acts between consenting adults over 21 in private should be regarded as criminal', and 63 per cent disagreed. Such a sampling of figures could be taken as indicating a mild drift towards increasing permissiveness, but there are difficulties in interpretation which even the opinion-pollsters themselves recognize. Thus, one survey (British Market Research Bureau, 1963: 4) commented:

> Many people's views about homosexuality were [found to be] vague and fluid, not to mention inconsistent. Few had thought out their ideas at all – most reacted largely in terms of feelings mixed with (often contradictory) 'okay' opinions probably borrowed from reading matter. It is thus likely that opinions are liable to be extremely vulnerable to propaganda – in either direction and especially if the propaganda has some authoritative backing.

It is difficult to draw any conclusions from this material.[5] More important, though still inadequate empirically, are those studies that have attempted to place attitudes to legal changes in a theoretical

105

context. In England, for example, Walker surveyed Oxford under-graduates and others with a view to testing the declaratory theory of the law – the theory that the law symbolizes the values of a society and serves to strengthen any one individual's commitment to that moral order. To change the law is to change the moral order; to maintain an unenforceable law on the statute book may thus be justifiable to maintain certain moral standards in a society (Walker and Argyle, 1964; Leiser, 1973). These studies tested the declaratory theory by asking respondents for their attitudes on the morality of certain acts, including homosexuality, while modifying their legal status. There was little support for the theory, but it could be argued that such small-scale studies fail to take into account the broader time dimension[individuals may still see homosexuality as immoral even when the law changes, but they may come to view it as less immoral over time. Asking students at one point in time in experimental situations is not a sufficient refutation of the theory. More important then would be an ongoing historical study of changing attitudes before and after the law change in England in 1967.

(b) General traits: Several recent studies suggest that the 'public' mistakenly approaches homosexuality with seriously misleading stereotypes. For example (Ruitenbeck, 1963: 81):

> In spite of increased information, the stereotype of the homosexual still colours people's ideas. The 'gay' boy is effeminate in manner: he knows more about dressing women than any women can and uses his knowledge to make women look grotesque, and so states his hostility to the sex. He inhabits the elegant, small art galleries, the showrooms of the interior decorator who fill the rooms of people too unimaginative to furnish their own houses, the expensive florist shops, the theatres . . . and, of course, he is neurotic.

These are overgeneralized statements, and what is now required is research that clearly tells us what images society's members actually do hold of homosexuals. Much work has been done on the stereotypes held of minority groups such as Jews and Negroes, but little has been done with deviant groups. The work of Jerry Simmons (1965; 1969) is a beginning in this direction. He had conducted a series of preliminary studies into stereotypes, using both student and adult samples. In a first study, he asked respondents ($n = 180$) to reply to the question: 'What is deviance?' A wide variety of responses were elicited which ranged from alcoholics to 'know-it-all professors', but the homosexual was the most frequently cited group, 49 per cent of the respondents naming homosexuals as deviants. Subsequently, he asked students in a social-problems class to characterize some of these deviant groups. The question was open-ended and produced a range of statements about homosexuals (among others), two-thirds of which were stereotypical. From these very general statements, Simmons devised a more systematic check-list of seventy traits for each deviant, and 134 adults were then asked to rate various deviants by these traits. The prevalent imagery for the homosexual was that of sickness and abnormality, the per-centage figures for each trait being as follows: sexually abnormal (72%), perverted (52%), mentally ill (40%), maladjusted (40%), effeminate (29%), lonely (22%), insecure (21%), immoral (16%), repulsive (14%), frustrated (14%), weak-minded (12%), lacking self-control (12%), sensual (11%), oversexed (10%), dangerous (10%), sinful (10%), sensitive (10%).

In another study, Simmons tried to examine the amount of public intolerance towards homosexuals (and other deviants) by giving respondents a social-distance scale, in which they were asked to rate homosexuals from scale point 1 (='might marry') through to point 7 (would not accept as a member of this country). The homo-sexuals were rated as the lowest group on the scale, the rating of 5·0 equalling the stage of 'accepting the deviant in the community but wanting nothing at all to do with him'.[6]

In sum, Simmons's limited studies serve as useful starting-points for more detailed research. He highlights some of the contents of the stereotypes of homosexuals (though there are clearly methodological difficulties here), and he demonstrates how (in 1965) homosexuals were generally regarded as the most deviant of groups and the least tolerated.

At about the same time, Rooney and Gibbons (1966) studied the attitudes of 353 citizens in San Francisco towards policy changes and victimless crimes. Looking at policies in the spheres of abortion, homosexuality and drugs, the authors found greatest tolerance in the former and least in the latter. They found two stereotypes of homo-sexuality widespread: that of psychological disturbance and that of 'adult homosexuals are dangerous because they often try to seduce young boys'. The 'pathological' notion was supported by 86·7 per cent of the respondents, and the 'dangerous' notion by 69·1 per cent. Interestingly, a considerably smaller number in the population held the notion that homosexuals were 'swish' or effeminate (39 per cent).[7]

The emergent stereotypes of 'sick', 'dangerous' and 'swish' have subsequently been taken up in the work of Steffensmeier (1970). His concern was to tap the determinants of the societal reaction towards homosexuals held by students, and he utilizes a sample of 373 re-spondents – half of whom were given a questionnaire about lesbians. Using the same stereotyped notions described above, he found that they occupied a similar rank order as the Rooney and Gibbons study. More than two-thirds of the student population held the 'sickness' stereotype, and about one-third (38 per cent) of the respondents held the 'dangerous' stereotype. About one-fifth of the respondents held the 'swish' stereotype. At the other end of the scale – the direct rejection of stereotypes – he found that 12 per cent rejected the 'sickness' view, 39·1 per cent rejected the 'danger' view and 52·2 per cent rejected the 'swish' view.

All the studies mentioned above are American, and draw a broadly similar conclusion about the 'prevalence of the "sickness stereotype" of the homosexual'. This is not surprising, given the tremendous impact that psychotherapy and psychiatric ideologies have had in the States (Berger, 1965). But it may not be possible to generalize from these studies to England, where psychiatric ideologies are not so prevalent. The little relevant work – from very simple question-answer surveys – suggests a wide range of stereotypes, only some of which have close connections with 'sickness'. Schofield, for example, in a follow-up study of nearly 400 young people in 1970, found that only 21 per cent of his respondents felt homosexuality was a 'sickness to be pitied', and Gorer's market research involving 2,000 randomly sampled respondents found that only 10 per cent of the men and 13 per cent of the women perceived homosexuality as a sickness or mental illness. These figures may well be different as a consequence of different methodologies, but they are large enough to suggest some cultural differences.

If these researches do not indicate such a prevalent 'sickness' imagery, what images are held in England? Some feeling of the diversity of the views held – if indeed they were held – can be seen from the findings of Gorer (1971: ch. 9), shown in Table 5.

TABLE 5   *Reactions to homosexuals in a sample of English respondents*

	Male (%)	*Female* (%)
1 Revulsion, disgust	23	25
2 Moral disapproval	5	4
3 Dislike, against it	10	6
4 Odd, queer	14	12
5 Ridiculous	4	2
6 Sick	10	13
7 Can't help it	5	9
8 Need medical help	3	2
9 Pity and sorrow	16	28
10 Tolerance	16	8

Put like this, it is clear that possibly nearer one-third of Gorer's sample hold views that are near to the sickness viewpoint (categories

6–9). At the same time, his sample has a high proportion of respondents who view homosexuality in quite strong negative terms of disapproval (over one-third). It is possible, on this basis, that England has more negative stereotypes and America has more sickness notions.

But then there is Schofield's work, and this throws much of the previous discussion into confusion.[8] His sample of respondents was not a random one – it was a subgroup of 2,000 people in their mid-twenties who he had previously interviewed in the early 1960s – but it emerged generally as a very tolerant one. While 14 per cent of his respondents were disgusted by homosexuality, and 21 per cent saw it as a sickness – some 58 per cent viewed it in a favourable or stoically accepting light. The 58 per cent may be broken down into four subgroups: 5 per cent who were 'generally tolerant', 30 per cent who were 'stoically tolerant', 16 per cent who were 'happy if they just kept to themselves', and 7 per cent who viewed it 'favourably'. Further, in answer to the question 'What needs to be done about it?', only 7 per cent responded in a punitive fashion, while some 70 per cent responded in a permissive fashion. In answer to the question 'Do you think it is a problem these days?', 42 per cent viewed it as a problem, while 48 per cent did not see it in this light. These are quite large figures for a society that is generally perceived to be hostile to homosexuals, and it may well be indicative of an age variation – given that this study tapped the views only of a particular age set and one that is generally considered to hold the most permissive views.

In addition to these somewhat general attitude surveys, a little work has been done on the attitudes of specific groups. Thus, for example, Coleman in a survey on homosexuality conducted among members of the Church Assembly in England discovered that 90 respondents saw homosexuality as sinful, 60 did not always see it as such, and 26 were undecided (Oberholtzer, 1971: 185–99). Studies conducted among the police have also provided materials on police attitudes towards the homosexual: Niederhoffer, for example, in a study of 186 policemen, asked them to rank sixteen groups – including juvenile gangs, psychos, bohemians, drug addicts and prostitutes – according to which they disliked most and which they liked most. Homosexuals were the second most disliked, figuring only after 'cop-fighters' who came first (Niederhoffer, 1969: 130).

(c) Relationships: A third area of inquiry straddles attitude and situational studies: it asks respondents about their interaction with homosexuals. The seminal study here is that by Kitsuse (1962), who interviewed more than 700 students, found from this group 75 who had known a homosexual, and subsequently explored their responses and relationships. The study documents the manner in which the respondents discovered they were interacting with homosexuals (through indirect evidence, direct evidence and over sexual propositions); how they imputed meaning to the situation; and how they responded to the awareness that their interacting partner was a homosexual. Four kinds of response were noted: explicit disapproval and immediate withdrawal; explicit disapproval and subsequent withdrawal; implicit disapproval and partial withdrawal; no disapproval and relationship sustained. What is interesting about this study is the surprising number of students who gave the last response – and this in the early 1960s. As the author comments (Kitsuse, in Becker, 1964: 100):

> In none of the interviews does the subject react with extreme violence, explicitly define or directly accuse the deviant of being queer, a 'fairy' or other terms of opprobrium nor did any of them initiate legal sanctions against the deviant. In view of the extreme negative sanctions against homosexuality that are posited on theoretical grounds, the generally mild reactions of our subjects are striking.

It is important to bear in mind of course that his respondents were students, and that the norms and values of such groups may be somewhat different from the rest of the population. As part of my exploratory research in this field, I interviewed twenty social-science students in their first years at two London colleges and found they all displayed in the interview context the same kind of general 'permissiveness' towards homosexuals in the first instance. Even one boy who told me that a pass had been made at him by a homosexual in the preceding days – a pass which he had explicitly rejected – could still say that: 'I think it's abnormal. But let them get on with it, as long as they don't bother me. If you want to go out with a girl you have to ask her – it should be the same with a boy.' One girl, however, provided me with a range of dutifully liberal answers for over half of the interview before frankly admitting that she felt 'sickened by homosexuals' and she 'couldn't conceal it from me any longer'. The interview had provided initially a context in which 'student attitudes' ought to be presented: but over the course of the interview she had altered this definition, and gave me quite different attitudes. This strengthened my belief in the importance of situated analysis, and was one reason why I did not consider it a worthwhile enterprise to develop the small-scale interview any further.

Correlates of attitudes towards homosexuals: In the section above, I have depicted a range of possible attitudes. One is now led to ask the question: are they randomly distributed throughout the population, or are they systematically more likely to be found among particular groups? Simmons, for example, in the studies mentioned earlier, found that the more educated groups and the more liberal groups were less likely to hold stereotypes. Smith (1971) in a study of 130 undergraduates found that those who reacted hostilely towards homosexuals were more likely to be sexually rigid, authoritarian and have higher status consciousness than those who were not hostile.

Before discussing a specific piece of research that has dealt with this problem, some very general hypotheses about possible links between homosexual attitudes and social variables can be made, drawing from a number of studies both of attitudes towards homosexuals and more general attitudes. It can be suggested that hostile reactions towards homosexuality increase as one moves down the social-class scale, up the involvement in religion scale, up the age scale, from the town to the village, from the South – especially London – to the North – especially Scotland, from the opposite sex to the same sex[9] and as one moves from permissive/liberal groups to authoritarian groups.

Such general statements are not meant to demonstrate discovered correlates, but rather only to imply that such correlations given current knowledge seem likely.

To discover the correlates of societal reactions will need careful and systematic research. Steffensmeier's work is an important step in this direction, emerging as potentially the most useful statement to date on this subject. His thesis sets out on the quest for 'determinants' of societal reactions, but I think it is more accurate to depict this quest as one for correlates rather than determinants. The author examines three important areas for their links with attitudes: demographic variables, general permissiveness, and respondent's perceptions of dangerousness. Using these three variables, Steffensmeier makes three main hypotheses:

1   Rejection of deviants will increase as their behaviours are perceived by the social audience as threatening or dangerous.

2   Rejection of deviants will increase relative to the degree of conventionality of the social audience.

3   Rejection of deviants will be related to certain background factors of the social audience.

His evidence strongly supports the first two hypotheses, but is more ambiguous on the third. Thus, for example, he suggests that students who hold stereotypes of the homosexual as 'sick' or 'dangerous' are more likely to reject the homosexual than those who do not hold such stereotypes. He also suggests that students who move in highly 'conventional' networks are likely to shun homosexuals. But his work did not generally find support for the notion that demographic variables such as class, age or religion were particularly significant correlates. One could, of course, argue with regard to this last variable that college students are highly similar in the first instance.

Steffensmeier uses his findings to make a plea for further analysis of an interactional kind. He argues that his research findings generally show the important role that interpersonal networks and significant others play in building up reactions, and the lesser role played by static social-demographic variables. He writes (1970: 93):

> Perhaps our research underlies what the interactionist sociologists have been saying, namely, that we need to look at the ongoing processes a person experiences if we are to succeed in understanding and predicting behaviour. The suggestion here is that when doing 'favourite native' research, sociologists might find it fruitful to place less emphasis on demographic variables, such as social class, commonly employed in mainstream sociology. Rather, a more fruitful approach might be to 'tap' the ongoing processes of a student's interaction network, part and parcel to the college scene.

Such a suggestion underlines the argument of this book.

Reactions to homosexuals: future research

The above research review demonstrates that, while beginnings have been made, there is a long way to travel before valid generalizations may be made. Although varying in sophistication, most of the studies described above avoid the kind of interactional analysis that Steffensmeier concludes would be most useful. Instead they assume that 'the public' holds specific attitudes or images of homosexuality which may be simply 'released' in the interview situation, and which may be validly depicted through summation. Such quantification of a highly fluid and variable phenomenon subsumed under the rubric of an 'attitude' makes little sense. Blumer (1969) has for a long time commented upon the way such studies defectively assume the existence of an entity called 'public opinion' which gives equal weighting to a large number of disparate individuals in many different social contexts who, in this instance, place homosexuality in varying degrees on a relevance hierarchy. Thus, for some members of the public, attitudes to homosexuals are non-existent and are socially created for the pollster; for others, attitudes may be clearer but weakly held; while, for a few, not only are the attitudes highly articulated but they are also effectively directed into paths of social action. This latter group constitutes effective public opinion, but is inevitably only a small section of the whole.

Not only do most of these studies suffer from an oversimplified notion of attitude, most of them fail to take into account the discrepancy that is likely to arise between words, deeds and feelings: 'What people say does not necessarily reflect what they do, and what they do does not necessarily show how they feel about it' (Grunwald, 1964: 2). The studies described above only tap what 'people say' and this in the highly atypical situation of the interview: they may not even tap what people 'say' in any other context (Matza, 1964: 48).

Even more worrying is the tendency for these studies to accumulate into a reified, solidified picture of hostility which serves as the basis for a self-fulfilling prophecy. The reactions presented above become globally packaged and presented in a way which conceals the variations in intensity and form they take in the day to day world. Such reactions purport to describe what is actually going on in society, what 'people' actually think, and may subsequently be fed back into society to influence what people do think and how homosexuals do perceive the situation. Indeed, homosexuals may come to see what was originally an uncrystallized, contradictory, ambiguous, ever-changing, weakly focused and highly variable individual reaction towards homosexuality as a unanimous, stable, well-defined, consistent and powerfully strong form of hostility. They may even come to perceive hostility where none exists.

The crux of these criticisms is a plea for detailed situated analyses of reactions towards homosexuals, consistent with interactionist principles. Instead of looking at abstracted, reified attitudes in non-relevant interview situations, research is required which depicts the ways in which members actually perceive, respond to and reflect upon homosexuality in face to face encounters. There is practically no research of this kind, only a few journalistic essays.

The few studies which do exist are very limited. Gerrassi (1966) has provided a useful, but journalistic, account of the reactions of one community (Boise) to a homosexual scandal – although it was written ten years after the event. Gallo et al. (1966) have provided a very full, but primarily legalistic description of the working of Los Angeles police departments in encounters with homosexuals, while Williams and Weinberg (1971) have looked at the reaction of military officials in their broader study of less than honourable discharge among homosexuals. These are modest beginnings indeed. Yet if the understanding of homosexuality in society is to advance, there must be an accelerated growth in studies akin to these. There must be a turn around from the obsessive concern with the homosexual that has characterized the field in the past, and a reorientation of researchers towards situated, contextual analyses of the ways in which specified groups perceive and respond towards homosexuality. We must eagerly await studies that show us how the media treat homosexuality; how control agents, teachers, parents, 'queer-bashers', employment agencies, moral crusaders, communities and friends respond to a 'homosexual in their midst'.[10] When such data are in, we will be in a better position to understand the situation of homosexuality.

The sources of homosexual hostility

While it is important to locate and describe the nature of societal reactions towards homosexuality, it is more important to explain such reactions. Bearing in mind the cautions made above, it can nevertheless be assumed that one pervasive reaction to homosexuality in this culture is that of hostility – 'homophobia'. The key question to ask here is why such a phenomenon should exist.

From an interactionist perspective any answer to this question may be viewed in two ways: first, simply as a socially constructed 'account', used to legitimate and justify hostility, and, second, as a valid portrayal of why people actually respond in this fashion towards homosexuals. The two are always intermeshed, and the relationship between them is often a mystified one. Mystification occurs when the 'institutional order is so interpreted as to hide, as much as possible, its socially constructed nature' (Berger and Luckmann, 1967). Thus, a particular kind of domination relationship – one built upon oppression (Humphreys, 1972: ch. 2) – is obscured by a series of 'accounts' which give meaning to the relationship and render it part of a natural, taken-for-granted, 'objective' order. Members of a society not only can, but also should, respond hostilely to homosexuals because 'it's against God's law', 'it's unnatural', 'it's against the law', 'it's a sickness' and so forth (Berger and Luckmann, 1967).

Around the subject of homosexuality, then, has emerged a vast superstructure of beliefs and imagery which help to conceal an underlying relationship by which dominant heterosexual groups tacitly but persistently oppress and attack homosexual groups. Whether this domination takes the form of being burnt at the stake as a heretic or murdered on a common by 'queer-bashers'; whether it takes the form of penitentials in medieval cloisters or exclusion from employment and country; whether it takes the form of being pilloried in the market square or mimicked and mocked on television and radio; whether it takes the form of trial and imprisonment or psychiatric examination and therapy; whether it is devalued as sin, sickness, crime or simply a sorrowful state – in each and every case the structure of the relationship is politically similiar: a dominant group, probably unwittingly, coerces and controls a subordinate one. The system of sexual relationships may thus be viewed as political.

Of course, it may be instantly objected that such a statement is itself an 'account' – socially constructed in a society which increasingly views deviance as a political phenomenon (Horowitz, 1968). In a society dominated by religion, homosexual hostility is justified by reference to God-made laws; in a society dominated by the fear of heretics, homosexual hostility is linked to the persecution of witches; in a society that views homosexuality as a sickness, hostility towards them is also explained in 'personality' terms; in a society with growing political consciousness, hostility then enters that arena of debate. 'Accounts' of hostility can thus always be socially situated, and the account which follows is likewise a social product.

Towards an interactionist account of homosexual hostility

While a number of accounts of homosexual hostility do exist, many of them contain assumptions that an interactionist remains sceptical about.

On a psychological level, homosexual hostility is often attributed to an instinctual feeling of disgust,[11] ambivalence about one's gender and/or one's bisexuality,[12] scapegoating by those suffering from authoritarian personalities and/or deprived backgrounds (Cory, 1953: ch. 2), and moral indignation from those suffering from a loss of status (Gusfield, 1963). Such theories – instincts, ambivalences, deprivations – are similar in form to those which social scientists would now have doubts about if applied to the 'deviant', but can be still evoked without much controversy to explain 'reactors'.

On a sociological level, homosexual hostility has been explained by reference to an ideational theory of matrist–patrist cultures (Taylor, 1965b); a functional theory of sexual norms which suggests that hostility serves to regulate an explosive drive, and maintain the familial system and the gender role system (Davis, 1971) and a functional theory which suggests that de-eroticization of everyday life serves to facilitate the economic productive system (Reich, 1969; Marcuse, 1969; Altman, 1971). Such theories provide only the most general of accounts and swerve dangerously between absolutism and tautology. While much can be learnt from the above theorizings, the loose assumptions upon which they are built remain a challenge to the interactionist. Thus, while the interactionist works from a notion of essential world open-endedness, much of the above assumes implicitly the existence of an all-powerful, energy-conserving sexual drive in need of control. While the interactionist works from a notion of inherent asexuality, the extant theories often assume bisexuality – and an ever-present tendency for such repressed bisexuality to erupt into 'homosexual panic'. While the interactionist sees man as busy imposing meanings upon his world, the existing

115

theories suffer frequently from an absolutist assumption that global laws of hostility exist independently of man's construction. Such laws usually overpredict the amount of hostility to be found. Further, while the interactionist assumes a learning model of socialization, many extant theories see hostility emerging through personality malfunctioning. Thus, while the interactionist would account for individual hostility largely in terms of (a) internalization of societal norms of hostility towards homosexuality, and (b) conscious consideration of the issues at hand, most of the extant theories assume that such hostility is due to personality deficiencies. It may even be that 'society's' hostility to homosexuals is much more rational than liberal social scientists would have us believe.

An interactionist model: As Lemert has noted, the symbolic interactionist perspective that stems from Meadian theory is not very helpful at explaining the origins of societal reactions (Lemert, 1972). Nevertheless, in constructing a model of homosexual hostility there are a number of related theories that can be drawn upon (Berger and Luckmann, 1967; Douglas, 1970; Erickson, 1967; Long, 1958).

The starting-point of such a model is with the three dialectical moments discussed by Berger and Luckmann – of men creating 'reality', internalizing that 'reality' and having that 'reality in turn define and create them'. Any one of these 'moments' may be used as taking-off points, but will always involve looking at the others. The previous section of this chapter has described aspects of this 'reality' that members hold, but in that discussion I only looked at the more directly obvious area of attitudes held about homosexuals by heterosexuals. This is a very myopic view since, as I have suggested previously, there are a number of direct and indirect elements that need considering in any given 'reality'. Furthermore, I have so far spoken as if reactions to homosexuality include only those specific images, etc., directed towards homosexuals, but this clearly entails a serious omission. For as well as these direct reactions, there are also indirect reactions which define the world-taken-for-granted views with regard to non-homosexual but closely related matters. Thus, the family as a social institution does not of itself condemn homosexuality, but its existence in certain forms may implicitly provide a model that renders the homosexual experience invalid. Likewise, a gender-role system does not of itself condemn homosexuality, but again may do so implicitly. Studies of the 'objectified reality' into which individuals are born requires analysis of both the positive and negative aspects of the sex elements mentioned above.

Such a reality must be accounted for as the end-product of a series of historical incidents, incidents which do not necessarily reflect systematic conflicts or possess underlying logic. Indeed, given the complexities of modern society, it seems unlikely that they should display any rational fit. The model of historical development which an interactionist model favours is that suggested by Long (1958) and developed by Buckner (1971): order becomes the outcome of many historical processes, not of planning. The only way to comprehend the 'objectified reality' of homosexual oppression is to take each of the elements located above and to trace their historical emergence – an emergence which may take one through analyses of economic conflicts, status conflicts, personal interests, philosophical debates, religious quarrels, chance outcomes, government reports, pressure-group politics, organizational dilemmas and rational decision-making (e.g. Bailey, 1955).

For example, legislation against homosexuality in England may be seen as the outcome of a series of shifting and often ill-defined interests. The legal sources of homosexual oppression in England seem to stem partly from the continuation of ecclesiastical law into secular law, and partly from what may be considered as political or chance factors extraneous to the issue of homosexuality itself. From the accounts given of the emergence of the Sodomy Laws in 1533 under the rule of Henry VIII, it seems possible that the law was 'incidental to the principal anti-clerical measures of the session' and that it was used primarily as a means for Henry to gain strength against the church (Hyde, 1970: 39). The later central Act, the Labouchère Amendment in 1885 – which legislated against homosexuality *per se* rather than just acts of sodomy – emerged as a peripheral amendment to a bill which aimed at 'the protection of women and girls and the suppression of brothels'. It was introduced by Henry Labouchère, a man who 'was in the habit of tabling amendments of substance to nearly every bill that came before the house', and who had, 'it seems, no special interest in the subject of the bill in question', and was passed with a minimum of discussion. 'It is extremely doubtful if either parliament or the government of the day were aware of the substantial change they had directed in the law against homosexuality' (Robinson, 1964: 453–4). If these commentators' reflections are valid, then the emergence of homosexual laws in this country cannot be seen as the direct result of an intensive moral crusade. More recent changes in the law, still awaiting detailed study, impressionistically seem to be the result of a highly successful pressure-group campaign – that is, the work of the Homosexual Law Reform Society. It is difficult to find in these three, admittedly ill-analysed and tentative, examples of legal change, evidence of the systematic oppression of one economic class over another, or one status group over another. The picture is much more complex and subtle than that.

Nevertheless, to say that the interactionist model in general de-

117

picts the construction of realities as the end-product of many, criss-crossing interests and chance factors is not to imply that power is equally distributed or that it is held equally by groups in different areas of debate. 'The idea that no single group organizes everything should not obscure the fact that there are differences in power be-tween differently situated individuals and groups' (Buckner, 1971: 40). Thus *some* groups are likely to dominate others in *some* areas, the economic sphere being only the most obvious example. But the domination should not be seen as automatic and all-encompassing, as it is in some models.

It certainly seems likely, although analyses of this are just begin-ning, that the sphere of sexuality is one area where domination of one group by another has been very pronounced. As the Women's Liberation literature increasingly suggests, men have constantly dominated women. Further, one may suggest that heterosexuals have dominated homosexuals, married couples have dominated single people, and a range of erotic minorities have been oppressed by groups of 'restrictive' heterosexuals. Little is really known about these kinds of conflicts – only very recently have they become at all explicit in discussions (Altman, 1971). But if one is to understand the ways in which the 'objectified' sexual realities have been built up, I am suggesting that this can only be done if one conducts detailed historical analyses of sexual conflicts – along with the criss-crossing conflicts of interests I have depicted earlier. This area is worthy of prolonged analysis.[13]

'The natural order': It is important to stress that the sexual world into which any individual is born is merely the end-product of historical actions of real, living men, and not some inevitable, God-given, nature-inspired order, and further that this reality is a *social con-glomerate* constantly subject to change rather than a social system (Douglas, 1971b: 275). This said, however, for any individual member of a society, there is tremendous pressure upon him to apprehend his reality as if it were inevitable, absolute and unchanging. To fail to do so, is to live in a Kafkaesque nightmare of uncertainty, flux and diversity. He cannot constantly question the historical origins of each element of reality that he is confronted with; he cannot constantly question the validity of the legitimations provided to 'explain' and 'account' for the existing reality; he cannot con-stantly consider alternative paths of actions to those he is routinely given. What was once, and still is, a man-made order becomes mystified as a Natural Order. Such a 'natural order' is clearly deeply conservative and resistant to change. Scott (1972: 20) writes:[14]

To most people it is reality and therefore not a thing that is subject to change. [It] serves as a kind of 'protective cocoon' shielding us from realities that are harsh and even intolerable. There is an understandable reluctance on the part of most people to permit anyone to alter this cocoon. Moreover, [it] is resistant to change because it functions in a kind of self confirming way. Its 'validity' is proven each time we use the categories of perception embedded in it to view reality, since that reality is arranged in our minds by the categories with which we view it. These experiences lead us to believe that our way of viewing the world is natural and correct. Finally, [it] is resistant to change because it is a public order. As Mary Douglas put it: 'It has authority, since each is induced to assent because of the assent of others. But its public character makes its categories more rigid – a private person may revise his patterns of assumptions or not. It is a private matter. But cultural categories are public matters. They cannot so easily be subject to revision.'[15]

This man-made and man-making 'order', then, contains within it a series of public, standardized categories which members take for granted. These categories have emerged in historical situations and provide clues as to what dominant political groups have held in high regard or found functional. Yet clearly, and especially in complex societies, social experiences are rarely so neat and orderly as to be exhausted by the prevailing system of classifications. Experiences will always arise that fall outside of the prevailing system, and which thereby serve as a threat to the stability of that order. If they cannot be accounted for, neutralized or disposed of, they stand as evidence for all to see that the world is not as it seems. The system comes under attack: order is threatened.[16]

Given the widely held public categories of this society, homosexuality exists as an anomaly that potentially serves to disrupt the order unless it can be accounted for. Three sets of categories seem particularly challenged by the existence of homosexuality – though undoubtedly there are others.

First, classification systems surrounding the family and marriage come under threat – the 'natural order' takes it for granted that the family is universal, that the family is the only appropriate context for childbirth and child-rearing, and that every member of society will belong to a family. It is one of the central statuses ascribed to individuals. Furthermore, it is closely linked to the 'natural' tendency of members to seek and sustain couple relationships – 'that for every boy and every girl, there's just one love in this whole world'. Whether these phenomena are seen as instincts or institutions, they come to be taken for granted; their original man-made nature is lost. The existence of homosexuality is an anomaly which threatens these institutions – by showing that people do not have to live in family units, do not have to have children, do not have to 'fall in love' with one partner alone, indeed do not even have to 'fall in love'. The prevailing categories could be irrevocably damaged if the existence of such anomalies are not eliminated.

A second important classification system challenged is that of gender. As Garfinkle has described, members function with notions of 'natural, normally-sexed persons' – one important component of which is that the world 'is populated by two sexes and only two sexes, "male" and "female"' (Garfinkle, 1967: 122). The homosexual stands as an example that the world may not be quite so dramatically simple – there may be shades of gender, rather than absolute entities. Again, such anomalies have to be reckoned with if the 'natural order' is to retain its credibility.

Third, classification systems exist around the area of sexual experiences. In the past especially, a utilitarian meaning of sexual experiences – sex linked to procreation – was taken as an objective reality, and the existence of people who were clearly involved in sexuality of a non-procreative kind must have served as a challenge to the existing order. Today, when I suspect sexual categorizations are much less clear anyway, the homosexual may not serve as such a threat in this sphere – although, following Erickson's discussion of the functions of deviance, homosexual hostility may become more necessary in situations of ambiguity in order to sharpen some boundaries of normality. There must always be 'deviants' for there to be definitions of normality, and when existing boundaries become blurred, 'group members may single out and label as deviant someone whose behaviour had previously gone unnoticed' (Erickson, 1966).

In any event, the existence of homosexuality in this culture does pose a series of threats to the prevailing systems of classification about gender, family and sexuality. Such threats are partly coped with by noting the anomaly as 'deviant' – evil, dangerous, heretical, malfunctional, pathological, sick and so forth. By rendering homosexuality as 'strange', as something outside the 'normal', a first step towards eliminating the anomaly has been taken. It is seen now as a peculiarity outside of the everyday world – still requiring explanation, but already discredited in any claims it may make for legitimacy. A second step is to provide explanations for its existence, using the vocabulary and taken-for-granted axioms of the existing 'natural order'. Among the strategies employed here may be denial, normalization and conversion. *Denial* involves a failure or unwillingness to recognize the existence of homosexuality, and thereby to make it appear so uncommon that the phenomenon can be dismissed as 'something not worth bothering about', 'a freak of nature'. Given

120

the generally low visibility of homosexuality, denial may be quite a frequent mechanism for coping with the anomaly. *Normalization* involves the effort to force anomalies to change so that they fit the prevailing categorization, or at any rate so that they can be explained as part of them. Thus, for example, the homosexual may be explained in terms of being a 'woman in a man's body', or as 'really a woman even if he looks like a man', and so forth. The conventional categories of 'normal-sexed' persons are retained. Some of the more disturbing features of homosexuality – the promiscuous threat to the family, for example – may be normalized by suggesting that even homosexuals really wish to achieve stable couple relationships and 'gay marriages'. In doing this, the 'natural order' may become strengthened by deviants. *Conversion* involves demonstrating the ability of the 'natural order' to control and contain alien forces – homosexuals may be cured through therapy, for example. Such visible control of deviance becomes another effective means by which a social order tangibly displays its potency. In all of these cases, a potential anomalous threat is brought back into the conventional order and that order demonstrates its viability and validity. The existence of homosexual hostility may thus come to serve important functions in maintaining the existing social order.

Conclusion

In this chapter I have attempted to bring together existing materials that have dealt with two crucial problems: the nature and sources of reactions towards homosexuals. In reviewing the existing sparse literature, I have revealed its limitations and argued the need for situated descriptive analyses of reactions, and for historical studies of their origins. All of this can only be seen as a preliminary therefore to systematic and detailed research. However, without this kind of research it is unlikely that an understanding of homosexuality can advance very far. For, as I am arguing throughout, the homosexual experience in this culture must be seen as very largely a creation of the society in which it is enmeshed.

7 The individual reaction to homosexuality: the homosexual career

For the clinician, the manufacturing of homosexuals takes place at birth or in childhood: certain individuals placed in particular familial situations or endowed with particular biological properties are unconsciously, unwillingly and often unhappily driven towards homosexual motivations, motivations so all-encompassing that they may be termed 'conditions' or 'personalities'. The account of becoming a homosexual effectively begins and ends in childhood.

Not so for the sociologist. For him, the process of becoming is seen as a life-long activity involving the interaction of self with others, while personalities and conditions are transformed into 'roles' strung together by a slender thread of memory and entailing various degrees of commitment. Such a process normally passes through two phases – one where emotions are nurtured and a relatively stable 'base world' is carved out for the individual, and a later one where the base world is constantly modified and new roles and knowledge are learnt (Berger and Luckmann, 1967: 149–66). At each stage, 'what a person becomes, including how he behaves, will depend in large measure on the way he has been and continues to be assessed and defined by others' (Quinney, 1970: 244). The sociological portrait of becoming a homosexual is thus altogether wider in sweep: childhood experiences may be seen as preconditions for adult experiences, but the main focus of analysis shifts to the contingencies confronted in adult life. While very little research has been conducted into such contingencies, much work has been done in the other sphere.[1] Many variable biological and psychological traits have been cited as causal, and while it will serve no useful purpose here to discuss them at length, I propose to briefly consider their general limitations before moving on to the main task of this chapter: an analysis of the processes involved in assuming a homosexual role.

Primary aetiology: problems and limitations

1 Methodological: Several studies have demonstrated how easy it is to plunge a knife right into the very heart of most homosexual research on methodological grounds (Hoffman, 1966; Schur, 1969a; Warren, 1972). Such studies work from non-representative, non-random samples. They uncritically adopt unwarranted assumptions. They believe too much in the power of the interview. They work from highly preselective questionnaires. They believe in the validity of the retrospective interpretation of their respondents. And so one may continue discrediting much research that has been conducted in a spirit of earnest inquiry.

Yet such methodological problems as I have raised above would, if taken seriously, not only throw into doubt the findings of homosexual research, but practically all research into deviant groups where sampling is difficult (Polsky, 1967; Habenstein, 1971). It is very easy to criticize these studies and very hard to provide alternatives. Rather, then, than simply abandoning such methods – a route that I have largely taken – research needs to be conducted that will highlight the nuances that surround such works, in an effort to bring into sharp focus their limitations, while allowing for the development of subsequent research programmes. Bieber's work, for example, looked at 106 homosexuals who volunteered for psychiatric treatment in the 1950s and explored the reasons for the emergence of homosexuality, concluding that 'A homosexual adaptation is a result of hidden but incapacitating fears of the opposite sex' (Bieber *et al.*, 1962: 303). The study provided a series of heterosexual controls, and was greeted by some as a 'well grounded statistical study',[2] 'the most authoritative study of its kind'[3] and as 'one of the very few scientifically oriented and revealing studies of homosexuality'.[4]

Because of its claim to fame, it has also received some of the most severe beatings of any study into homosexuality. I do not wish to go into these criticisms here, though it can be remarked that all of the 'aetiological errors' to be discussed here may be found within its pages. My point, criticisms notwithstanding, is simply that such a study has produced a considerable degree of discussion and refinement – a necessary condition for scientific progress. For example, the central challenge to its argument – that its findings were only applicable to a small, highly preselected group of psychiatric respondents – has produced a number of studies in which 'non-psychiatric' homosexuals were the respondents. The Bieber questionnaire has been reapplied to non-psychiatric samples, and the ambiguities noted (Evans, 1969; Gundlach, 1969; Hooker, 1969b). This kind of argument has also led to research with contrasting sampling sources, observing differences in response (Schofield, 1965a; Wein-

123

berg, 1970b). Thus, while most studies are open to criticism, these very criticisms hopefully lead towards an improvement of the methodological foundations; a task whose successful undertaking seems far away at present.

2 *Theoretical:* In homosexual research, as in much criminological research,[5] an empirical eclecticism has resulted in the production of much *ad hoc* listing of variables which contribute to the emergence of homosexuality – 'causes' ranging from an atavistic brain structure to 'the concealed attempt to experience the self in the penis of the other' (Hornitra, 1967). Westwood (1960: 17) relegates a list of such factors to a footnote:

> A summary of the theories on the cause of homosexuality would have to include: a biological anomaly; a hereditary defect; an immature form of skeletal development; endocrine imbalance; a child from a degenerate stock; pre-Oedipal aggression and the oral trauma of weaning; the castration complex; mother fixation; identification or rivalry with the parent of the opposite sex; faulty training during elimination learning; emotional excesses from a maladjusted upbringing; early dominance by one parent; absence of male influences in the home; regression to or fixation at an earlier libidinal level; ignorance in matters connected with sex; seduction during childhood or adolescence; early onset of adolescence; painful sex experiences at puberty; segregation of sexes during adolescence; fear of the opposite sex caused by feelings of inferiority; restraints on premarital intercourse; lack of sexual success.

This kind of causal nihilism has to be rejected. If there is ever to be an adequate scientific theory of the causality of homosexuality, causal propositions will have to be developed which demonstrate that some large but specific variables interact in certain ways to produce homosexuality. To say simply that there are hundreds of 'causes' does very little to aid scientific understanding, for it tends simply to indicate correlation factors rather than causal variables and minimizes the importance of theory. This does not mean, of course, that the many variables listed above may not be significant in developing a theory, nor that a theory has to explain homosexuality by means of a single factor. Rather, it means that the necessary variables for the emergence of homosexuality have to be formally integrated into a higher-level general theory, and that to be content with anything less is to simply produce a correlation porridge – where we have some idea of the factors involved, but little idea of how they interrelate in a causal nexus.

3 Substantive: Every theory of homosexual aetiology has its critics who can point to the flaws in the argument and suggest alternatives. The genetic evidence for homosexual causation is put forward with evidence from twins, but is soon rebutted by those who favour environmental explanations (Kallman, 1952; Ellis, 1963). The role of the mother is announced as a causal factor, and is soon rebutted by those who emphasize the role of the father (Bene, 1965). Further, depending upon the fashionable scientific endeavours of the day, theories may be put forward, die and then be revitalized. The current vogue in biological theories is an instance of this.[6]

The listing of causal traits also results in the presence of factors which contradict and compete with each other. It seems almost any combination of family factors has been shown at some time to have aetiological links – mothers may be weak or strong, dominant or submissive, and fathers may too; mothers may be causal on their own or with fathers, and fathers may be causal on their own or with mothers.[7] Likewise in the biological sphere, Ellis (1963: 170) has shown some of the contradictions:

> Lichtenstein's and Dickenson's claims that lesbians have large clitorises are directly contradicted by Havelock Ellis's contention that they usually have small clitorises; and all three are contradicted by Henry who insists that lesbians have both over and underdeveloped labias and clitorises. Weil's data showing that male homosexuals have larger hips than non-homosexuals are directly contradicted by Henry's data, which indicate that they have relatively narrow hips.

In the end, the listing of so many factors and contradictory hypotheses in a 'Heads I win, Tails you lose' fashion is likely to make the researcher feel impotent. At the very least it is not very helpful.

4 Applied: While such theories may not be very helpful to the person trying to understand homosexuality, they may in fact be positively harmful to those who experience it. For when such causal studies, in spite of their prematurity and apparent inadequacies, become the basis of policy and treatment, they may give rise to several dangers. They may become the basis of self-fulfilling prophecies; they may generate unnecessary guilt for the hypothesized causal agent; and they may provoke spurious 'treatment orientations'. Thus, on the first point, the fact that certain variables (such as possessive mothers and weak fathers) are 'known' to give rise to homosexuality may help to sensitize an individual to view himself as 'homosexual' when confronted with such variables.[8] On the second point, those human agents – usually the parents – who have been designated as 'causal' in the aetiological theories may unnecessarily incur much suffering and guilt – blaming themselves for precipitating homosexuality in their children. Third, some of the causal theories have given rise to 'treatments' which are supposed to 'cure' or 're-move' homosexuality, and while under certain conditions it may be possible that some of these 'treatments' are successful in their goals, in many if not most instances, they not only fail – but involve the 'patients' in more suffering, confusion, pain and anxiety (not to mention possible financial loss) than may be justifiable.[9] Clearly, one cannot wait until 'all the facts are in' before one starts building up policies; but one should at least endeavour when theories are only vague to avoid any further suffering.

5 Ideological: Perhaps the most important criticism that needs to be directed at the extant research into aetiology is the *ideological* one. The condemnation of the homosexual experience that arises in society is implicitly transferred to the scientist when he looks for the faults, flaws and follies that lead people to be homosexuals. Our understanding of homosexual causation reads like a long list of failings. Because homosexuality is 'odd', the explanations for it must be too. Thus, for example, one recent and very competent study by Hatterer cited earlier attempts to draw together in a summary statement all those 'aetiologies popularly advanced in the up-to-date psychiatric literature'. He lists seventy-seven variables, and this list is an indictment very largely of family failings. I cite the first ten factors on this list (Hatterer, 1970: 34–5) as illustrative below (my italics):

1 An early development of a strong *fixation* to the mother and the consequent life-long *inability* to leave her together with a continuous *wish* and *dread* of rejoining her.

2 An *overidentification* with and *submission* to the mother and the feminine passive role accompanied by the development of an overwhelming Oedipus complex which is *unresolved*.

3 An *excessive dependency* upon the mother and her own dependency upon her son with *distorted mutual overidentifications*.

4 A *life-long negative effect* on her son's relationship to women caused by either the mother's *dominant, binding, seductive, overprotective, passive-aggressive controlling or possessive* behaviour. Her son's *repressed hostility* towards and/or *fear* of one or many of her *hypercritical, hostile, aggressive, emasculating, demanding* attitudes and behaviour.

5 *Exploitation* by the mother of her son whom she uses as a *substitute husband, confidant, alter-ego or as a bolster to her own security*.

6 Transference of the mother's own *passivity, anxiety, and fear of men* and/or *hatred, distrust* of other women to her son.

7 A mother's *hostile* and/or *competitive reactions* to all men, or frigidity and/or *inhibited, prohibitive* sexual attitudes and behaviour.

8 Her *criticism* and *subsequent inhibition* of her son's attempt to introduce himself into *normal* social and sexual relationships with other women.

9 An *absent* mother, or the existence of too many *overwhelming mother figures and/or surrogates.*

10 A mother who has a *lesbian, bisexual, or asexual* adjustment.

Such a list clearly points to the causes of homosexuality as lying firmly in certain failings. The need for a wider and more general understanding is overlooked and the immersion in value statements is ignored. The way in which the aetiological questions are being asked at present largely prejudges the issues. Simon and Gagnon (1967a: 179) suggest an alternative:

> The problem of finding out how people become homosexual requires an adequate theory of how they become heterosexual; that is one cannot explain homosexuality and leave heterosexuality as a large residual category labelled 'all others'. Indeed, the explanation of homosexuality in this sense, may await the explanation of the larger and more modal category of adjustment.

In effect, then, Gagnon and Simon are criticizing current aetiological theorizing for divorcing their analysis from the wider context of heterosexuality, and for implicitly assuming the problematic nature of homosexuality. They attack the notion that homosexuality is problematic while heterosexual conformity may be taken for granted. It is just such a line of attack which has underlain the branch of criminological theorizing known as 'control theory', and it may thus have some relevance for the study of homosexual aetiology.

Control theorists such as Box (1971a) and Hirschi (1969) start out with different aetiological questions. Instead of asking why it is that men violate certain rules and norms, they ask the question why men conform to rules. They reverse the conventional assumptions, and take as their new main assumption that 'men are born free to break the law, and will refrain from doing so only if special circumstances exist'. They then set about trying to understand what these special circumstances are. Now given that man is born with an essential biological open-endedness and builds up sexual meanings through interactions with significant others, any individual could become 'homosexual', 'transvestite', 'ascetic' or 'sado-masochistic' unless there are good reasons not to. The problem has shifted: why, one is led to ask, do most individuals narrow their world down into one of heterosexuality? Why, when there are so many potential sexual roles available, do so many elect for heterosexuality as a predominant mode of sexual experience? The answers to such questions may provide a potentially more fertile starting-ground in the quest for homosexual causation.

6 *Sociological:* While most studies have been concerned with explaining the existence of individual homosexuality, a sociological account should also be able to explain the existence of variant *rates* of homosexuality. This is a question of causation, but of a quite different order. It starts out from the hypothesis that the incidence of homosexuality varies considerably from time to time, society to society, and within different contexts in the same society, and then seeks structural explanations of such variance. Now given this as a prime sociological concern in the study of deviance since Durkheim, it is surprising that so few sociologists have considered it. Again there is little research existing and much work required; but it is possible to suggest four areas where useful hypotheses could be generated:

(a) The nature of gender roles: It has been argued by Kardiner (1963) that in a society which places exaggerated emphasis upon the proper performance of polarized gender roles, anxiety is more likely to build up and inhibit the development of adequate relationships with the opposite sex. This may well lead to an increase in homosexuality. Conversely, however, it has been argued that a breakdown in well-defined gender roles may lead to increasing ambiguity and confusion in appropriate sexual behaviour, with perhaps a concomitant increase in homosexuality. Thus both rigid gender roles and more flexible ones can be hypothesized as leading to higher rates of homosexuality in a society. Only research and detailed argument can demonstrate the validity of such hypotheses.

(b) Symmetry of accessibility between genders: Ashworth and Walker (1972: 148) have suggested that homosexual rates are likely to increase 'when the access of members of one sex to members of the opposite sex for erotic, companionship or marriage purposes is persistently obstructed by features of the social structure'. Such features of the social structure may be highly visible (e.g. single-sex institutions where access to the opposite sex is clearly limited (Ward and Kassebaum, 1964)) but may also be covert. In this latter group, Ashworth and Walker suggest that stratification may be important, in that erotic groups who figure in a low position in the class structure may not be able to find partners of the opposite sex. Their argument is an interesting one, backed up by illustrations from the theatre, striptease, Moslem societies and institutional life, and is worthy of further exploration.

(c) The nature of deviancy definitions: While it is popularly assumed that by outlawing homosexuality in a society, its incidence will become minimal, it could be, as Schur (1965; 1969a) and others have suggested, that such outlawing actually encourages the growth and stabilization of a polarized sexual role known as 'the homosexual'. Schur (1969a: 13) comments: 'In a society where intense concern about this matter is publicly and constantly expressed and felt, one may find arising in many individuals strong anxieties which could generate the very pattern toward which the concern is directed.'

The existence of a stereotype which stresses that there are really only two kinds of people – the majority who are heterosexual, and the fringe who are homosexual – forces people to take one or the other and to shun the idea of a range of diverse sexual experiences. It may be then that in a society which renders homosexuality as taboo, the rate of stable, exclusive homosexuality will increase; and that in a society where it is more freely encouraged, the rate of bisexual experience will be much greater.

(d) The nature of the family structure: Finally, and most obviously, the manner in which a society or group develops varying family structures may provide an important clue as to the varying rates of homosexuality. While I have previously criticized the 'family aetiology' theories, I suspect there is more than a modicum of truth in the idea that overidentification with the mother figure precipitates homosexuality in many instances. And what is important for a sociologist is that a society (or group within that society) may be characterized by a family structure that is more likely to facilitate such a female identification pattern—Parsons's 'female-dominated' family, for example, is supposedly a characteristic family structure of industrialized societies, and it also corresponds in many ways with the psychiatrists' 'modal homosexual family' (Parsons, 1964).

In sum, this error of most aetiological studies is one involving the level of explanation. The question is always asked as to why individuals should be that way: a sociologist should ask also why structures arise with varying rates of homosexuality.

7 *Philosophical:* One of the main features of most studies of homosexual aetiology is their strong commitment to determinism. Whether due to genetics, brain structure, birth order or parental influence – homosexuality always arises without the slightest element of choice or consciousness on the part of the homosexual. To suggest that anyone should actually choose to be a homosexual is indeed a heresy.

Such a commitment to hard determinism as a model of explanation has dominated the field of criminological thinking. But in the past decade it has come in for some sharp criticism, especially in the work of Matza (1964; 1969). Earlier criminological theories, he suggests, viewed deviance as contagious. Individuals, if sufficiently exposed and properly placed, must 'catch' a deviation – as pre-ordination, as hard determinism. Alternatively, more recent developments – as exemplified in Becker's statements of becoming a marijuana smoker (Becker, 1963) – demonstrate the process of choosing to be a deviant; of being ordained, not preordained; of being converted not contaminated. Becker begins his study with a willing subject – one who wants to try marijuana. Thereafter, a whole series of meanings, perceptions and objects flow into his field and a series of choices have to be made. 'It becomes apparent', says Matza, 'that anybody can become a marijuana user and that no one has to' (Matza, 1969: 110).

If I were to apply that last observation to homosexuality, one would have an idea so totally alien to every analysis and discussion of homosexuality over the past few decades that one would feel like instantly dismissing it. People just don't choose to be homosexuals; they might choose to be pot smokers, but then that is a fundamentally different form of experience.

Now, it would be dangerous to suggest a fully voluntaristic picture of the origins of homosexuality. But the great contribution of the interactionist perspective is that it moves away from a hard deterministic picture of the homosexual, and suggests areas of choice. After all, becoming a homosexual – like becoming a nudist, stealing a car or joining a church – can be enjoyable, exciting, rewarding. It can be banal, boorish or beastly. By assuming a traditional conception of a hard determinism, homosexual studies never look at the processes of decision-making, of balancing cost and reward, of choosing to be a homosexual. There are few studies that consider the first homosexual feelings and responses, and then relate these to future socialization routes; the decision to stop, to savour again or to become committed.

The notion of determinism in homosexuality has been a highly influential one, but a pernicious one too. It has had the consequence of suggesting that nobody could ever choose to be 'gay', and has hence robbed the behaviour of its own validity. I am not suggesting that homosexual behaviour is as free as Matza suggests hash-taking is, but I am suggesting that there are many areas where choice enters and it is the researcher's task to explore these.

In conclusion, then, the plethora of clinical aetiological studies on homosexuality are open to a number of serious limitations: methodological, theoretical, substantive, applied, ideological, sociological and philosophical. For many years, individual aetiology has been the central concern of homosexual research and an impressive list of variables has been correlated with homosexuality, many of which have only a spurious connection with aetiology. No doubt many researchers will add to this list in the future. It is noticeable, however, that in the recommendations made by the American Task Force on Homosexuality for future research, the 'problem of aetiology and determinants', while recognized as an 'ultimate concern', were placed last in a list of thirteen research priorities (Hooker, 1969a: 8).[10] This may indicate a 'problem-shift' within the realms of scientific inquiry that could have significant consequences.

The making of a homosexual

While there are many studies of early childhood experiences, there are very few that have concerned themselves with adult processes. It is such processes that concern me in what follows.

Some elements of adult socialization

At least five elements need to be considered in any 'dense' analysis of adult socialization: the underlying processes, the content, the agents involved, the stages and the properties of the status passage.

First, it is clear that the selection of a theoretical paradigm will affect the task of analysing *processes*. In looking at the emergence of homosexuality in the past, two main paradigms have been used – one drawn from Freudianism, the other from behaviourism. The former has focused upon the emotional preconditions for sexual development and highlighted the processes of introjection and identification. The latter has focused upon stimulus-response learning and highlighted the process of conditioning. In both cases, scant attention is paid to the role of meanings, symbols and significant others which are the hallmark of the interactionist approach. Further, both perspectives essentially seem to be very heavily rooted in what Allport has called the Lockean tradition in psychology (Allport, 1955: chs. 2 and 3). Man is seen here as essentially a receptor, rather than a self-conscious reactor. From what has gone before, it is clear that this is not my approach. Instead, the underlying process that guides human action is assumed to be an ongoing interaction between selves and significant others, in which life is constantly built, altered but never completed. The concept of stable personalities is not consistent with others advanced here. Rather, I prefer to talk of 'personality drift';[11] of individuals constantly striving but never arriving; of change, flux and modifications; in short, of becoming. While, therefore, there may be emerging commitments and perspectives that maintain a person within the homosexual role, even this role will constantly be changing and modified through interaction with others. It is with this never-ending interaction as a source for understanding socialization that I will be concerned in what follows.

Second, in analysing the *content* of the homosexual socialization process, the interactionist perspective is at odds with much that has been written in the past. For the central concern of most earlier studies has been with depicting the contents of homosexual socialization almost exclusively in terms of homosexual orientation and sexuality. The sole concern has been with how an individual comes to be attracted towards his or her own sex. But it should be clear that there is much more to homosexuality in our culture than sexuality. Indeed, some of the primary attributes of homosexuality are derived from its stigmatizing properties. Homosexuality is always only one small part of an individual's total life experience, and it is dangerous to rip it entirely from its broader context. As Gagnon and Simon, with customary insight, have remarked (1973: 142):

> Like the heterosexual, the homosexual must come to terms
> with the problems that are attendant upon being a member of
> society: He must find a place to live with or without his family,
> be involved or apathetic in political life, find a group of friends
> to talk to and live with, fill his leisure time usefully or
> frivolously, handle all of the common and uncommon problems
> of impulse control and personal gratification, and in some
> manner socialise his sexual interests.

Thus, interactionism focuses upon a wider range of materials than those simply of sexuality.

Third, previous studies have looked at only a limited range of *agents* – notably the mother and father. But in the analysis that follows, these are widened to include all those significant others – real or imaginary – with whom one has contact over one's life span. At different phases, groups will play lesser or greater parts, the family being particularly influential in the early stages, and others playing more significant parts later. Thus access to other homosexuals may be of considerable importance in providing a series of socially learnt 'accounts' which validate homosexuality, as well as providing a series of socially learnt strategies for homosexual encounters. Again, access to a control agency may provide a guiding series of expectations as to how homosexuals behave and what they are like, while the constant exposure to stereotypes of homosexuality presented in the media are another important source for learning the homosexual role.[12] Only a narrow understanding of the process of becoming a homosexual can come from looking solely at the influences of the family.

One important agent of socialization – often overlooked – is that of the self, and the self-initiating process. In line with my earlier argument, socialization cannot be viewed merely as a pouring process, by which external agents of socialization pour into the individual the social roles he is supposed to enact. Rather, the individual has considerable say at a large number of 'turning-points' as to which path or direction he will take (Strauss, 1959). As Brim has observed: 'The person himself has many self initiated ideas and prescriptions for his own personality and behaviour change, and in many cases the self initiated socialization is a greater source of adult personality change than are the demands of other persons' (Brim, in Clausen 1968: 186).

The most obvious example of a self-initiated learning process for many homosexuals occurs when they actively decide to seek out other homosexuals. As I shall argue later, few homosexuals 'stumble' accidentally upon the existence of other homosexuals; discovery of their whereabouts often depends upon a quite painful experience of searching.

Fourth, as Glaser and Strauss (1971) suggest, *properties* of status passages need to be considered. So far they have listed seventeen properties – including legitimacy, inevitability, clarity, respectability and centrality – and confess the list is not exhaustive. Their argument suggests that most earlier discussions of status passages – Becker's medical students, Goffman's mental patients, Davis's polio victims or Garfinkle's degradation ceremonies – are limited because they fail to look at the full range of properties (Glaser and Strauss, 1971: 9):

> Our contention is that unless a researcher is explicitly sensitive
> to multiple properties of status passage, he can be expected to
> make a relatively incomplete analysis of his data. . . . We suggest
> that anyone who wishes to develop a substantive analysis about
> any phenomenon that might also be fruitfully conceived of
> as a status passage can considerably tighten up, as well as
> make more dense, his systematic formulation by guiding his
> research with a sensitivity to the kinds of properties listed
> above.

Key properties for understanding the status passage to homosexuality as a way of life are that it is usually seen as an *undesirable* passage; one which, once embarked upon, is generally *irreversible* (although it may stop dead in its tracks): one which for the most part (and certainly in its earlier stages) is conducted in relative *isolation*; one which is marked by a lack of *clarity* of signs, and which finally can become a *central* passage for an individual undergoing it.

Finally, in looking at the *stages or sequences* of socialization, the concepts of 'status passage' and 'careers' are both useful in pointing to the sequential phases in the movement from, say, seeing oneself as asexual to homosexual. Lemert (1967: 51) puts the career concept at its broadest level as: 'the recurrent or typical contingencies and problems awaiting someone who continues in a course of action.'[13] Such a concept is not meant to imply that all people in the same course of action are necessarily going to face all these contingencies, let alone in the same sequences as described in the typical career trajectory. Nor is it meant to depict features of individuals; rather, it is a property of social systems. Further, it is a heuristic device and not a concrete one (cf. Davis, 1968).

In the analysis that follows, I have emphasized the stages through which some homosexuals pass in adopting homosexuality as a way of life. In summary, these are depicted as sensitization, signification, 'coming out' and stabilization; and together they may be taken as an 'ideal type' of career route for that homosexual who lives his life primarily as a homosexual in contact with other homosexuals. Such a trajectory is obviously less applicable in the later stages to those homosexuals who do not enter the subculture or who 'fight their tendencies all life long'. For them, only the early stages are applicable. There are several important things to notice about the career type of analysis. First, attention is drawn to the continuity of experiences, how one experience builds upon the other and how 'an identity once gained is never lost'. At any stage of analysis, an individual can be seen to lie at the mid-point between his past experiences (latent culture) and his future one (anticipatory culture), and it is not possible to divorce him from these wider experiences. Second, the socialization process is seen as essentially a problem-solving mechanism; individuals in their daily round are constantly facing problems and having to resolve them as best they can. Often the solutions are highly unsatisfactory, but it is through this cumulative problem-solving that socialization takes place. Third, the concern is placed upon the 'turning-points' at which crucial decisions are taken. Man, of course, is not invariably 'rational', does not possess full knowledge and is not always clear even about his immediate goals; and he thus acts at these 'turning-points' in an unreflexive mood. The sociologist, with his desire for clarity and precision, armed with his analytic and conceptual baggage, often loses sight of this important characteristic of 'turning-points' and, although, in what follows, it may appear at times as though the homosexual is acting very self-consciously, in fact he is doing this in a semi-slumbering mood.[14]

With these cautions in mind, I can move on to consider the four problem stages in becoming a homosexual mentioned above.[15]

Career stages and the homosexual role[16]

Sensitization

From an interactionist viewpoint, the most appropriate take-off stage in understanding the process of 'becoming homosexual' rests neither with the unconscious psychodynamics of an individual, nor with the myriad other biological, psychological and structural factors. Rather, the initial concern rests with those first conscious and semi-conscious moments in which an individual comes to perceive of himself potentially as a homosexual: with the general process of constructing sexual meanings, modifying them, and in many instances neutralizing them. One cannot see the individual 'automatically' and 'intrinsically' 'knowing' that he is a homosexual – as the simple interpretation of prior elements. Rather, one must analyse the social situations and interaction styles that lead to an individual building up a particular series of sexual meanings, a particular sexual identity. It is with those factors that create a potentiality for 'homosexual identification' that an interactionist analysis most suitably starts.

A number of potential sources for homosexual identification are readily discernible because they lie in the spheres of genitality and emotionality which are so closely identified with sexuality in this culture. Thus, for example, any actor who commits a genital act (e.g. masturbation) with a member of the same sex, who develops a strong emotional attachment to a member of the same sex, or who spends time daydreaming of his own sex in fictional erotic encounters, develops an apparent source for subsequent ponderings over potential homosexuality. Less apparent may be those situations in which there arises a 'spillover effect' – the linkage of one series of meanings in which there may be no clear sexual connotation with others where the sexual meaning is clearer. An individual may become attached to, interested in or fascinated by a number of 'objects' – penises, bottoms, football boots, and other male-orientated objects – which may subsequently come to symbolize his whole being as homosexual.

Less obviously, a series of explicitly social events may be interpreted as 'homosexual'. For example, some actors may well find a base created for subsequent homosexual interpretation through gender confusions – a child coming to see his bodily self as in some ways inappropriate to the cultural definitions of his gender: a small, frail, fragile boy may come to perceive himself as 'not like other men', and go on from this belief to build up a definition of being a homosexual.[17] Others may develop a sense of 'differentness' – only later to be translated into sexual differentness – which cuts them off from everybody else: the boy who prefers to be alone, or the boy

135

whose interest is in the arts and literature finds himself distinguished markedly from his 'football crazy' peers. As one respondent to Ross commented: 'I thought I was different because I wanted to become an artist and not because of homosexuality' (Ross, 1971: 387). This sense of 'differentness' is a fairly common experience in homosexual case histories (Schofield, 1965a: 28; Wildeblood, 1955: 11). As a simple example, four working-class homosexuals interviewed revealed a highly sensitive childhood – playing violins, visiting art museums, developing taste in the arts, literature and music, taking an interest in fashion and clothes to an extent that seems strangely at odds with the traditional working-class male culture in which they were brought up. They were all incidentally characterized by very slender and frail physical frames. I am *not* saying here that 'homosexuality' gives rise to these interests or physiques. Quite the contrary: the interests and physique may well provide a subsequent base for interpreting oneself as a homosexual. They provide clues for retrospective interpretation.

In each of these early *social* experiences, a potential base is created for a subsequent *sexual* interpretation. Gender confusion, feelings of apartness, partialism or even genital acts are not 'intrinsically sexual', but can later be defined as such. Each of the above examples is similar in that a source is provided for subsequent homosexual self-indication. Some sources, however, may not be derived reflexively from the self; they may be thrust upon one. Consider the following interview response, relating a homosexual incident at school (Hauser, 1962: 147):

> I was told, when I got myself into trouble, that I was a dirty, filthy, queer. I did not even know what this was so I was told that this meant that I would never be able to love a girl, that I could never have kids, that I had 'had' it, and would most likely end up my life in prisons for having been caught interfering with small children. These were the crimes of Sodom and Gomorrah, for which they were destroyed by God, and for the rest of my life I would have to expiate this filth and wickedness. I was half hysterical and I simply could not understand what they meant, as all that had happened had been weeks ago, I had forgotten it all by then, but somebody was made to blab by the Coppers and the Head had been brought in.

Thus labelling by parents, teachers and even peers may have manifest consequences for an individual's self-conception. A child who is constantly being told that he is 'not like other children', a boy who is caught *in flagrante delicto* with another boy, or a boy accused of being a 'cissy' or 'mother's boy' may subsequently incorporate these hostile reactions into his own self-conception. Not only may he be given a notion of being 'queer' – he may also be provided with a full-blown stereotyped imagery, as in the case cited above.

In sum, then, the sources for interpreting oneself as possibly homosexual are many and varied. They can arise at many points in an individual's life history. While I have spoken above of sexual labelling arising at adolescence – that most critical period of sexual identification – it may also take place at other times. From a small initial sensitization the experience may become heightened and signified, and it is this process which I wish to examine shortly. But, before doing this, a crucial problem must be raised.[18]

Neutralization: a note on 'not going homosexual': The previous discussion has suggested a wide range of situations that potentially lead to homosexual identification. Such situations are, however, so many and so widespread that they can hardly serve as a useful explanation of why some individuals adopt homosexuality as a more or less permanent life style. A question that thus arises is: why, when so many people are potentially available for homosexual experiences and identification, do so few enter stable homosexual roles?

The answer to this question depends upon the theoretical orientation adopted. Clearly, to an extreme behaviourist, much of the previous discussion will be irrelevant, and the reasons why some people become 'exclusive homosexuals' will be analysed in terms of drive strength, hormonal strength or conditioning strength. The stronger is the 'push' of each of these in a homosexual direction, the more likely that an individual will become exclusively homosexual; the weaker, the less likely. From an interactionist perspective, however, an important part is likely to be played by identification with significant others who enable an individual either to neutralize his homosexual potential or to build it up. The 'strength of the drive' is less important than 'access to supportive others'.

In discussing this point, I propose for simplicity to restrict my argument to those 'potential sources' of homosexual identification that are most explicitly 'sexual'. That is, genital acts between members of the same sex. Whenever this occurs, one suspects that there is a firm base for subsequent interpretation as being homosexual. Yet, if Kinsey's figures are to be relied upon, 37 per cent of the male population have such an experience to the point of orgasm – and only 4 per cent become stabilized from this into homosexual roles of a permanent kind. With an enormous potential for sensitization, most of the population avoid such labels. What plausible explanation may the interactionist provide for this?

The answer may be given in two parts. First, the strategies by which homosexual sensitivity is neutralized and heterosexual sensitivity strengthened, and second the strategies by which homosexual sensitivity develops.

Homosexual disavowal: Speculations as to the manner in which individuals may neutralize their homosexual sensitivities may be derived from empirical studies of people who behave homosexually but who remain inoculated from a homosexual self-conception. Four examples may be cited here.

First, the classic study of neutralizing a homosexual label is that provided by Albert Reiss in his study of delinquent boys who 'hustle' adult male homosexuals. Such a boy regularly commits acts of homosexual fellatio, but 'develops no conception of himself either as a prostitute or as homosexual' (Reiss, 1961). The mechanism for insulating himself from a homosexual self-conception, suggests Reiss, lies mainly in the social organization of the peer network. Adolescent delinquent boys develop norms which prevent homosexual identification while still permitting homosexual acts. Reiss points to a number of norms that underpin this process. First, 'a boy must undertake the relationship with a queer solely as a way of making money; sexual gratification cannot be actively sought as a goal in the relationship'. Second, 'the sexual transaction must be limited to mouth-genital fellatio. No other sexual acts are generally tolerated.' Third, 'both peers and queers, as participants, should remain effectively neutral during the transaction'. Fourth, 'violence must not be used as long as the relationship conforms to the shared set of expectations between queers and peers'. These four norms insulate the boy from seeing himself as a homosexual. He is not 'really a queer', because he always performs the male role, only does it for money, and shows no emotional feelings. This study highlights the role of the peer group as a reference group in shaping a heterosexual identity and preventing a homosexual one. At the same time, the study has some unsatisfactory aspects. For example, there has been no follow-up on these boys, and it is feasible that some of them were not effectively insulated from homosexual self-conceptions, that some have subsequently adopted stable homosexual roles. Further, the boys' comments may be 'accounts' constructed by them to provide insulation from blame by a middle-class researcher, and not 'accounts' that actually serve to insulate their private self-conceptions. The existence of numbers of other boys who were visibly involved in the same acts makes it likely, however, that reference group support was available to neutralize the homosexuality latent in the act.

Another group which seems capable of insulating itself from homosexual self-conceptions are the Greenwich Village Beats described by Ned Polsky. He writes (1967: 159):

> What one would not necessarily expect is the peculiar pattern
> that homosexual behaviour takes among the beats.

Proportionately, the amount of such behaviour seems as high as in the non-beat world even though the beat whose outlets are entirely or almost entirely homosexual is proportionately very much rarer than his non-beat counterpart. In other words, an extraordinary number of male beats . . . are fully bisexual or in some cases polymorphous perverse [an unusual clustering of Kinsey points two, three and four]. They accept homosexual experiences almost as casually as heterosexual ones. Even beats with numerous and continuous post adolescent homosexual experiences typically do not feel the need to define themselves as homosexuals and create some sort of beat wing of the homosexual world. Beats not only tolerate deviant sex roles but, to a much greater extent than previous bohemians, display a very high tolerance of sex-role ambiguity.

Now Polsky was writing about a particular 'beat scene' as it functioned some time ago, and his observations may not therefore have general validity. A number of '1970 London hippies', for example, commented that the 'Head scene was a bad one for gays' – that there was not the increased tolerance in some sections of the underground in London that Polsky speaks of in Greenwich Village. Nevertheless, his discovery is valid for his group, and it is plausible that the normative organization of the 'beat world' provided differential sexual meanings that served to insulate actors from taking on stable homosexual roles.[19]

Perhaps the most widely cited example of homosexual neutralization is that which occurs in the prison context. Cut off from 'normal' sexual access, most men are confronted with a three-fold sexual choice: abstinence, masturbation and homosexuality. A considerable minority opts for the latter, and members commit homosexual acts within the limited confines of a prison context. On release they revert to their 'heterosexual' roles.[20] The normative organization of the prison seems to function to maintain these kinds of homosexual experiences – the experiences of the 'wolf' or 'jocker' – as not stigmatizing and, in effect, not homosexual. Basic to this normative system are two criteria (Kirkham, 1971: 331):

(1) The homosexual acts must represent only a situational reaction to the deprivation of heterosexual intercourse, and (2) such behaviour must involve a complete absence of emotionality and effeminacy – both of which are regarded as signs of 'weakness' and 'queerness'. An inmate who engages in homosexual activity must present a convincing façade of toughness and stereotypical 'manliness' in order to escape being defined as a homosexual.

At times, of course, such homosexual acts may actually serve to strengthen their perceived masculinity.

The examples given all refer to quite specific and fairly uncommon groups and situations, in which specific norms emerge to neutralize homosexual acts – where one may commit homosexual acts without becoming 'a homosexual'. But the more common example is that in which a boy or a man 'just happens' to commit homosexual acts – at school, at college, with a good friend, flat-mate or even a stranger who makes advances. Under such conditions the actor has to develop suitable 'accounts' which may serve as 'excuses' or 'justifications', and which simultaneously insulate him from seeing himself as a homosexual. He may, for example, view it simply as a 'passing phase', as an 'experiment', as a 'broadening of one's experiences', as a 'favour for a good friend' and so forth. Sometimes actors may have recourse to situations which release them from moral constraints, and which thus allow temporary 'lapses'. Drink is one good example of this. Michael, in the play *The Boys in the Band*, describes this as the 'Christ-was-I-drunk-last-night' syndrome (Crowley, 1968: 14): 'You know when you made it with some guy in school and the next day when you had to face each other there was always a lot of shit-kicking crap about "Man! Was I drunk last night! Christ! I don't remember a thing!"'

Humphreys's study revealed a considerable number of married men who regularly had homosexual acts in public conveniences, but unfortunately he provides little information as to their self-conceptions or their accounts. One does not know therefore quite what mechanisms are at work here, or what the end-product is. Perhaps indicative of some of his men, though, is Dwight who he quotes as follows (Humphreys, 1970: 119):

> I guess you might say that I'm pretty highly sexed (he chuckled
> a little), but I really don't think that's why I go to tearooms.
> That's not really sex. Sex is something I have with my wife
> in bed. It's not as if I were committing adultery by getting
> my rocks off – or going down on some guy – in a tearoom. I
> get a kick out of it. Some of my friends go out for handball.
> I'd rather cruise the park.

In all of these instances, then, men are able to commit homosexual acts but neutralize the potentiality for labelling themselves as homosexuals through the employment of 'accounts' and through access to reference groups. These mechanisms are not of course sufficient to explain the divergences that arise, because one is forced back an analytical stage to ask why they have these reference groups, and why they need to produce such 'accounts'. Answers to these questions may well be derived from control theory. That is, most individuals might become attached and committed to heterosexual groups because of the way society is organized, and such commitments may become increasingly difficult to sever. This being so, 'accounts' have to be provided to justify homosexual acts, and attachments to reference groups become not only sources of support, but also barriers to further interaction with new groups.

Homosexual deference: This last point leads to the significant question of how the minority sensitive to homosexuality become stable homosexuals. The answer, following from above, lies mainly in their access to supportive groups, their attachments and their commitments. I will discuss attachments and commitments in the section on 'coming out' below, but here I shall consider the notion of supportive reference groups.

Many people may become potentially sensitive to the fact that they could be homosexual, but develop attachments to heterosexual groups through which they may be able to accommodate homosexual experiences which are insulated from self-labelling implications. Others however may well find themselves having access to reference groups that do not provide any sexual meanings, or which actually provide some homosexual ones. They remain relatively isolated from the orthodox conventional heterosexual structures in which many boys grow up. They may, for example, mature earlier than their peers – or later, and in either case find themselves with few significant others who can help them to build up sexual meanings. In these situations, they may evolve meanings from cues that they find around them; cues which, as I have already suggested, may have considerable homosexual potential. Not all actors who have no access to well-formed heterosexual reference groups are likely to become homosexuals, because not all actors have the initial predisposing sources for homosexual identification. But when such sources do exist, and there are few reference-group supports for heterosexuality, homosexual sensitivity is highly likely to occur.

Signification and disorientation

Signification begins where sensitization ends. It entails all those processes which lead to a heightened homosexual identity: subjectively, from the nagging inner feeling that one may be 'different' through to a developed homosexual identity, and objectively, from minor homosexual involvements through to the stage known as 'coming out'. For some these changes are passed quickly; for others they groan through the life span. For some, the awakening sense of homosexual identity comes as a positive relief; for others it is an issue to be constantly debated, challenged and surrounded with ambiguity. This process of high anxiety and confusion in coping with one's life situation may be termed 'disorientation'; the process of heightened self-awareness and meaning about the experience of homosexuality may be termed 'signification' (Lofland, 1969: 178; Matza, 1969: ch. 7).

Disorientation and signification arise not simply because of personality factors, but rather because of the structural propertics of the wider society in which the neophyte finds himself. Both the positive and negative elements of the societal reaction to homosexuality give rise to particular sets of problems and the consequential signification of the homosexual experience. On the negative side, the devaluation of homosexuality may lead to problems of secrecy, guilt and access; on the positive side, the importance attached to gender roles and the general privatization surrounding sexuality may lead to problems of identity and solitariness respectively. Through these various problems, an actor's random and fortuitous homosexuality may become crystallized and signified. A minor sensitivity may be rendered all-important, and the path towards secondary deviance, pivotal deviance or role engulfment may be seriously embarked upon.

I wish now to look briefly at a few elements of the societal reaction, and suggest ways in which problems may emerge and signification ensue.

First, the homosexual experience is, in Matza's fine phrase: 'bedevilled by ban'.[21] As a homosexual spokesman commented (Cory, 1953: 12):

> A person cannot live in an atmosphere of universal rejection, of
> widespread pretence, of a society that outlaws and banishes his
> activities and desires, or a social world that jokes and sneers
> at every turn without a fundamental influence on his personality.

It is not surprising that such influences begin from the earliest moment of sensitivity for many actors. The condemnation and degradation of the homosexual experience by society renders the individual 'worried' and 'guilty'. Confronted with stereotypes of sin, sickness and sadness when not veiled in silence, the neophyte comes to perceive his initial experience with increasing anxiety and possible guilt. In *Giovanni's Room*, James Baldwin (1963: 11) vividly recounts the first childhood experiences of his homosexual hero, David:

> I awoke whilst Joey was still sleeping. . . . I was suddenly
> afraid. It was borne in on me: *But Joey is a Boy.* . . . The power
> and the promise and the mystery of that body made me suddenly
> afraid. That body suddenly seemed the black opening of a cavern
> in which I would be tortured till madness came, in which I would
> lose my manhood. . . . The sweat on my back grew cold. I was

ashamed. The very bed in its sweet disorder testified to vileness. I wondered what Joey's mother would say when she saw the sheets. Then I thought of my father who had no one in the world but me. . . . A cavern opened in my mind, black, full of rumour, suggestion, of half heard, half forgotten, half understood stories, full of dirty words. I thought I saw my future in that cavern. I was afraid. I could have cried, cried for shame and terror, cried for not understanding how this could have happened to me, how this could have happened *in* me. And I made my decision. I got out of bed and took a shower and was dressed.

Such sensitivity will increase the potential homosexual's attentiveness to the negative imagery of homosexuality in society at large, an imagery which he may only remotely have been aware of formerly. At school, at home, in the media, what others may ignore he will find increasingly important. And, at each point, the message will be the same: homosexuality is, at the very least, odd.

An important part of the process of becoming sexual is sex education, and for the sensitized homosexual, this is invariably negative. Schofield, in England in 1963, suggested that two-thirds of boys learnt about sex from their peers, about 12 per cent from school and 7 per cent from books (Schofield, 1965b).[22] Each source reinforces the 'abnormality' of homosexuality and the normality of heterosexuality. By evasion or by devaluation, the homosexual experience is always shown to be inferior. For the peer group, homosexuality is possibly only mentioned at the level of the 'queer joke', and for the teacher it will be limited to that part of the lesson that deals with 'perversions, abnormality and deviation', if it is discussed at all. In sex-education books it is often not mentioned: only 11 out of the 42 books discussed by Hill and Lloyd-Jones (1970: 20) dealt with the topic. When it is raised, however, it is couched in the language of abnormality. Barnes (1962: 166–7), by no means atypical, defines homosexual acts as 'abnormal sexual acts between two persons of the same, not opposite, sex . . . usually thought of as immoral', and comments in a well-known Penguin handbook (his capitals, my italics):

It is *normal* for people to pass through a STAGE in growing up that can broadly be termed as homosexual. *Ordinarily* they *grow through* this homosexual stage and out of it, later falling in love and marrying *normally* . . . at present it is a fact that an adult who is *deeply* homosexual, either because of his *bodily make up* or because of *wrong treatment in his early life*, is very difficult to *help*. He *cannot deliberately* change himself by turning his attention towards girls.

143

Likewise, Dawkins (1967: 76), in a textbook designed for 'club leaders, teachers, clergy . . . all who have to face the problem of sex education with the young', advises:[23]

> Homosexuals must be regarded *compassionately*. Many of them are *suffering from a psychological disturbance*, and none of them can ever find the *happiness* of raising their own family. There is evidence that homosexuals have not, *from a very early age*, been *able to accept their own sexuality*: consequently they *cannot love* a member of the opposite sex (my italics).

Here again homosexuality is located in almost entirely negative terms.

In the main, then, wherever the sensitized homosexual turns, he is likely to find his potentiality devalued and denounced in various guises. Clearly, under these conditions there is a firm basis for casting guilt, shame and even hatred on to the self.

Yet another important consequence flows from the act of ban: the transformation of homosexuality into a secret. Homosexuality, perhaps more than other sexuality, is a furtive exercise. Neither spoken about openly, nor immediately visible, it is something that can be kept to oneself, debated inwardly and defended from public gaze. And like most secrets, 'what is private becomes even more private', an inward spiralling takes place. As Simmel (in 'Wolff, 1950: 333) observes:

> From secrecy . . . grows the typical error according to which everything mysterious is something important and essential. Before the unknown, man's natural impulse to idealise and his natural fearfulness co-operate toward the goal: to intensify the unknown through imagination, and to pay attention to it with an emphasis that is not usually accorded to patent reality.

In other words, secrecy once again leads to signification. In part the problem that emerges at this stage is one of not being recognized, of not becoming transparent, of keeping the secret (Matza, 1969: 150). And as will be shown in chapter 9, there are several structural features in society that render this task relatively easy. The point, however, for the neophyte, is that he will increasingly feel that others suspect, that they 'must have guessed by now', even when the 'objective situation' has not changed and nobody is actually aware. As Matza says: 'Conscious of ban, and conscious that he has flaunted it, the subject becomes self conscious. Little else need be assumed to raise the possibility of human transparency' (Matza, 1969: 150). And with such transparency comes further signification.

Keeping a secret raises a further and very serious problem for the neophyte homosexual: the problem of access. For as long as he guards his secret well, people will probably not know he is 'one of them'. But as long as he does this the chance of ever meeting somebody else who experiences the world in the same way remains slight. Flowing from this then, and closely linked to the more general process of the privatization of sexuality, a third factor which contributes greatly to signification arises: that of solitude.

Partly because homosexuality is perceived as deviant and partly because it is a secret, the neophyte will typically confront his initial sensitization experiences alone. When he has access to supportive reference-group structures, as I have earlier depicted, the experience may be considerably less stressful and less significant. But where he is confronted with these worrying doubts about his sexuality in isolation from helpful others, signification proceeds apace. Hours, days, even years may be spent wondering and worrying about it. Sometimes the secret and the solitude are carried with the 'homosexual' to the grave.

There are two sides to this isolation process. One comes from a lack of contact with other homosexuals, the other from a lack of support from heterosexual companions. The first source of isolation may mean that the neophyte comes to perceive himself as 'the only one in the world', or as one respondent said to me 'it was me and a lot of dirty old men'. If one is confronted naïvely with a societal reaction that says homosexuality is odd and that nobody should be engaged in it, it is difficult for the neophyte to actually believe that many people are so engaged. But to this feeling of 'uniqueness' must be added the related feeling of pain for, after all, the base of the homosexual experience is a longing for homosexual contact – emotional or physical contact with the same sex. And the devaluation of homosexuality and the privatization of sexuality make it extremely difficult for the neophyte to find legitimate sexual expressions. Elements of frustration may thus add to the signification experience.

The second source of isolation comes from a (justified) unwillingness to broach the subject with family, peers or 'officials'. As Westwood's respondents commented: 'I was much too scared to tell anyone about it'; 'I daren't mention it to anyone. It was very difficult in those days' (aged 58); 'Until quite recently I wouldn't talk to anyone about it' (aged 23).

Not only are peers and families generally inaccessible on the subject, official agencies have not developed any well-defined and 'well-known' paths to offer 'help'. Recently, of course, there has been an increase in organizations developed to help homosexuals and to provide forums for discussion; but in the past such bodies were non-existent.

In addition to the unavailability of others with whom one can talk about homosexual experiences, there may also arise over time a gradual exclusion from heterosexual contacts: 'As his friends start to go out with girls and eventually marry, he finds other interests and gradually drifts away from their company' (Westwood, 1960: 183). Not only then is he cut off from homosexual experience and contact, he is slowly pushed away from heterosexual ones.

One of Westwood's (1960: 38) respondents illustrates much of the above discussion, and anticipated what is to follow, when he remarked:

> Round about my early twenties I went through an agonising period. I thought I was the only one in the universe – struck down by some terrible fate, I watched others getting married, settling down and I hadn't the slightest interest in any girl. By then I knew it wasn't a passing phase; it had been there from the beginning. I got a book on psychology out of the library, but it was not much help. It was only when I met others, after a long period of struggle, that I became first resigned, then adjusted, and now happy with my situation.

A final factor which contributes to signification may be briefly mentioned. Homosexual sensitivity touches upon a core identity. In our society, the positive elements of the societal reaction stress the importance of gender distinctions, of appropriate male-behaviour and female-behaviour, and such gender identities become (in Everett Hughes's oft-quoted phrase) 'master-determining status traits'. Now, deviant traits are often likely to become 'pivotal' to an individual's life style; but, when they are, not only is there an issue of deviant identity, there is also a problem of gender identity. The sensitivity to being a potential homosexual thus goes right to the very heart of the matter of identity. 'Who am I?' becomes a key problem that leads to signification.

In summary, then, the homosexual experience is likely to become highly significant for the individual through its linkages with guilt, secrecy, solitariness and central identities. And such features of the early homosexual experience are derived very largely from the broader structure of society: from the hostile imagery of homosexuality, the privatization of sexuality, and the emphasis placed upon appropriate gender behaviour. The homosexual experience becomes significant because society largely renders it so.

From such matters as ban, secrecy and solitariness flow particular problems which every homosexual neophyte must face, and resolve more or less satisfactorily. Three problems can be identified as crucial:

(a) The problem of access: how to remove the solitariness of the earlier experiences, find both social and sexual partners, and companions willing to talk about homosexuality.

146

(b) The problem of guilt: how to cope with the doubts and anxieties, guilts and fears that one experiences as a consequence of knowing homosexuality to be 'deviant'.

(c) The problem of identity: how to evolve a satisfactory self-image and sense of identity.

Such problems as these, if unresolved, serve to heighten disorientation and amplify the significance of the experience; and for many homosexuals such problems may well linger on for long periods, if not the entire life span. These homosexuals may well appear before a psychiatrist, a social worker or a priest as disturbed and maladjusted. But, equally, large numbers of individuals confronted with such problems attempt to evolve resolutions in a number of different ways. I wish now to turn to one particular way that is fairly common and seems fairly successful: the path of taking on homosexuality as 'a way of life'.

'Coming out'

At least three different meanings have been given to the phrase 'coming out' in a homosexual context. Most social scientists favour the one given by Simon and Gagnon as 'the point in time when there is self-recognition as a homosexual, and the first major exploration of the homosexual community' (Simon and Gagnon, 1967a: 181). In other words, two elements are seen as central: an identity, and contact with other homosexuals.[24] Alternatively Dank (1971), in the only systematic study of homosexual 'coming out' to date, suggests that this is not how the term is used by homosexuals themselves. Rather, for the homosexual (and concomitantly for Dank), 'coming out' refers to the process of 'identifying oneself as a homosexual', whether or not such identification occurs within a homosexual context. Dank's definition would be helpful if it were true that most homosexuals used the term exclusively in this way. But I suspect that this is not the case; and it is not possible to use members' definitions without problems of ambiguity. A third meaning – quite different to the two given above – is the one used by members of the Gay Liberation Front, for whom it means 'going public' – letting oneself be seen in the 'straight' world as homosexual. In the homosexual world, then, there are at least two meanings for this phrase, and probably more.

I shall use the term 'coming out' for the process by which individuals pass out of the moratorium just described, and are 'reborn' into the organized aspects of the homosexual community – a process during which they come to identify themselves as 'homosexuals'. It is neither an inevitable nor a necessary stage in becoming a homosexual – one may develop self-conceptions as homosexual

147

without contact with this world (as Dank rightly points out) – but it is crucial in taking on homosexuality as a 'way of life', the kind of homosexual experience that is the concern here. Thus, at this point in the homosexual career, the individual defines himself as homosexual and through interaction with other self-defined homosexuals begins to resolve the previously mentioned objective and subjective problems that emerge through signification. Thus, an identity is rebuilt and involvement with others may lead to an enhanced self-image and self-valuation.[25] Through such interaction patterns, access is found to socially constructed 'accounts' which may serve to legitimate the homosexual experience and neutralize feelings of guilt.[26] Further, one gains access to partners – both sexual and social. The individual moves from a world characterized by secrecy, solitude, ambiguity and guilt to a subworld where homosexual-role models are available, where homosexuality may be temporarily rendered public, where 'coaches' are willing to guide him into homosexual roles (Strauss, 1959) and where a belief system is on hand to legitimize the experience. A highly diffuse, unstructured experience, somewhat akin to anomie, becomes translated into one that is more clearly socially organized and ultimately stabilized. The first experience of 'going social' can have an enormous impact (Dank, 1971: 187):

> The time I really caught myself coming out is the time I walked into this bar and saw a whole crowd of groovy, groovy guys. And I said to myself . . . that not all gay men are dirty old men or idiots, silly queens, but there are some just normal looking and acting people, as far as I could see. I saw gay society and I said 'Wow, I'm home'.

Not all experiences are as sudden as this, and some may take place in other contexts. Respondents have related how their first homosexual contacts arose in work situations, in public places, through pen-pal magazines, through homophile movements, at public meetings, etc., as well as the gay-bar system. Surprisingly, Dank's study – which provides an empirical analysis of the coming-out contexts of 180 homosexuals – suggests that the gay bar was not as frequent a context as some other researchers have thought. Dank's findings, however, may reflect his different definition of 'coming out'. Following that definition, it is possible for 15 per cent of his sample to 'come out' simply by 'reading about homosexuality for the first time'. There is little doubt that an individual can become aware of his homosexuality before gaining access to other homosexuals (one respondent of mine spent nearly twenty years in this state), but such self-awareness is hardly 'coming out'.

Sometimes the experience of coming out is a relatively simple one – a chance contact on a railway platform turns out to be a homosexual who is willing to introduce the neophyte to the 'scene'; more typically the experience is a prolonged and often stressful one. For, even assuming that the neophyte is aware of the existence of other homosexuals and has decided to locate them, they may not be readily available for him. As Cloward and Ohlin have noted in the broader context of subcultural theory, access to illegitimate cultures cannot be assumed but must itself be seen as problematic (Cloward and Ohlin, 1960). Further, even assuming that there is access to this illegitimate opportunity structure, an individual may be unable to avail himself of it.

Thus, in 'coming out', the neophyte has to have both the *knowledge* and the *ability* to mix with other homosexuals. Neither of these factors may be present. In the past, knowledge of where to meet other homosexuals was particularly difficult for many individuals, but there is evidence that it may be becoming slightly easier for today's younger homosexuals with their widely advertised meeting places and organizations. Once one has entered the subculture, a snowballing process enables one to discover many other places where homosexuals have contact with each other. But in the first instance the problem is one of locating such a source – a problem that may be particularly acute for those with restrictive (geographical and social) home backgrounds.

Knowledge, however, is not enough. Also crucial is the ability of the neophyte to mix with other homosexuals in these social settings. Much may depend here upon the previous cultural and socialization experiences that the neophyte has undergone. Sometimes, far from the initial contact with other homosexuals being a satisfactory experience for coming to terms with oneself, it can be an experience in which guilt and worry are accentuated. One homosexual for example related how much difficulty he had experienced in buying a homosexual handbook:

> I was just looking in some window around Piccadilly and saw this homosexual guide, and I thought this is it – that'll tell me where to meet them. But I just couldn't get up courage to go in and buy it straightway. Do you know I went back to that shop five or six times before I finally plucked up courage enough to go in. And when I finally did, the man [behind the counter] didn't think anything of it at all (author's research notes, 18.10.70).

Another young homosexual commented that although he had been to a club once it was raided by the police and that he just couldn't go back to them: 'I can't relax in clubs. I keep thinking I might see someone from work, or that the police might raid.' Earlier he had commented: 'It's my problem and I've had to live with it for the past seven years, I think of it all the time – every day. I just can't see where it's all going to lead – I wish I was dead' (author's research notes, 27.9.70).

This homosexual seemed permanently lodged in the signification and disorientation stage, even though he had been to a club on one occasion. Many other homosexuals have related their difficulties in going to homosexual meeting-grounds of all kinds. Many fears exist – fears of being recognized, fears of shame, fears of the unknown, of possibly becoming involved in the criminal underworld, of being 'bashed up', of getting into trouble with the police. And even if these general fears do not exist, the neophyte may find himself quite simply unprepared and unable to cope with the norms and values of the homosexual world. The requirements of sociability, youthfulness and attractiveness in the bar setting for example may disqualify a shy, unattractive old man and simply render him a double failure: a failure in the heterosexual world and a failure in the homosexual world.

'Coming out', then, is by no means a simple, automatic or immediate process. Nevertheless, for a sizeable group of people who confront the homosexual experience, its occurrence marks a significant change in life style.

Stabilizing homosexuality

The process so far depicted has led individuals from a situation in which the homosexual experience was merely a fragile potential through a series of shifting choices towards the adoption of a permanent homosexual role. In a series of steps, the individual has developed a commitment to homosexuality as a way of life. A serious problem now arises: if, as has been argued throughout this study, man is capable of exercising choice – is in essence free – why is it that he does not retrace his footsteps more often and become a heterosexual or even a bisexual; why does he allow himself to become 'role-imprisoned', and deny himself access to a wider sexuality? Why does the label stick? Why does he accept the label?

Now apart from the value stance that such questions make (it is rarely asked why heterosexuals remain heterosexuals), they also ignore the narrowing of perceived choices of action available to any person as an identity becomes stabilized. As Lemert (1967: 55) says: 'Once deviance becomes a way of life the personal issue often becomes the cost of making a change rather than the higher status to be gained through rehabilitation or reform.' It becomes easier, more attractive, less costly to remain a homosexual.

There are many reasons why individuals should be both *unwilling* and *unable* to leave the homosexual role once entered. Unwillingness arises not least because of the intrinsic delights of being a homosexual: the acts of falling, making and being 'in love' with a member of the same sex can be both pleasurable and satisfying. Such a pleasurable state is generally ignored by scientific and lay imagery alike, which more typically renders the homosexual experience meaningless and unsatisfying, concentrating only upon its dangers and disadvantages. Now while it is true that there are obstacles to overcome in becoming homosexual, once these are overcome the experience itself may be pleasurable enough to provide a basis for its continuation. And while it is true that many homosexuals experience worry and misery in their day to day lives, so too do many heterosexuals. One does not really have to seek esoteric reasons then for individuals staying in the homosexual role: homosexual experience is persistently sought because it is pleasurable in itself.[27]

Further, once one has entered the role other advantages may accrue that are positive, even if unintended.[28] Magee (1968) has listed some of the advantages arising because homosexuals are independent and without ties,[29] while Hoffman (1968: 155) has described the advantages of being young and 'gay':

There is a very seductive quality about gay life in the large cities which is extremely attractive to the kind of young man who wants to be admired and sought after by other individuals. For in that community, he can find a kind of attention, from a large number of individuals, which he simply cannot get from a large number of women. . . . There are always bars to visit and parties to go to; there is a certain routine about settling down with one sexual partner which can entirely be obviated by taking up a promiscuous homosexual life. The whole scene is very seductive and glamorous, especially when one has first entered it. It is a constant source of meaning and one's self esteem is continually buoyed up.

Not all the blocks to 'normal' identity are voluntarily imposed, however: there are also external constraints to change. Thus, even if a homosexual should desire to leave the homosexual role, he may find that he is increasingly unable to do so. As he becomes older and more encircled by the homosexual experience, so he may find it increasingly difficult to make or maintain heterosexual contacts and increasingly disturbing to contemplate the idea of heterosexual activity. His earlier problems of access and identity may re-emerge in reverse if he should contemplate departure from the homosexual role: the secure world now is the 'deviant' world, and the problematic world becomes the 'straight' world. How does one make contact, for example, with a potential female partner at the age of thirty, if one has never attempted to do so before, and knows no heterosexuals; and, still worse, how does one set about having a hetero-sexual coital experience for the first time at this age? Further, not only will obstacles be set up to restrict a return to a 'normal' role, but punishments may be imposed from within the world for all who attempt to 'go straight'. Every homosexual who attempts to return to the heterosexual world constitutes a threat to the stability of other homosexuals. If one person can be reconverted to hetero-sexuality, why not all? Thus pressures may be brought to bear upon the miscreant. One respondent related to me several personal in-stances of this, when he occasionally sought contact with girls with a view to 'going straight', and was rejected – first verbally then socially – by his homosexual friends. They returned, of course, with tales of 'I told you so' when the various relationships came to an end, the threat having been removed and their position as 'exclusive homosexuals' actually strengthened (Ray, 1964).

One further factor that may lead to 'role-imprisonment' is that of official labelling and public degradation. (Erickson, 1966; Garfinkle, 1956). To come before a court in the blaze of a public scandal – as did Wilde, Wildeblood and Harvey[30] – is to be publicly ushered into a deviant role, with few chances of receiving official declarations of exit. This is, of course, the most apparent instance of the functioning of deviant labels, but it is also with regard to homosexuality today possibly statistically the least significant (Weinberg, 1969; 1970a).

Later stages

I have traced the process of becoming homosexual through four central stages: sensitization, signification, 'coming out' and stabiliza-tion. A full analysis should not stop here, however, but should go on to consider the other modifications to the experience that take place over the life span. Indeed, the process of 'reaching middle age' and 'becoming old' as a homosexual are two areas where little is known and much needs to be known. But such issues must lie outside the scope of this book.

Conclusion

In this chapter, attention has been focused upon that most researched of topics: the process of becoming homosexual. However, the em-phasis has been placed not upon the aetiological factors that con-tribute to homosexuality in the first instance (primary deviance), which is the conventional and most researched path. Rather, after a critique of such theories, the discussion has been concerned with the processes involved in adult socialization; the processes involved in learning a homosexual role. Four particular stages were highlighted as worthy of prolonged analysis in the future: sensitization, signification, 'coming out', and stabilization.

My intention in this chapter has been to show the role that the social context plays in shaping homosexual socialization. Especially in the early stages of sensitivity and signification, the societal reaction of hostility plays a crucial role in bringing about an exaggerated concern with matters of homosexuality, and a strong potential for polarization. But a concluding caution is in order. The recent signs of change in our sexual mores may well mean that in the distant future, the process of becoming a homosexual will be a less significant one and a less painful one. This may result in a decrease of polarization so that individuals come to see themselves as simultaneously occupying homosexual and heterosexual roles, with an accompanying decrease in rigid, exclusive forms of sexuality. This remains conjecture.

8 The collective reaction: the subculture of homosexuality

The concept of subculture has already been highlighted at several points in this book, and in this chapter I propose to take up a number of matters relating to the subculture of homosexuality in greater detail. Once again, and perhaps surprisingly, there is a serious lack of data available. The core of knowledge in this field is contained in a handful or so papers, none of which relate to the English scene. My comments will thus be sketchy, although I will draw both from this literature and my own direct observation of homosexual life in London between 1968 and 1970. I will begin by considering the nature of the subculture of homosexuality, describe some of its features, locate it structurally, and then put forward some explanations for its emergence. [1]

The subculture of homosexuality

Subcultures are consequences of complex, pluralistic societies where the existence of a unitary value system among societal members can no longer be taken for granted. While there are many problems involved in the use of such a concept, [2] it may be taken to refer to any life style involving shared norms and values that differ in significant ways from a dominant culture – the culture generated by the dominant political groups in any society. Clearly, they are always part of a larger culture and the dialectical relationship to that culture needs constant attention. At the same time, to see the world as it is constructed by the subcultural group, and not as it is constructed by the dominant group, is one of the main tasks of subcultural theory.

The subculture of homosexuality, then, refers to a relatively stable life style involving a number of interactants around the homosexual experience. As with any culture, it comes to develop its own 'designs for living' – but such elements are neither homogeneous, well organized and stable, nor fundamentally different from other cultures. Rather, the subculture is a constantly changing and loosely organized phenomenon displaying varying forms, whose members vary considerably in their involvement and commitment. I wish to expand some of these points before going on to consider the distinctive features of the homosexual subculture.

First, then, the subculture is not homogeneous, but expresses a diversity of forms, all of which may be seen as 'variants' of the main subcultural elements to be described in the next section, but all of which are distinctively divergent. Several earlier attempts[3] have been made at describing the subcultural variations, but two levels may be usefully distinguished: the public and visible levels organized around specific behaviour settings and institutions, and the private and less visible forms of homosexual life organized around relationships and friendship cliques. Not all discussions would agree with my inclusion of the latter level within the rubric of subculture. Hooker (1967), for example, distinguishes three social levels that are not a part of the subculture – closely knit groups, larger groups and very loose networks – but all of these could, by my account, constitute subcultural forms. It is true that these three kinds of relationships may only constitute networks of acquaintances, and in this case they cannot be seen as subcultural; but, in general, such networks also develop a life style that accompanies them, and this life style is the critically important variable. Too much research in the past has overstressed the well-defined, publicly accessible facets of the subculture, whereas for most homosexuals this is the least significant part. They may only occasionally visit bars, but most of their homosexual lives are spent with friends and acquaintances in networks.

These two levels of the homosexual subculture themselves display variations. On the institutional level, at least four forms have been studied by researchers: the bar life, the public places, the hustling market and the homophile movement. Each of these variants has a different emphasis and particular characteristics, but I cannot discuss these here.[4] The bar is primarily a social institution; the public places are primarily locales for impersonal sex; the hustling market is the source of homosexual prostitution; and the homophile movement is comprised of a number of bodies organized around the task of legitimation. Involvement of the 'homosexual' in any of these areas does not automatically implicate him in the others – many homosexuals, for example, may become involved in bars, while remaining totally uninterested and even unaware of the existence of homophile movements. Indeed, Sagarin and others have commented that the homophile movement remains only marginally supported by homosexuals (Sagarin, 1969). Furthermore, each of these forms may exhibit great variety in their turn: male prostitutes range from adolescent boys who indulge in a 'moonlighting' for extra cash, to those who develop stable 'street-corner' hustling roles; to the homosexual boy who becomes a call boy in a 'house of male prostitution'. Similarly, places of public sex may vary immensely – from the patterns described by Humphreys in toilets to others that take place in cinemas, baths, parks, streets and department stores.

While these four variations are important and serve crucial functions for many homosexuals, to stress them at the expense of more general relationships is as valid as describing heterosexuality purely in terms of pubs and bars, swingers and public sex, prostitution and pressure groups for sexual liberation; they are simply some of the more visible forms of heterosexual life. The homosexual's situation in a hostile society may well mean that these four variations assume a somewhat greater significance in his world, but they should never be seen as *the* homosexual world. Rather, the crux of the subculture – tucked, as it is, away from sight and thus much less accessible to study – is the homosexual relational network. Much of the homosexual world is better characterized as a series of friendship cliques only loosely connected with the public institutions just described. Thus, homosexuals may occasionally go to a gay bar, or the local 'cottage', but most of their life is spent among friends and acquaintances, as indeed is a heterosexual's.

Sonenschein's (1968) study of homosexual relationships in America has discussed their nature around two main themes – the sexual/social nature of the relationships, and the duration of the relationships. By tabulating these variables, he is able to construct a six-fold typology of relationships in the homosexual world ranging from the 'one night stand' to the 'permanent affair'. The full typology is given in Table 6 (taken from Sonenschein, 1968: 71).

TABLE 6   *Sonenschein's typology of male homosexual relationships in the subject community*

| Sexuality | Duration | |
	permanent	*non-permanent*
Social	First-order friendships	Second-order friendships
Sexual	Extended encounters	Brief encounters
Socio-sexual	Mateships	Circumstantial encounters

Sonenschein's discussion highlights the range of possible relationships in the homosexual world, relationships that are not so dissimilar in range (though highly different in incidence) to those found in the heterosexual world. I have discussed one of these relationships (that of mateships) in detail elsewhere (Plummer, 1974a).

Second, the subculture of homosexuality is not so very different from the dominant culture – but is continuous with it. This is true in an obvious sense – no member of any subculture, except perhaps those in total institutions, can be hermetically sealed off from the dominant culture in his daily round: homosexuals, like everybody else, generally clean their teeth in the morning, drive on the left-hand side of the road, work for a living and sleep in beds with four legs, a mattress and sheets (McCall and Simmons, 1966: ch. 2). In a less trivial sense, even the elements of the homosexual subculture that serve to mark it off from the dominant culture have most of their roots in that culture. Most of the values that I shall be describing in the next section, for example, are really only those values commonly associated with courtship in the heterosexual culture; and most of the material forms of organization of the subculture have their basis in capitalism and the 'market mentality'.

Third, within the subculture, individual members vary in their degree of involvement and commitment. At one extreme, there is the highly 'camp' and very 'obvious' homosexual who spends most of his time by day in the company of homosexuals at work, say, in a theatrical occupation, and by night in gay bars and gay public places, and retires to his home which he shares with two other homosexuals: such involvement is almost complete, effectively his whole life is spent in interaction with other homosexuals. At the other extreme, there is the 'respectably married man', who may just occasionally go to a gay bar or a public convenience when away from home on business: the involvement and commitment to the homosexual subculture is minimal. Both these types are empirically observable, but represent polar ends of a continuum of subcultural involvement. Individuals should be seen as subscribing with different degrees of commitment to the subculture. In order to assess the degree of involvement of any individual in the homosexual subculture, some measures need to be taken of his familiarity with the main elements of the homosexual culture.

These elements can be reified for the purpose of analysis into an ideal type or parent form of subculture, a form which does not exist in reality. While it is possible to list them as if they had an existence of their own, it must again be stressed that they are placed in a constant dialectical relationship with the dominant heterosexual culture. As Matza (1961: 105) says: 'There is an ongoing dialectic between conventional and deviant traditions and in the process of exchange, both are modified.' The homosexual bar, for example, modifies and is modified by the wider bar system.

With these cautions about the variability of the subculture, its continuity with the wider culture, and the differential attachment of

157

members to it, I turn now to some elements of an ideal type of subculture.

Elements of the homosexual subculture

At the risk of gross reification and crude stereotyping, I wish to outline in this section a number of elements which my fieldwork has led me to believe are particularly identifiable with the homosexual life style. Such a task is clearly one that is plagued with hazards for, as I have already stressed, the homosexual subculture cannot be seen as a phenomenon quite apart from other cultures: it must be related to these cultures with which it has much in common. Nevertheless, it must have some distinctive elements for it to be worthy of the name of 'subculture', and it is some of these that I wish to consider here.

Since 'subculturalness is a continuum not a dichotomy' (Goode, 1968: 54), one way of considering the elements below is in terms of the extent to which any one individual conforms to them, or is involved in them. To the extent that he is, one may talk of this individual as being highly involved in the subculture. To the extent that he is not, one may say he is not involved in the subculture. The following elements could be constructed as rating scales for measuring homosexual subculturalness with more specific scales being devised to tap the degree of involvement in a specific variant of the subculture. In summary, if a researcher wished to assess the degree of subcultural involvement of an individual, he would need to know about: (a) the actor's symbolic world; (b) the normative organization of the actor's world; (c) the language and argot of the actor's world; (d) the interaction network of the actor; (e) the behaviour patterns of the actor; (f) the self-conception of the actor; (g) the material organization of the actor's world. There are other elements, but I wish to look at these briefly in turn.

a *The symbolic world:* Central to any comprehension of the homosexual subculture, indeed the central element, is the existence of a quite distinctive perception of the world. To put it simply: male homosexuals are 'boy' watchers.[5] In contrast, and as simply, male heterosexuals are 'girl' watchers. No comprehension of the homosexual world is possible unless this point is grasped.

Such a pivotal distinction means of course that people in the homosexual subculture regularly and routinely apprehend other men as erotic objects: at work, watching television, walking along the street, at parties, in moments of 'time out' and reverie, the young man's fancy turns to other men. It is the world of the waking heterosexual man in reverse – with all the variations in kinds of objects and intensity of attraction that this implies. An example, recounted to me by one student, may make this clearer. The student, John, was a 'homosexual' and was 'known about' by one particular hetero-sexual friend, Bill. John explained how on one occasion he was walking down a corridor at his college with Bill, when he saw a young man walking by whom he 'fancied'. He swung his head around as the attractive stranger walked by, and commented to Bill that he 'fancied that'. Bill – being a hot-blooded man! – subsequently swung his head around, but couldn't see anybody in the corridor. A little later he realized that there was in fact somebody else in the corridor, another male student. But there was nothing worthy of the label 'fanciable'. Subsequently Bill realized that John was referring to the other man, and that there was no woman in the corridor. The same objective situation – three men in a corridor – thus took on quite different meanings according to the symbolic world of the actor.

The above discussion has raised only the most significant aspect of the homosexual's symbolic world. There are others; for example, a whole series of material artefacts may become symbolically signi-ficant for the homosexual, while remaining insignificant for the heterosexual. The sight of a tube of KY cream – used officially for surgical instruments, but widely used too as a lubricant by homosexuals – may mean very little to most heterosexuals, but a great deal to any homosexual who has had only minimal sexual con-tact with other homosexuals. Similarly, the functioning of public conveniences for acts of public sex may figure quite significantly in a homosexual's symbolic universe, while remaining unnoticed and un-dreamt of in the symbolic universe of a heterosexual (Humphreys, 1970: 61). These symbolic variations – variations in the way one perceives the world round about – are some of the most distinctive features of the homosexual subculture.

b *The normative organization:* The most apparent and frequently cited element of a subculture is its normative system. It is also per-haps the hardest of all to measure, since, as I have constantly stressed, subcultures are often closely continuous with wider cultures. There are no rigidly separate values, except in the polar care of contracultures. Rather, there are values and norms which are slightly distinctive.

Several studies exist which demonstrate some of the ground rules of organization for specific aspects of the subculture. Reiss, for example, has discussed the normative organization of delinquent hustling boys; Pittman has shown the rules of the 'house of male prostitution'; Humphreys has described the rules of 'pick-ups' and public sex; and Cavaan has discussed some of the 'standing behaviour' patterns of the bar (Reiss, 1961; Pittman, 1971; Humphreys, 1970;

Cavaan, 1966). Such norms as these may be partially distinctive, but they also overlap with their heterosexual counterparts in many ways.

It is, therefore, dangerous to suggest that there are any very general norms around which the homosexual subculture functions. I would, however, briefly like to indicate four themes that I found particularly prevalent during my fieldwork, and which, while not separate from many themes that emerge in the heterosexual world, nevertheless capture the 'feel' of the norms as they exist in the gay world.

1 Sexuality: Since, in the first instance, homosexuals have really only one feature in common with each other (their erotic preference for the same sex), it is not surprising that this should be a major concern of the homosexual subculture. Overtly, there is both a lot of talk about sex, and not an inconsiderable amount of activity. Covertly, there are a lot of secret yearnings and thoughts about sex. Many of the major institutional forms – bars, hustling, 'cottages' – function with an emphasis upon sexual partners, and many individual homosexuals spend a considerable time involved in the pursuit of a stable lover. None of this is really so very different from large sections of the heterosexual world – where workmates endlessly talk about their 'good screw'; where dance halls are used for 'pick-ups'; where a lover is necessary to avoid being 'left on the shelf'. Sexuality may be central to the homosexual subculture; but then it is central to many others too.[6]

2 Appearances: The concern with appearances is true in two senses. The first is trivial and not widespread – involving the concern of many homosexuals to render themselves as physically attractive to other homosexuals through the use of appropriate dress, hair styles, etc. The second is fundamental and widespread – involving the concern of most homosexuals to present an appropriate and non-stigmatizing 'personal front', to carefully control the impressions that others have of them lest they be discovered as homosexuals. The first arises largely from the importance of sexuality; the second arises largely from the fact that homosexuality is a stigma label. A consequence of the concern with appearance is, as Williams and Weinberg (1971: 15) point out, that the homosexual is likely to become a 'practical methodologist'. Thus, homosexuals come to see how the world is socially constructed and become aware of some of the rules by which it is so constructed, being placed as they are in positions of constantly having to consciously perform roles. Being stigmatized results in the uncommonsense knowledge of commonsense social structures (Garfinkle, 1967; Goffman, 1963a).

3 Youthfulness: Many homosexuals occupy less 'responsible' positions in the social structure – in the sense of lacking family commitments and duties – and in this parallel the position of some young people. They may thus be expected to develop some of the

attributes commonly linked to this group. Further, in a society that places considerable emphasis on the values of 'being young' (concomitantly devaluing 'the old'), it should not be surprising that many people (including the heterosexual culture) should wish to emulate the young. Since unmarried homosexuals are not tied into the 'age-grading system' in the same way that their married peers are, they may well become more mobile between the generations. For such reasons there appears to be an emphasis on youthfulness in the homosexual world. Bennet Berger has argued that 'youth culture' should designate the normative system of youthful persons, not necessarily young ones. 'The definitive characteristics of youth culture are relevant to groups other than the age-grade we call adolescence' (Berger, 1963: 320). This being so, the homosexual culture seems to have much in common with the youth culture. There is an emphasis on expressive behaviour – entertainments, parties, fashion, pop music, 'irresponsibility', romance, 'rating and dating' and other hedonistic pursuits – prevalent in *some* sections of the homosexual world, especially the bar system. Hoffman (1968: 54) writes:

> In the gay world there is a tremendous accent on youth and this is reflected in the composition of the bar clientele. Youth is very much at a premium and young men will go to the bars as soon as they have passed the legal age limit. . . . Along with the younger men, there are somewhat older men who are trying to look young.

And later, and more dramatically, he comments (p. 155):

> Since virtually the sole criterion of value in the homosexual world is physical attractiveness, being young and handsome in gay life is like being a millionaire in a community where wealth is the only criterion of value.

Certainly Hoffman's comments are valid if one is talking about some of the more public aspects of the homosexual community, but they cannot readily be generalized to the whole homosexual subculture.

4   Problematics: On two counts homosexuality may be seen as a 'problem'. First, as a personal problem and second as a social problem. As I have shown in chapter 7, many homosexuals will find the sensitivity to being homosexual an intense personal problem. Equally, I demonstrated that many homosexuals will move out of this problematic stage and become stabilized (and 'well-adjusted') homosexuals. So while some members of the subculture may have their personal 'hang-ups' about being gay, this need not be as widespread as is sometimes assumed. However, the social problem is ever-present – arising as it does from the existence of a hostile

societal reaction. Homosexuals have homosexuality defined as a problem for them by society's members, and while they may not agree that it is a problem, they nevertheless have to respond to such a challenge. Thus many parts of the homosexual world are characterized by norms that help members to cope with this problematic nature of the experience.

c *Argot:* A third element in subculturalization is the degree of familiarity an individual exhibits with regard to the specialized linguistics forms that develop within the subculture. Lerman has suggested that a reliable indicator of an adolescent boy's familiarity with the delinquent subculture is his awareness of the spoken argot (Lerman, 1967). Likewise, the more an individual displays familiarity with homosexual slang, the greater the probability that he will be involved in the homosexual subculture. At one end of the continuum of subcultural involvement are the homosexuals who display full knowledge of homosexual language, and at the other are those who are even unacquainted with common words in the homosexual lexicon such as 'gay' and 'camp'.[7]

Very little research has been conducted into the nature, extent and functions of the homosexual argot, although its existence has been acknowledged for a long time. A few speculative generalizations may however be in order.[8]

The language appears to exist in two related forms – one that is 'full blown', all-encompassing and stable over time and place; and one that is piecemeal and constantly changing. The former called 'palare' rests on a particular syntactic construction rather like rhyming slang and is known by only a few homosexuals. The latter is essentially a situational language – a language where meanings are largely dependent upon the context in which they are spoken and which is known by many more homosexuals. It is transmitted in day to day interaction in the subculture and is forever in a state of flux. The words in the homosexual argot are likely to exhibit wide differences over regions and contexts. A West-coast homosexual may have a very different rhetoric from one in the East coast, and a homosexual involved in 'Gay Lib' may have a markedly different language style from that of his 'Gay Brother' in other 'straight' sections of the homophile world.

Within this argot, Sonenschein (1969) suggests four main processes at work which help to characterize (though not define) it. These are effeminization, utilization, redirection and invention. The first process marks the way in which the language typically feminizes nouns, adjective, pronouns, names and phrases: a man may constantly be referred to as 'she', David converted to Daisy, and interjections such as 'honey' and 'darling' flow freely. Utilization refers to the borrowing of terms used in other groups, and here Sonenschein suggests the homosexual may borrow from other sexual subcultures where a langugage has developed around sexuality. The male hustler, for example, has some similarity in his language to that of the female prostitute. In addition, the language may also borrow from cultures that are closely related to it: the Gay Lib activist, for example, utilizes a language that may have at least as much in common with the 'underground' as it does with the homosexual world. Redirection occurs when the form of the word remains the same, but the meaning changes; as when a homosexual is called a 'bitch' to indicate unpopular characteristics but not necessarily those of effeminacy. Finally, invention refers to 'words . . . taken and given a new and unique meaning, the use of which in a slang sense is not to be found outside the homosexual circle'. As an instance of this, Sonenschein cites the use of the word 'Nelly' to mean effeminate. These four processes may be seen as influencing the content and form of the homosexual language.

The functions that such a language serves seem at least three-fold. As with most minority languages, there is a heightening of group awareness and consciousness. One of the most widespread distinctions in the language, for example, is that between 'straights' (sometimes even called 'normals') and 'us'—the 'gays', and this may serve to heighten group identity. Some words given to homosexuals by this 'straight world'—such as 'queers'—seem to be used only by those homosexuals who have little contact with the homosexual world; those who become totally committed to one or other aspect of the subculture may quite explicitly reject any words given to them by the 'straight world' and emphasize, even exaggerate, their own.[9]

A second function of such language is that it may serve as a means of secret communication, a possible source for locating and identifying other homosexuals in the company of 'straights', or in conversations where one member is not sure of the other's identity. Through a casual inclusion of the word 'gay' in a conversation, one member serves to sensitize the other if he too is a homosexual, while remaining immune if the other is not. Such a 'secret' process however is not always reliable, since some words may be known by the 'wise' or, as with the word 'gay' in recent times, by so many 'outsiders' as to render its potency rather weak.

Another function which the homosexual language serves is common to language generally: it serves to structure perception and experience. Thus, it highlights particular 'types of people' in the homosexual world ('camp', 'chickens', 'queens', 'butch', 'trade', 'tricks', 'leather', 'closet queens', 'rent' and so forth); locales ('cottages', 'cruisy scenes', 'trolling grounds', 'meat-racks'); mannerisms ('swishy', 'camp') and acts ('blow-job', 'one-night stand', 'daisy chain', 'brown') among other things that non-homosexuals may not be aware of. A detailed understanding of the homosexual world most certainly requires an understanding of the forms and functions of its argot.

d *The interaction network:* Network is a measure of relationships not culture, and thus has only a limited applicability in understanding homosexual subcultures. Nevertheless, knowledge of any individual's contact with others who call themselves 'homosexual' may be quite a good indicator of the degree of subcultural involvement. An individual who knows only one or two other homosexuals is not very likely to be highly involved, while at the other extreme some homosexuals boast that there is not a town in the country that they could not go to without knowing and meeting other homosexuals. In less common instances, the 'homosexual brotherhood' may function on an international level.

e *The behaviour pattern:* Every culture brings with it recurrent behaviour patterns that are taken for granted by members but which may remain highly problematic to non-subcultural actors. Whether one is poor, a church-goer, a janitor, a student nurse or a nudist – specific behaviour patterns will emerge with which the members will become familiarized. For the neophyte homosexual or for the heterosexual, there may seem to be a number of problems associated with being a homosexual on a purely behavioural level: 'Is it not, for example, very painful and difficult to commit acts of anal intercourse?'[10] 'Is it not very difficult to know how to meet partners and friends? How does one cope with threats from 'queer-bashers', the blackmailer or the police?' As one moves into the subculture, however, these kinds of problems begin to disappear as one routinizes patterns of behaviour. Subcultural homosexuals thus develop distinctive styles of behaviour.

f *Self-concept and identity:* One key measure of subcultural involvement (a socio-psychological one) is an individual's identity, which is learned from the reaction of others (Kinch, 1963). As one moves further into a subculture, so one 'develops a stronger identity with the category' of people in it, and such identities become more stable (Hall, 1966). Those in the sexual subculture may thus have clearer, more stable self-conceptions of themselves as homosexuals than homosexuals who do not become so involved.

g *Material organization and artefacts:* Finally subcultural involvement may be assessed through familiarity with the material and organizational forms that the subculture takes. Any culture comes to develop special institutions and equipment which serve to facilitate the smooth running of the social order associated with the subculture. In the homosexual world, material organization may emerge in the form of sauna baths, gay bars or homophile organizations which may have premises and sometimes quite complex organizational structures surrounding them. Further, in the homosexual world, a range of artefacts may become available to cater for specific homosexual needs – gay-guides for those who don't know their way around the homosexual world; homophile journals and newspapers whose functions are many and varied; gay films and film clubs; gay Christmas cards and even gay colouring books. Much of the material organization of the homosexual world follows closely the material organization of the heterosexual world, utilizing, for example, the market mechanism and conspicuous consumption. Some of it serves as an example of what Lemert has termed the 'exploitative culture' by which 'sharp practices' may be employed to exploit those in marginal roles (Lemert, 1951: 65–8). Clubs may recruit subscribing members and never open; film theatres showing homosexual films or shops selling homosexual pornography may charge excessive prices; sexual accessories which fail to live up to their extravagant claims may be distributed at great cost to the client 'under plain cover'.

The structural location of homosexual subcultures

Homosexual subcultures are not randomly distributed throughout societies and are not equally available to all. Within England and America, for example, subcultures become more pervasive in larger cities and develop only rudimentary structures in smaller communities. For men, the world is much more organized than for women; for the young, it is much more public than for the old; for the poor and lower class, it may be harder to gain access.[11] Further, different forms of the subculture are differentially available: gay bars seem to need large populations (perhaps over 50,000 to flourish (Karlen, 1971: 513); while public conveniences available for sex develop even within the smallest community.

Two factors seem especially likely to affect the distribution of socially organized homosexual experiences: the need for tolerance and anonymity, stemming from hostile reactions, and the need for cultural continuity, by which the homosexual subculture remains endemically tied to the wider order.

Cultural continuity: Homosexual groupings are likely to arise with features broadly paralleling those found among heterosexual groups in the wider society. Thus, membership of homophile movements such as the Campaign for Homosexual Equality or Mattachine parallels the middle-class membership of any heterosexual voluntary organization; membership of movements such as GLF parallels the student, 'beat', politically-aware membership of any heterosexual radical or militant group; and involvement in the world of male prostitution parallels involvement in the heterosexual counterpart.

One of the clearest examples of this 'cultural continuity' thesis is the relative lack of involvement of women in the public aspects of the homosexual subculture. In comparison with males, there are very few women involved in the homophile movements, very few 'lesbian' bars and clubs, and an almost total lack of women involved in public sex'. It could be argued that this is a consequence of a lower incidence of homosexuality among lesbians, but even allowing for some validity in such an observation, it could hardly be held to account for the very wide variations. Rather, the cultural continuity thesis makes considerably more sense. Simon and Gagnon in several papers have suggested how many features of lesbianism are continuous with femininity and the cultural definitions of the female role (Simon and Gagnon, 1967a, 1967b). Thus, unlike the male who is reared on notions of dominance and aggression, the woman is reared to be submissive, domestic and romantic. She is much more likely than the male to seek a permanent, loving partner and then to devote her time to developing her 'nest'. The lesbian mirrors this belief system. She becomes much more concerned with the issues of establishing and maintaining a stable love relationship with another woman than she is with 'casual sex' or 'cruising bars' (Wolff, 1971). There is small ground for surprise at the fact that there are few lesbian bars, for the world of taverns, pubs and bars has traditionally been the province of the male, and the lesbian world merely reflects this historical claim (Knupfer and Room, 1964; Cavaan, 1966; Pittman and Snyder, 1962).

Further, the subculture also reflects the youth concerns of the dominant society. There is, as already remarked, a premium placed upon youthfulness in the gay world, and it is not surprising that many segments of it – such as the bar, the hustling markets, the liberation movements – tend to be youth dominated. Weinberg (1970a) has produced evidence which suggests that as homosexuals age, they tend to withdraw from the organized, more visible and more sociable forms of the gay world. This could be seen as simply continuous with the broader ageing process of disengagement.

The search for anonymity: Subcultures are also likely to arise in 'protective places' which afford a measure of security and anonymity.

Homosexual bars, for example, are only likely to arise in larger towns and even there will not readily be open to public gaze – they will arise in areas of transient and floating populations,[12] and will develop strategies to restrict public entry. Locales for 'public sex' are less likely to be limited exclusively to the larger towns – indeed, almost every small community is likely to have developed its casual sex spot away from the public eye. Such places are generally shielded by protective barriers: toilets are selected for public sex when they lie in the remotest corner of the park (Humphreys, 1970: ch. 1) or when they lie in side streets that are seldom used by the public at large; open spaces are selected when they are hedged in by trees and shrubbery;[13] and turkish baths are selected that do not display signs of ready accessibility to the public. In addition, some such places are shielded by sheer numbers – where crowds render the activity of a few individuals invisible, as in the activity that takes place in public conveniences at main railway termini.

The emergence of the subculture of homosexuality

Nobody to date has tackled the task of explaining the emergence of the subculture of homosexuality in any detail, although a fair idea of what such a theory would look like may be found by considering some of the accounts given to explain the emergence of subcultural delinquency. One prominent theory suggests that it can be seen as arising as a solution to problems faced by individuals collectively in the social structure (Cohen, 1955; Cloward and Ohlin, 1960). Another suggests that it may be largely a consequence of a hostile societal reaction which results in segregation and isolation of deviant groups (Wilkins, 1964). A third suggests that it may be seen as a consequence of direct cultural transmission (Miller, 1962). This latter theory differs from the first two, in that it is more concerned with the processes by which individuals become socialized into an already existing culture. All homosexuals who become involved in the subculture of homosexuality experience the transmission of the existing 'gay culture' in part – though this is not a direct socialization experience but rather a resocialization experience (DeLameter, 1968).[14] Since I have dealt with this in chapter 7, I will restrict my attention here to the first two kinds of theory which I have separately dubbed the 'push' and the 'pull' theories: one theory stressing the 'pull' of the gay world as problem-solving, the other stressing the 'push' of societal reactions towards the gay world. The theories are complementary.

A 'pull' theory: According to the 'pull' theory, 'the 'crucial conditions for the emergence of new cultural forms is the existence, in

167

effective interaction with one another, of a number of actors with similar problems of adjustment' (Cohen, 1955: 59). The subculture thus comes into being because it provides solutions to particular problems faced by homosexuals and becomes attractive in itself. I have described the kinds of problems homosexuals face in chapter 7: those of guilt, access and identity. And I also highlighted there how as one moves progressively into the subculture, so one gains readier access to sexual and social partners, to a series of legitimations about homosexuality, and strengthened sense of identity. This is not to say that each variant of the subculture is equally competent at solving all these problems. The bar seems to be particularly effective at most of them; whereas the cottage and hustling systems seem to be efficient primarily at solving the sexual problems and dysfunctional in some other respects.

I have observed a number of individuals 'coming out' in the bar system, and noted the changes that have taken place over a couple of months. Typically before entry to the bar system, the individual was 'sexually frustrated', alone, worried about being 'queer' and ashamed. After a few weeks, the individual outlook had changed radically – he had met sexual partners, gained social friends and learnt a series of legitimations for his homosexuality. Sometimes the change had been a very accentuated one – resulting in the individual, often temporarily, assuming an extremely 'camp' and effeminate role-style. While not all individuals can cope with the threats of gay-bar visiting – threats that I have discussed in chapter 7, pp. 148–50 – many use bars as a multiproblem-solving device.

The 'public-sex' system, on the other hand, primarily resolves the problems of sexual access. Here, indeed, it is remarkably efficient, evoking admiration from some 'wise' heterosexual respondents:

> The homosexuals seem to have got themselves a lot better organized for a quick bit of sex than we have. They've got their bogs and their commons – and their pubs too – and they know when they go there that they're going to get some sex straight, and no messing. We've got to hang around bars for some time, and then we can't be sure after chatting a bird up that we'll get anything.

This subculture then provides instant, accessible and impersonal sex (Humphreys, 1970). At the same time, it is not very competent at providing social contacts or legitimations for homosexuality – indeed, since the games of public sex are typically conducted in silence, there are few means of communication. For some homosexuals, public-sex contact is supported by relational networks and perhaps contacts in the gay bars – so these side functions are not important. For others (Humphreys's heterosexually married man, for example), sex seems to be the only problem actually confronted – and no social contact with homosexuals is desired. Yet for some, the 'cottaging' experience is particularly distressing because it fails to meet needs other than the purely sexual and may even provoke such reactions as guilt. One respondent said:

> I must have been cottaging since I was 20 [he was now forty] and I haven't made a single friend out of it. Mind you, I've met quite a few people, but we either have it there on the spot or we go back to his place for a 'quicky' and we never meet again. . . . I don't really think the sort of people who go there are nice to make friends with.

A 'push' theory: This theory, as developed by Wilkins, suggests that from a small initial deviation generated by a problem (in this case, the personal problems of homosexuality described above), there is a spiralling process which culminates in a crystallized sub-culture that is 'cut off' from the mainstream of culture. The crucial factor in this spiralling process is the 'push' of the hostile societal reaction which condemns and acts against the initial deviation, causing it thereby to become reinforced, alienated and divorced from the wider structure. Such a dynamic is implicit throughout my argument.

Now both these theories stress the importance of the 'societal reaction' notion. Thus, the 'pull' theory suggests that certain problems arise for which the subculture is the solution, but that these problems are largely those generated by a hostile societal reaction; while the 'push' theory suggests the subculture arises through a social reaction process which serves to segregate homosexuals from wider involvements. Given this, then, the explanation of homosexual subcultures could be tentatively depicted as in Table 7.

TABLE 7   *The creation of the subculture of homosexuality*

	Immediate problems:	Pull:	
	→ Guilt, identity, acces	→ problem-solving	
Structural features: Societal reactions to homosexuality			Subculture of → homosexuality
	Segregation process: → Deviancy amplification	*Push:* → rejected	

Such a picture rightly puts considerable emphasis upon the existence of a hostile societal reaction in the creation of deviant subcultures. But, regretfully, it is too one-sided – viewing the subculture entirely as a response and ignoring its dialectical relationship with

169

the society. As Young has suggested, the notion of subculture has frequently been used too statically, ignoring the dialectical interplay between deviant action and reaction. While subcultures provide solutions to problems, such solutions subsequently 'create new contradictions and new responses, and the change in the latter represents a new environment – and therefore problems – for the group' (Young, 1974).

Further, viewing the subculture entirely as a response serves to conceal the positive aspects of the homosexual experience which may lead to the existence of such subcultures, even if society no longer devalued it. A group's distinctive way of life can never be seen solely as a reflection of the dominant forces that have oppressed, excluded and alienated its members from a wider society; they must also be seen as having some positive elements of their own. Thus, the 'homosexual culture' is sometimes seen as a consequence of a 'homosexual temperament' – that its forms are derived from the nature of the homosexual condition. One author suggests that the homosexual temperament is characterized by a 'high degree of introspection, imagination, abstraction, subjectivity generally, preoccupation with mood and fantasy, and a number of other qualities', and goes on to suggest that if a homosexual culture exists it would have to demonstrate these qualities (Crowther, 1960). This view supports those writers who suggest that 'homosexuals are creative' and that such creativity finds an outlet in the homosexual culture, which itself is highly influential in shaping the dominant culture.

Such views must remain suspect because there is little evidence for the existence of such a phenomenon as the 'homosexual temperament'. At the same time, there are some aspects of the homosexual experience which may well give rise to the need for a subculture, even if society's hostility were to diminish. It is plausible that even if 'homosexuals' did not confront problems of guilt, identity and hostility through societal reaction, they would still face some problems of access and indeed that the nature of the homosexual experience leads homosexuals to seek other homosexuals. In other words, the subculture could be seen simply as the consequence of homosexuality *per se*. In the same way as people who like surfing, medieval dancing or stamp collecting band together with similar enthusiasts, so homosexuals would choose to band together even when there exists no hostility.

Two factors need to be stressed about such an argument. First, the form of the subculture under such conditions would probably be considerably different. At present many of the features of the subculture highlight problems of identity, legitimacy and guilt management, but most of these aspects would no longer be present.[15] Second, if the societal reaction were to be *totally* eliminated, it is plausible that subcultures would not even be necessary for the purpose of joining with mutual enthusiasts. For it is part of the argument of this book that in a non-repressive society, homosexuality would most probably not take the exclusive form that it currently does – there may well be no 'homosexual condition', only homosexual experiences available to everyone. If this were the case, then there would be little need for homosexual congeries, since all would have ready access to homosexual partners.

Stability and change in the subculture

Unlike some subcultures of recent origin (Arnold, 1970), the subculture of homosexuality extends back historically through at least several centuries.[16] From the perspective of a contemporary homosexual, there is little need for him to 'create' a subculture, rather he may be enlisted into an already well-developed world. The subculture has evolved historically, and now confronts him as an 'objective reality', even if a counter-institution that flies in the face of the conventional objective reality (Buckner, 1971: ch. 10).

Many reasons exist for the persistence of the subculture of homosexuality over time – not least of which is its ability to incorporate elements of the changing dominant culture. After the war period, for example, the bar system in London began to change in order to incorporate more elements from the emerging 'youth culture';[17] it was quite radically transformed during the 1960s when dancing and drinking clubs of the discothèque variety emerged to correspond with the 'swinging London scene'.[18] In America, the emergence of 'go-go girls' and bottomless dancers in the straight bars have been accompanied by 'go-go boys' and bottomless dancers in the gay bars. More recently, Humphreys suggests that changing attitudes to manliness in America have led to changing features of the 'gay world' (Humphreys, 1971). The subculture thus displays a remarkable durability and adaptability.

One aspect of this adaptability is the recent emergence of a range of militant homosexual groups – the most famous of which is the Gay Liberation Front – and I wish to discuss this briefly here as an example of subcultural emergence and subcultural change.

The Gay Liberation Front: The GLF and other militant groups could be classified generically with the homophile movement, but they differ markedly from it. While the homophile movement has quite a long history, the radical movement has its origins in the very late 1960s. While the homophile movement adopted a cautionary, liberal attitude to change, the radical movement emphasizes the need for revolutionary social change. While the homophile movement

171

adopted a largely 'apologetic' rhetoric, the radicals adopt a rhetoric which legitimizes homosexuality in its own terms, not those provided by a 'liberal society'. While the homophile movement adopted a clandestine, conservative and often élitist approach, the gay militants have 'come out of the closets' and confronted society's members with their homosexuality. The two movements should not therefore be confused, though they are related.

There are two important questions that need to be raised about these new groups: why have they arisen at this particular time, and what will their consequences be? The latter question will be briefly addressed at the end of chapter 9, and elsewhere; here I wish to take up some explanations of the emergence of a new subcultural form.

There have already been a number of journalistic and personal accounts of the emergence of the Gay Liberation Front, and no doubt there will soon be a number of more scholarly discussions of the rise of this movement.[19] Here I merely wish to suggest three plausible interpretations of this emergence – none of them excluding the others, each of them tentative, and each reinforcing the cultural-continuity thesis which I have stressed in this chapter.

The first draws from the thesis of *relative deprivation*. For some observers, it seems ironic that GLF should have emerged to fight oppression at the very time when the sex laws began to be changed, homosexual literature became popular fare and discussions of homosexuality moved out of the shadows; at the very time, in short, when oppression seemed to be weakening. Yet the critical issue here is not *absolute* oppression but *relative* oppression. Runciman (1972), for example, has suggested that militancy among unions is greater at precisely those times when affluence is increasing, when the perception of possible wage increases becomes heightened. At those times of economic depression and brute poverty, reference groups and aspirations are lower. So it could be with homosexuality. At those times of severe oppression – when the laws are hostilely rigid, when the literature is censored and discussions are taboo – the homosexual is willing to put up with that little bit of security that he can carve for himself in the gay world; at those times when oppression becomes less severe – when it is publicly spoken about and accepted in many groups – the homosexual may feel his oppression to a greater degree. He can articulate the oppression more readily.

A second plausible explanation for the emergence of Gay Power highlights the changing political awareness that has been taking place in society during the past few years, suggesting that homosexual liberation is a continuation of other kinds of revolutionary and liberatory consciousness. This is the argument put forward by Altman, who views the emergence of Gay Liberation as a concomitant of a countercultural consciousness. Seeing close links between GLF and other militant groups, such as Women's Liberation and Black Power, he comments: 'Without the example provided by the blacks, the young radicals, the women's movement, gay liberation could not have been born' (Altman, 1971: 175). In the same way as the gay-bar scene in the 1960s mirrored the change in the broader youth culture, so the homophile movements of the 1970s mirror the revolutionary consciousness of their time.

Horowitz and Liebowitz (Horowitz, 1968), among others, have suggested the importance of this politicization process for deviant groups. They comment how some political groups have recently been transformed into deviant groups, and how some deviant groups have been transformed into political groups. Thus, the politicization of deviants is not peculiar to homosexuality: it has affected drug users, the mentally ill, imprisoned criminals and many others. There is, then, a new political consciousness, and homosexuality is but one part of this.

A third explanation for the GLF returns to the basic precondition for subcultural emergence suggested by Cohen: namely that there must be a sufficient number of people with similar problems in effective interaction with each other. Apart from their homosexuality, GLF members have two other factors in common: a political awareness and a disillusionment with the existing homosexual subculture. This latter may be seen as an important problem. They dislike the bars ('they exploit us'), condemn the 'cottages' ('they are the signs of a sick society'), are angered by the existing homophile movements ('they are patronizing and too apologetic') and pour scorn upon homosexual marriages ('they idealize the "straight world" ') (Teal, 1971). They have either tried the existing homosexual world and found it ideologically unsound, or they have tried it and found themselves unable to succeed in it. Such 'misfits' of the gay world have no doubt always existed, but possibly never in such numbers until recently, when students, political deviants, hippies, yippies, flower children and so forth are becoming marked in their criticisms of conventional 'plastic' life styles. The making of a counterculture has become a significant goal of many more individuals. Whereas in the past the presence of such individuals was numerically insignificant, now they constitute a large enough group to form a collective solution to their problem, rather than an individual one as may well once have been the case.

Conclusion

This chapter has aimed to provide a number of cautions about the homosexual subculture, and a few general observations. On the cautionary side, it has stressed that the homosexual subculture is not stable, well defined, homogeneous or apart from the rest of society; rather it must be seen as containing a number of variant forms, as being continuous with the dominant culture in many ways, and that any homosexual will display differential commitment to it. On the side of general observations, some remarks have been passed about the main elements of homosexual culture, some possible explanations of its existence and some directions of change.

9 Some interaction problems of the homosexual[1]

Homosexuality in this culture is a stigma label. To be called a 'homosexual' is to be degraded, denounced, devalued or treated as different. It may well mean shame, ostracism, discrimination, exclusion or physical attack. It may simply mean that one becomes an 'interesting curiosity of permissiveness'. But always, in this culture, the costs of being known as a homosexual must be high.

It is the knowledge of the cost of being publicly recognized as a homosexual that leads many people to conceal their sexual identity. A central fact of the experience thus becomes the necessity for the homosexual to manage a discreditable identity; to present a suitable non-homosexual front; to play down the homosexual self; to 'pass'. In the words of Goffman (1963a) the problem becomes: 'to display or not to display; to tell or not to tell; to let on or not to let on; to lie or not to lie; and in each case, to whom, how, when and where'. More dramatically Wildeblood (1955: 32) draws from his life experiences:

> The strain of deceiving my family and my friends often became
> intolerable. It was necessary for me to watch every word I
> spoke and every gesture that I made in case I gave myself away.
> When jokes were made about queers I had to laugh with the
> rest, and when the talk was about women I had to invent
> conquests of my own. I hated myself at such moments but there
> seemed nothing else I could do. My whole life became a lie.

The problems of 'passing' and 'identity' management are common to many deviant groups, although for those groups whose deviance is manifestly visible the problems are of a different order (Davis, 1963). The purpose of this chapter is to suggest some of the interaction problems confronted by the homosexual who attempts to conceal his identity, and some of the strategies he employs to prevent discovery.

175

Homosexuality as a dramaturgical experience

In 'dramaturgical' analysis life becomes theatre, people become role-players, and events become performances. Thus any everyday routine may be analysed as a performance, and the analyst may question the nature of the audience, how the actor performs his part and presents an appropriate self, how he handles his 'props' or sign equipment, and how he moves from scene to scene. Such analysis recognizes that this is not the way people actually see the world, but rather that it is simply a theoretical device useful in focusing upon the strategies and consequences of interaction. Messinger writes (in Truzzi, 1968: 13):

> In viewing 'life as theatre', the dramaturgical analyst does not present us with a model of the actor's consciousness; he is not suggesting that this is the way his subjects understand the world. Instead, the dramaturgic analyst invokes the theoretical model as a device, a tool, to permit *him* to focus upon the consequences of the actor's activities for other's perceptions of the actor.

Men, in their natural attitude, do not behave generally in a state of dramaturgical consciousness. They are not usually aware of 'being on', of 'playing a role', or of 'presenting a self'. At moments of crisis, or when a novel situation arises, individuals may well find themselves consciously 'acting' a part: but, in general, while the analyst may perceive them as 'acting', they themselves do not. However, a few groups do come quite close to viewing much of their daily routines in these terms, a good example being the 'celebrity', whose fame means that he constantly runs risks of being recognized and who senses as he walks through a busy street that he is 'on'.

Homosexuality may be viewed in this light, too.[2] It is certainly true that for many homosexuals interaction problems become routinely resolved over time, and techniques of coping thus become habitual. But it is equally true that at many times homosexuals self-consciously become involved in presenting a 'respectable and normal' self to audiences while playing down if not concealing that most worrying of matters: their homosexual identity. Daily, problems of their identity may be publicly raised and need to be publicly resolved; crisis points emerge when failure to 'pass', failure to maintain a convincing heterosexual front, failure to keep one's 'cool', may have dire consequences (Lyman and Scott, 1970). No homosexual can keep up such an 'act' indefinitely in a state of waking consciousness; at crucial moments his dramaturgical skills will have to be mustered with all his might if he is to retain a creditable public image. For some homosexuals, the act becomes simply routine; for many, it becomes an occasional 'self-conscious drama',[3] and for others, it may pose insurmountable difficulties – the skills of dramaturgy simply being beyond them.[4] In this chapter, my concern will be less with the two extremes of routine interaction and insurmountable difficulties, and more with the moments of stagecraft, the moments when an actor has to play his part well or be discovered as a homosexual. In the next section I shall discuss some of the situations likely to be problematic to the homosexual; subsequently I shall discuss some of the stagecraft strategies available to cope with these problematic situations; and finally some comment will be made in relationship to social change.

Homosexuality and awareness contexts

A useful analytical tool for discussing the structural aspects of information distribution is that of the 'awareness context', a concept first introduced by Glaser and Strauss (1965) in their substantive analysis of dying. They define awareness contexts as 'the total combination of what each interactant in a situation knows about the identity of the other and his own identity', and use it primarily to show the evolving and problematic nature of most day to day interaction. Such contexts attempt to define situations by the nature and degree of distribution of social information, and take into account not only the simple questions of actual identity and information, but also those of imputed identity and information – the metaperspectives of Laing, Phillipson and Lee (1966) (Scheff, 1967: 1970). Thus any social situation may not only be characterized by whether Alter knows that Ego is a homosexual, but also by whether Ego knows that Alter knows this fact. Indeed, what is sometimes more important in understanding action is not the actual situation, but the imputed situation: the homosexual takes as his basis for action his definition of the situation, not the 'actual' situation. Thus his inference that other people know he is gay becomes more important than the fact that they do not, in actuality, know he is gay.

Classifying situations as awareness contexts has many complexities. Apart from the problems involved in describing and locating metaperspectives, difficulties become increased in multiperson encounters (as contrasted with simple dyadic situations). Thus the homosexual in a group situation may simultaneously be confronted with people who know his true identity, people who suspect it, people who do not know it and so forth; and he may be presented with the problems of 'teamwork' – of flashing cues to some while maintaining a straight self with others. Complexities increase, too, because the context may be constantly changing: at one moment nobody may know that Ego is a homosexual – but one small slip can transform the situation to one where his homosexuality becomes highly suspect. Indeed, the

177

analysis that follows highlights this issue of transformation of awareness contexts – the conditions that bring about 'crisis points' of public identity.

Two extreme states of 'awareness context' have been described by Glaser and Strauss as the 'open' and 'closed' awareness contexts, and the transformation of homosexual awareness may be depicted through a shift from the latter to the former. Other things being equal, the homosexual is most likely to find himself in a closed-awareness context – 'when one interactant does not know either the true identity or the other's view of his identity', and here he will be confronted with the task of building up a 'normal identity' and playing down his 'homosexual identity'. At any point, however, the context may be weakened – so that the homosexual comes to feel that others are cognizant of the situation. Such situations, where information is only partially known, may be suspicion or mutual pretence contexts. When each interactant becomes fully aware of the other's true identity and his own identity in the eyes of the other, one may speak of an open-awareness context. If the conditions supporting a closed-awareness context break down, therefore, the homosexual is likely to find himself confronting a suspicion, pretence or even open-awareness context. What will follow is an analysis of some of the structural conditions that help to maintain closed-awareness contexts for the homosexual, and an analysis of some of the factors that may lead to the breakdown of closed awareness.

Structural conditions for closed awareness

A closed-awareness context exists when an interactant with a homosexual does not know the identity of his partner, and the homosexual knows that he does not know. For example, many homosexuals in their work situation feel confident that 'nobody knows about them', and it is indeed very likely that their workmates do not suspect their sexual identity.[5] Such situations, and similar ones, frequently occur because of the existence of at least four structural conditions: when all of these are fully present, the chances of being recognized as a homosexual are reduced; but as soon as one breaks down the potentiality for the awareness context to slip into a suspected, pretence or open context becomes marked. Of these four conditions (and there may well be others, my account is not exhaustive), two concern the nature of homosexuality, and two others are wider societal issues. In summary, these four conditions are:

1 Homosexuality is generally invisible. Unlike the physically handicapped whose overt stigma makes them a highly visible group, homosexuality is not usually open to public gaze.

2 Homosexuality is generally irrelevant. For most people and in

most situations, homosexuality remains outside of the 'domains of relevance' (Wagner, 1970: ch. 5). It is simply not given much thought.

3 Sexuality is privatized. The major parts of the sexual life of Western man are restricted to certain 'back regions' and excluded from everyday routines. Sexual experiences are delegated to the realms of the private.

4 Society is segregated. Much of the social life of complex society is characterized by extreme segregation, both of groups into subcultures and individuals into role segments. It becomes increasingly possible for an individual to 'slice' his life into parts – territorially, temporally and biographically. Only under a few limited circumstances – if any – need people be known in their totality.

The presence of these four factors may effectively eliminate awareness of homosexuality from many social situations, although it is clear that such preconditions are always precarious and may be easily toppled: a shift in any one can render a seemingly 'stable', 'closed' awareness context highly insecure and problematic for the homosexual. The question that needs to be asked here then is simply – under what conditions will the closed awareness break down?

The breakdown of closed awareness

Most generally, I wish to suggest that breakdown becomes more likely whenever (1) homosexuality increases in visibility, (2) homosexuality increases in relevance, (3) sexuality becomes deprivatized and (4) social groups become less segregated. Each of these hypotheses is interconnected. In what follows, I wish to isolate a number of variables which contribute to such changes.

1 Making homosexuality visible

Recognition of homosexuality depends upon both perception and action: somebody must identify a homosexual, and certain actions must be identifiable as homosexual. With the exception of being caught in the act there is nothing automatic and intrinsic about such recognition processes; they depend largely upon the mediation of certain patterns of socially constructed meanings. Given this, it becomes possible that some people who see themselves as homosexual will never become visible; and some people who are not homosexual will be identified as such. A potentiality for miscarriage of justice becomes possible (Becker, 1963: 20).

As Kitsuse (1964: 92) discovered in his study of the reaction of American students to homosexuals, identification of homosexuals may be direct or indirect. Directly homosexuals may be recognized by discovery, denunciation or declaration; indirectly homosexuals

179

may be recognized through stereotypical symmetry and rumour. I will discuss each of these variables briefly in turn.

Discovery as direct visibility: By discovery here, I refer to the chance of being caught literally with one's trousers down. Sexual acts between the same sex are relatively clearly definable as homosexual – though there is always the chance that an 'account' of some form can neutralize away the apparently explicit homosexual meanings of the act. Schoolboys may say that 'It's only a phase, sir', and teenage boy prostitutes may say they were only doing it for the money – and in both cases the homosexual act may be reinterpreted as 'not really homosexual'.[6] In general, however, being caught *in flagrante delicto* is sufficient to be tagged 'homosexual'.

Since homosexual acts, like heterosexual ones, generally take place away from easily offended eyes, such visibility is rare. At the same time, there are a number of public locales – parks and commons, cinemas, baths, public conveniences – where some homosexuals do meet to 'have sex'. While, as I will argue later, they are generally shielded from public surveillance, activities in these locales are more likely to be rendered visible (Humphreys, 1970: 156).

Denunciation as direct visibility: For a variety of reasons, some homosexuals who offend society's norms may find themselves ushered into a public role of infamy from which there can be little return. With fanfares and trumpets, witch-hunts seek out homosexuals, the media announces them, and the courts and prisons castigate them. A private identity becomes a public one, recognizable to all. Such denunciations may take place on a national level, as in the infamous English scandals of Wilde, Montagu, Harvey and Vassal, where a public figure became universally degraded and stigmatized.[7] Or they may take place on a much more local level, where, for example, local newspapers fill in the lurid details of local homosexuals who come before the courts. In both cases, individuals are ushered into deviant labels, visible to society's members. Once again, given the proportional infrequency of public prosecutions of homosexuals, most homosexuals evade becoming visible in such a manner.

Declaration as direct visibility: Under a variety of situations, the homosexual may actually decide that it is expedient for him to voluntarily declare his homosexuality. Not all homosexuals, for example, are able to withstand the pressures of leading a double life with their parents and a few therefore find it necessary to inform them of their sexual proclivities. Others, visiting psychiatrists, may again find it necessary to inform the analyst of their identity. Likewise the 'professional homosexual' who uses his public declaration to 'advance homosexual causes', the soldier who declares his homosexuality in order to get out of the service and the Gay Liberation Front member who publicly wears his badge and holds hands in the street may all find it expedient to reveal their identities and in so doing break down the closed-awareness context.

One especially important reason why a homosexual should declare his sexuality, albeit discreetly, arises from his need to locate other homosexuals. There is a paradox here: to the extent that the homosexual succeeds in making himself invisible, so he will cut himself off from contact with other homosexuals – who are, after all, potential lovers. The more successful he is at 'saving face', the less successful he may be at 'finding a trick'.

Stereotypical symmetry as indirect visibility: Although there is evidence to suggest that only a limited section of the population holds rigid stereotypes of the homosexuals (Simmons, 1965; Steffensmeier, 1970), and evidence to suggest that very few homosexuals actually match this stereotype,[8] the existence of homosexual stereotyping is beyond dispute. Such stereotypes provide 'cues' for some perceivers to interpret an individual who exhibits these 'cues' (whether homosexual or not) as homosexual. To assist the public in recognizing homosexuals, several accounts exist in both the academic and non-academic press of 'points to watch for'. The *News of the World* advised its readers in 1964 to be cautious of 'the man who has never married; the fussy dresser; the office or factory crawler with a smarmy grin on his face; the man with an excessive interest in youth activities; the man who cannot resist pawing you as he talks'.[9] These men, the article suggests, are likely to be homosexual.

Such lists are plentiful, and they are not restricted to the popular press. Clifford Allen, for example, writing in his *Textbook of Psychosexual Disorders*, tells the serious student (1969: 221):

> It is not necessary to be homosexual to be able to detect inverts in casual social life. Although I am normal I have seen many homosexuals and am able to observe them in a crowd by minute gestures, tones of speech, and so on. Even on the wireless one can tell them by their speech which is either excessively soft and slightly slurred or else grating and harsh.

Clearly, if an individual matches some of these stereotypical portraits, he stands a greater chance of being recognized as a homosexual – whether or not he in fact is. Such stereotypes could have disastrous consequences for the effeminate-looking heterosexual.[10]

Rumour as indirect visibility: In the study of students' reactions towards homosexuals by John Kitsuse, the author discovered that

181

many homosexuals were recognized through the aid of rumours and gossip; similarly in Schofield's recent work involving over 300 young respondents. The most frequent answer to the question 'How did you get to know that X was a homosexual?' was simply that 'others told me'. Such rumours may not be restricted to people; they may also be applied to places. Thus knowledge may become public about a homosexual bar or public convenience, or even a whole community, and all who frequent it become suspect. Students in one class at a Midlands technical college informed me of a homosexual bar nearby, and warned that anyone who goes there must be a 'poof'. Such knowledge then, once public, places a strain on the homosexual, particularly at those points of entry to 'bars' and 'cottages' where the public may see him and demand some kind of explanation.

Such of course is rarely the case but for the homosexual it may become a significant issue. One homosexual in Humphreys's study (1970: 82) commented on his departures from public conveniences:

> Sometimes when I come out of a tea-room, I look up to the sky just to make sure that some plane isn't flying around up there writing JOHN JONES IS A PERVERT.

2 Making homosexuality relevant

Most members of a society routinely face situations in which homosexuality is absolutely irrelevant. Even when confronted with information about it, they ignore or deny its significance. As Wildeblood (1955: 32) wrote:

> I had on several occasions discussed the problem of homosexuality with my mother and father, hoping to find some ways of telling them about myself. But it was impossible. Their attitude like that of so many people was not one of particular condemnation or of particular tolerance; it was simply that they had not given the matter much thought because they did not believe they knew any homosexuals.

Closed awareness can be generally maintained because homosexuality figures so low in most members' 'domains of relevance'. There are, however, some *people*, some *times* and some *situations* when homosexuality becomes an issue, and it is these that I wish to consider here.

People who make homosexuality relevant: Ironically, the most significant group to treat homosexuality as an issue are homosexuals themselves. Each situation a homosexual enters may, among other things, be briefly assessed for potential homosexual partners and for potential discreditors. To the homosexual, the secret identity looms so significantly in his consciousness that most situations will be briefly interpreted through it. This may well mean that seeing everyone as potentially homosexual and being seen by everyone as a homosexual becomes an implicit assumption of much homosexual interaction. And if such as assumption is held closed awareness breaks down to a suspicion awareness.

Homosexuals, however, are not the only group in society for whom homosexuality is a salient issue: there are also those who Goffman calls the 'wise' ('Persons who are normal but whose special situation has made them intimately privy to the secret life of the stigmatized individuals and sympathetic with it'), and the 'knowing'. Examples of the 'wise' may include the 'Gay Moll' (the 'straight' female who enjoys the company of homosexual men) and the 'straight' friend who, through contact with homosexuals, becomes sensitized to the world view of the homosexual without being one. Examples of the 'knowing' include both agents of control (such as the police patrolling a local 'cottage') and exploiting others, who are able to prey upon the homosexual's vulnerability (such as the blackmailer and the 'queer-basher'). All of these people then become aware of homosexuality as an issue and render situations of closed awareness highly vulnerable.

Times when homosexuality becomes relevant: Homosexuality may also become significant as an issue at certain critical times, particularly those that have been called times of 'moral panic' (Cohon, 1972). One such American incident is that of the 'Boys of Boise' reported by John Gerassi (Gerassi, 1966). On Hallowe'en night 1955, a witch-hunt hysteria began with the arrest of three men for homosexual offences in Boise, Idaho – a ('respectable') middle-class town with a population of about 50,000. Two days later the *Idaho Daily Statesman* published an incendiary story entitled 'Crush the Monster', clearly indicating that 'these arrests mark only the start of an investigation that has "only scratched the surface" ', and suggesting that the task of uncovering the homosexual underworld in Boise was 'too big and too sinister to be left alone to a private detective and an officer of the probate court'. About 100 boys and several adults were said to be involved by this time. Police, community and press panicked and within weeks a list of 500 names of suspected homosexuals had been constructed; before the scandal ended in 1956, some 1,472 men had been questioned. All men became suspect in this highly-charged atmosphere, where women would ring up the police and say: 'I've just seen so-and-so sitting by the high-school practice field with a funny look on his face', and men had to avoid meeting other men alone for fear of being labelled homosexual. One male respondent told Gerassi in 1965 (1966: 48):

> after they arrested that pianist fellow and Larsen, both of whom were charged with indecent acts against adults, well, let me tell you, every bachelor became jittery. I was a buyer then, so I had to travel a great deal. Everywhere I went, people started making jokes. I used to wear my school ring on the third finger of my right hand. Well, I had to stop that. I remember talking to a guy in Denver, a buyer from Salt Lake, a guy I had gotten to know quite well. And all of a sudden he starts kidding me about boys-y, and then he looks at my hand and says with the goddamest sarcastic smile, 'Hey, I see you're wearing a ring these days. . . .' Boy, I felt like punching him in the nose. He had seen that ring ever since we first met, three years before. Well anyway that's the way it went. It got so bad that every time I left Boise on business I was sure some dirty gossiper was spreading the word that I was going to see my boy friend who had left Boise not to get arrested.

Situations where homosexuality becomes relevant: Although in the past, homosexuality has been considered a taboo topic which could not be raised in 'polite company', more recently it has become eligible for public discussion and debate – both jocular and serious. University unions debate homosexuality, women's magazines run feature articles on it, and the entertainment media constantly depict it. For the homosexual today, then, there is the increasing probability that he will be confronted with situations in which 'straight people' in his presence will be discussing homosexuality – the 'queer joke' which embarrasses, the discussion in which he must conceal his expertise and insight, the gossip where his 'cool' must be kept (Matza, 1969: 153). In each of these situations, the homosexual may try to avoid the situation or else enter a situation which could be characterized as 'stage fright' – a situation where identity is severely at risk (Lyman and Scott, 1970: chs. 6 and 7).

3 Deprivatizing sexuality

Seeing homosexuality as largely invisible and irrelevant is a specific example of a more generalized phenomenon: the privatized nature of sexuality. Most sexuality lies well within the realms of privacy and concealment.

Wayland Young, among others, has described how sexuality has developed within a shroud of excluded imagery, language, actions and people: people are not provided with a language with which they can talk about sex, are inhibited by morals which prohibit sex from any form of public display and are denied access to most forms of sexual imagery (Young, 1965). In such circumstances it is easy for concealment to occur. Nobody can see, nobody can ask.

For the homosexual, then, the fact that sexuality itself is rarely openly raised serves as an insulating factor, protecting his sexual identity from public gaze. Once again, however, there are situations in which the homosexual may find sexuality becoming an issue, and at such times his identity becomes tentatively vulnerable. The most apparent examples of this are those direct situations when sex is spoken about or when sex activity is actually expected, for there are, despite protestations to the contrary, a number of situations in our culture where sexual activity is actually prescribed. The most noticeable examples seem to come from the imperatives of male culture, where men together may be expected to talk sex and boast of their exploits. This may be particularly strong at adolescence: adolescent boys 'clearly talk about girls and sex a good deal of the time they are together' (Willmott, 1969: ch. 3). Likewise, sexual jokes, 'stag-nights', work-talk and gang chat may all raise sex as a matter of course, and simultaneously raise problems of identity for the homosexual: is he, for example, to 'play along' with a group whistling at women and talking about sexual exploits, or is he to 'drop out' of the conversation or the group? In the first case, his flagrant lying may be a source of embarrassment while, in the latter, his silence will be suspicious. In either case, when sexuality is raised, his identity becomes a problem.

So far, I have spoken about sex as it relates to genital meanings: it clearly also has more broad gender and social (e.g. marital) ramifications. Here, sexuality is much less privatized. It is, after all, very much a matter of public knowledge whether one is a man or a woman, and whether one is married or not. There are times and situations when a man may be able to get away with not being masculine, and there are times too when a man may be granted celibacy or bachelorhood. But, in general, failure to publicly demonstrate that one is a *man* or that one is *normally married* will be regarded by others with suspicion: people will wonder, questions will be asked and gossip will spread. Turner (1970: 50) suggests that marriage is one of the cornerstones of our value system, providing an important basis for judgments of normality and masculinity. He writes of the:

implication of personal competence and normality associated with the married state, and the suspicion that the unmarried may be disoriented, incompetent, maladjusted – in some sense personally inadequate. . . . For the man there is . . . reflection of his masculinity. If the man is not especially attractive, then his failure to marry is identified with weakness and possible

185

impotence. If he is clearly attractive and holds on too long, the suspicion of homosexuality is often spread through gossip. The attractive man or woman with no discoverable personal deficiencies who fails to marry represents a continuing puzzle to those about him and is likely to be plagued constantly with questions or insinuations about why he or she has not married.

4 Desegregating society

It is a commonplace of social science that complex societies like England and America are characterized by differentiation and segmentation. Individuals may divide their lives temporally, territorially and biographically – hiving off the knowledge which they present in any situation to that which is strictly relevant for the purpose at hand, and avoiding being known in their totality. For the homosexual, this means that he may restrict the information that any group has about him merely by restricting his contact with that group. At work, he is known as the clerk; at church, he is the organist, in the street or on the bus, he is simply a stranger. Given the fleeting, impersonal and role-specific nature of most interaction in complex society, the homosexual need never be known as a homosexual in most groups. Closed awareness prevails.

Of course, in some parts of his world, the homosexual may well seek to be known as a homosexual. He may establish relationships where his role is specifically that of a homosexual, and he may move into protective, home territories where his homosexuality is taken for granted. By virtue of one's presence in certain bars, toilets and other public places, one may be presumed to be a homosexual. Open awareness prevails.

The gay bar[11] may be seen as one important 'home territory in a back region', a region invisible to the mainstream of daily activity where the regular participants enjoy a relative freedom of behaviour and a sense of intimacy and control. It is thus a place which permits many homosexuals the chance to drop the mask they wear during their working day and in relative security and anonymity to 'let their hair down'. A number of factors serve to protect such places from public visibility.

First, such bars are concealed from 'front regions'. They lie at the top of long flights of stairs, or below eye-level in basements; they emerge in the most remote bars in hotels, ones that are least likely to be wandered into by chance; or behind a 'protective front room reeking with respectability' (Cory and LeRoy, 1963: 106). Very rarely are highly luminous signs displayed, and then they assert only that it is 'members only' – I know of no club which labels itself publicly as a homosexual club. The point of entry to such meeting places then is rarely left to chance factors: in clubs, it is almost impossible to enter without being aware of the homosexual nature of the setting.

A second factor in territorial defence is the management's policy of 'insulation' – in which a barrier is erected 'between the occupant of the territory and potential invaders'. The most obvious technique of insulation is the policy of 'membership' – where membership cards are regularly checked at the door by a gatekeeper, with varying degrees of stringency according to the gatekeeper's familiarity with the patron, or the patron's 'tales'. In London, for example, continental visitors will be allowed in at most clubs on sight of a passport, but a lone stranger may well find it impossible to penetrate without knowing an insider or being a member. The policy may be taken to extremes, and in some instances remote speaking systems have been introduced into clubs in order to 'screen' visitors before even opening the door. One club gives all its members a key to the front door, which enables them – but only them – to come and go as they please.

Although barriers are set up to prevent territorial encroachment, there are occasions when 'outsiders' may find their way inside. This is much more likely to occur in the 'pub' sector of the gay-bar world, where techniques of insulation are not usually so well developed, and sometimes may well be acceptable to the habitués – in some bars the two worlds seem to exist side by side. But more generally, the habitués and management will need to employ further techniques of territorial defence. Thus the bartenders may well display aloofness and unfriendliness to 'strangers'. As Cavaan (1966: 229) recounts:

> There were only about sixteen people present when we entered,
> although they took up all the seats at the bar. I sat down at
> one of the small tables along the wall opposite from the bar,
> and [my husband] went to the bar to get our orders. The
> bartender was standing almost in front of him, more or less
> listening to the conversation between two patrons. It took the
> bartender almost five minutes to decide to take the order and
> another three or four minutes for him to make the drinks, which
> were very, very light.

The habitués themselves may well routinely try to make the 'outsiders' feel out of place, uncomfortable and embarrassed. This may arise simply through inattention, monopoly of the facilities available and so forth, or it may take the form of outright 'offensive' behaviour. Indeed while many 'straights' entering a gay bar may instantly feel threatened by the activity – 'You can spot the action straight away',

187

'There's no mistaking what's going on', 'Just takes a couple of minutes to tell' (Cavaan, 1966: 222) – there is some evidence that some gay bars are not immediately noticeable as such to an outsider. One contact in Westwood's (1960: 71) research commented: 'I once took a normal friend of mine there who said it might be the National Liberal Club. Everyone was so good mannered and quiet. He said he wouldn't have suspected a single one of the people there.'

Thus, if it is true that the bar does not instantly offend, one technique of territorial defence is to make it offend. Therefore, homosexuals may deliberately exaggerate their femininity, or make direct passes at heterosexuals when they enter the establishment. The segregated nature of complex society, then, helps to separate some situations which sustain closed awareness from others where open awareness is prevalent. The homosexuals may routinely move between the two worlds in relative security.

But while it is true that complex society is characterized by segregation, this insight must not be pressed too far. For homosexuals, like everybody else, are clearly also likely to build up a small group of primary relationships – among friends and family – where effective bonds may be established and interaction patterns intensified. In such situations, there may arise what Simmel has called a 'strain towards totality', through which the knowledge about one's self that is presented to close friends is constantly broadened. Further, in such situations, there may arise a constant questioning by others in which the homosexual is asked to account for his sexuality, his marital status, his use of time and so forth. The business of establishing 'full' relationships is a costly one for the homosexual. For some homosexuals, this dilemma may be resolved by restricting their primary group contacts to other homosexuals with whom the problem of concealing sexual identity does not arise. Thus, the homosexual may leave home and family, and maintain a simple working relationship with his colleagues at work, segregating his life into parts while keeping his full personal relationships for other homosexual friends. But for many others, such tactics are not readily available – it is not possible to leave the parental home and it would be a problem in itself to keep aloof from work colleagues. At these points, then, homosexuality may remain a constant potential threat to the relationship.

Preventing open awareness: some strategies

It should be clear that while there are certain structural features of society which underlie the existence of closed-awareness contexts,

188

these structures are fragile and precarious and may break down at many points. The homosexual often feels that he stands to lose a great deal by being publicly known as a homosexual. Thus, he may evolve a number of strategies in order to 'cope' with crisis points, some of which I now wish to briefly consider.

At the outset, two main choices – if that they can be called – exist for the homosexual: to 'go public' or to 'pass'. Clearly, because of the risks and costs attached to being publicly recognized as a homosexual, very few homosexuals – at least until recently – have opted for the former route. As I have indicated earlier, however, some adopt this course either by their own choice, or through some form of public 'scandal', and once this happens the problems that the homosexual faces become those of managing a discredited identity. Nevertheless, the path of 'openness' may often bring with it rewards which outweigh the costs. Wildeblood, for example, commented at the end of his public labelling: 'I was able to move out of a false position and take up a true one. There was no further need for pretence: I could discard the mask which has been such a burden to me all my life.' And a respondent of Westwood's (1960: 187) commented: 'I've told all my normal friends I'm queer and they say they wouldn't have me any other way.'

To date, we have very little research which indicates under which conditions homosexuals are willing and able to 'drop the mask' and 'go public'. One may speculate that access to supportive groups and avoidance or rejection of groups that are likely to condemn may be one factor that brings this about: the Gay Liberation Front, for example, having a policy which advocates (among many other things) that 'gay people should be free to hold hands and kiss in public' and which simultaneously has supporters who have rejected those parts of society most likely to condemn the homosexual experience (e.g. traditional business), seems to provide important preconditions for 'going public'.

Sagarin (1969: 21), writing in the more general context of voluntary deviant organizations, comments that 'in taking the step of joining with others who are similarly labelled deviants, an individual actually increases his stigma by enhancing his visibility as a member of a socially disapproved category; he thus calls public attention to his own deviant existence'.

But, in general, most homosexuals still seem to be involved in the 'passing' system. 'Passing' involves the presentation of a public identity out of harmony with a private identity, and is most frequently discussed with reference to the Negro or gender confusions (Stoller, 1964). But, as Goffman (1963a; 93) points out, it is relevant to all those individuals who possess a stigma and who try to conceal the discreditable identity from others, and thus may be discussed with reference to homosexuality. There are, in fact, a great many strategies that may be employed in 'passing', but below I shall discuss just a few of them.[12]

a *Avoidance strategies* are the simplest and most apparent of the strategies available: they simply involve the homosexual avoiding all those situations in which his homosexual identity is likely to become a threat. Referring back to my four preconditions for closed awareness, the homosexual will avoid any situation of his homosexuality being visible; will avoid any situation where it might become an issue; will avoid all sexual spheres; and will keep within the bounds of secondary groups. While some homosexuals may attempt to employ all these routes, it should be quite clear that in practice it is never possible to avoid all the situations completely. This is so for several reasons.

First, there are contradictions between preconditions, so that ability to avoid one may well result in the confrontation of another. Thus, for example, the ability to avoid suspicion of one's sexuality may lead to a position of marriage, which in turn will daily raise problems of identity before a spouse (Ross, 1971).

Second, some situations that lead to a breakdown of closed awareness are almost impossible to avoid. For example, it is very difficult for a homosexual to stop thinking homosexual thoughts throughout much of his waking day; and even if he is able to cut himself off from external contingencies, he will find it very difficult to make such a split in his consciousness. He will constantly be confronted with 'people he fancies' and with situations where he is worried about disclosure. And both of these, by definition, make it difficult for the homosexual to adopt avoidance strategies *in toto*. At any moment, homosexuality may become problematic.

A further complication arises from the fact that the adoption of avoidance strategies lessens the possibility of successful access to other homosexuals. Paradoxically, the better one is at passing, the less the chance of meeting other homosexuals! For example, in the extreme case of avoidance, where all homosexual contact is shunned and a 'normal' married life embarked upon, the individual may pass through life as a secret deviant, often wishing for just a cursory contact with other homosexuals, but partially unaware of their existence and partially frightened of such contact.

A final problem involved in avoidance is simply that the very act of avoidance may render one open to suspicion. Indeed, since one cannot control when sexuality or homosexuality are likely to be raised as issues in everyday life, homosexuals will inevitably find themselves in the presence of others talking about threatening matters and thus seriously confronted with problems of maintaining a 'cool'.

To leave the situation without good reason could well be interpreted as an admission of guilt.

It should be clear, then, that the total avoidance of homosexuality will be a difficult if not impossible task. Nevertheless, many homosexuals will make attempts to avoid dangerous situations, though to varying degrees. At one extreme, there is the 'secret loner' who effectively tries to avoid all homosexual contact; in the middle, there is the 'closet queen' who avoids many situations but nevertheless faces a number of problematic situations; and at the other end, there are the homosexuals who seem to take inordinately serious risks in pursuit of their homosexual experiences. Most 'subcultural' homosexuals seem to simply avoid situations that are too dangerous.

b   *Information control* is a very general term used to depict all those strategies by which a homosexual prevents others from discovering his true identity. In part this may be done by 'building up' some form of alternative fictional biography, and in part it may be done simply by selectively presenting only certain aspects of one's self to an audience.

One of the most apparent strategies of information control is that of avoiding the usage of 'stigma symbols', all those give-away signs that are typically associated with homosexuality in the popular stereotype. Such symbols may include many facets of personal front, ranging from dress – 'being too smart', 'a fussy dresser', 'wearing too many rings'; to demeanour – the swish gait, the mincing walk and the limp wrist; to bodily presence – the effeminate frame and the immaculate hair style. It is relatively easy for most homosexuals to avoid the adoption of such stigma symbols, and most probably do. Nevertheless, as any cursory contact with the homosexual world will demonstrate there are a number of homosexuals who deliberately cultivate the existence of such stigma symbols. The role of 'queen' may be a stereotype, but it is also an actuality. In part, then, the delights of being recognized (for some homosexuals) are greater than the costs. 'Stigma symbols' may also be found outside the personal front in behaviour settings. Thus, for example, the existence of one bedroom and one double bed in a flat shared by two men is open to suspicion. One homosexual couple interviewed commented that they had learned to live with two single beds in the same room, for the sake of family and 'straight' friends; however, they always slept together in just one! Such rearrangement of property to create a misleading impression is further evidenced in the discussion by Lyman and Scott (1970: 60):

A passing homosexual might invite someone who suspects his true identity to his bedroom where a seemingly casual and careless display of pictures of female nudes and his baseball cap and glove convey a contradictory impression.

Finally, stigma symbols may exist through the existence of 'with relationships', by which an individual is perceived as a homosexual because of the contacts he keeps. A stigma is attributed simply because one is 'seen with homosexuals'. For all of these situations then – the stigma of personal front, property, and 'with relationships' – the 'passing' homosexual may employ a series of strategies to prevent the stigma symbol being apparent. In many instances, such a process involves the use of disidentifiers – as in the examples listed above, and as in the case of the homosexual who deliberately cultivates a very rugged masculine appearance, dresses slovenly, leaves dirt under his fingernails and slouches!

Another technique involved in 'information control' is that of creating an alternative biography. This may be a largely truthful account, but selective and distorting; or it may be entirely fictional. Homosexuals are often placed in the situation where information is required of them, but when the giving of true information would be tantamount to disclosure. Thus, the homosexual who goes to gay bars nightly may find himself regularly asked to explain 'what it is he gets up to at night', and the homosexual who does not marry may find himself held to account for this. He may answer these questions and others by constructing a series of imaginary events – girlfriends, heterosexual parties, and relying heavily upon the segregation of his worlds to reinforce these 'lies' for his audience. Sometimes, he may even find partners who are temporarily willing to help him sustain these illusions – either wittingly or unwittingly. Thus, simply being seen around with a girl from time to time may allay suspicions in the eyes of others. On the other hand, and possibly more commonly, the homosexual may simply remain quiet on all sorts of key issues. He fosters what Robert Lindner has termed a 'sexless identity'. Writing of a case study, Howard, Linder comments (in Ruitenback, 1963: 64):

> Howard is sexless for all purposes of outer identification. Neither you nor I encountering him outside the gay world would be able to identify him as an invert. Nor for that matter would we receive any clue from him at all as to his basic sexuality and, what is more important, neither would we get from him an impression of *any* kind of sexuality. For Howard and his kind are sexually bland. In their public behaviour at least they have effaced all evidence of inversion, and more: they have obliterated, to an amazing degree, most vestiges of sexuality.

This 'obliteration of sex' may be explained by the homosexual in all manner of ways – 'I'm too busy for sex or marriage', 'I'm just not interested in that sort of thing' – but providing he can adopt this role confidently as a public posture, suspicions may be tentatively weakened.

Closely related to this point of constructing alternative biographies is the construction of alternative roles. Goffman (1963a: 117) points out how 'mental defectives apparently try to pass sometimes as mental patients, the latter being the lesser of two evils'.[13] Likewise, the homosexual may prefer to be seen as a criminal, as mentally ill, as suicidal, as inadequate, or even as a murderer – in preference to being seen as a homosexual. Sometimes, the role adopted may even be that of a polar opposite. Humphreys, for example, has suggested how several of his men who frequented public conveniences adopted a posture of moral crusader in public (Humphreys, 1970: 141). Thus, attention may be deflected away from homosexual roles by an exaggerated concern with other roles.

c *Role distance:* Goffman has defined role distance as 'actions which effectively convey some disdainful detachment of the performer from a role he is performing' (Goffman, 1961b: 110).[13] The concept can be applied to homosexuality in a number of ways, but here it is simply taken to mean the distancing mechanisms employed by the homosexual while enacting a heterosexual role.[14] In heterosexual situations the homosexual is typically imputed with a heterosexual role: it is 'taken for granted' that he routinely prefers the opposite sex to his own sex. This may provide a threat, and an ongoing one, to his sense of homosexual identity; and he may therefore indulge in variants of the role to alleviate this threat. Stebbins (1969) has distinguished at least six modes of role-distancing behaviour which can be employed in threatening situations. These are (1) presence of special vocal behaviour, (2) absence of ordinary vocal behaviour, (3) presence of special deeds, (4) absence of special deeds, (5) presence of special gestures and (6) absence of ordinary gestures. Thus, the homosexual may either behave in ways unfitting for a man or actually behave in manners associated with homosexual stereotypy. Indeed, several homosexuals have commented how they have overtly enacted homosexual roles – to the extent of making passes and putting their arms around other men – which have been interpreted by the audiences in part at least as 'joking behaviour'. Such distancing allows the homosexual the opportunity to behave homosexually while others assume he is basically heterosexual. As one homosexual put it:

> I put my arms around the boys, and I talk quite openly about my homosexual fancies. Sometimes I camp it up quite a lot. But nobody really takes me seriously. I think they think that I'm just joking. But most of the time, I'm not.

Conclusions: social changes and awareness contexts

In this chapter, I have analysed four structural conditions of closed homosexual-awareness contexts, suggesting ways they may break down and strategies employed by homosexuals to cope with some of these problematic situations. Building upon this it is possible to speculate about changes that may be taking place in the structure of society which could have radical consequences for the existence of closed-awareness contexts. What follows, therefore, is largely a speculative exercise based upon the hypotheses given earlier.

The paradox of homosexual secrecy

I have suggested that, at least until recently, most homosexuals have worked hard to conceal their sexual identity from public gaze and have employed a number of tactics to do this. They have estimated the cost and the stigma likely to befall them if their deviant identity was to become known and have decided to 'pass', carefully concealing their homosexuality in the company of 'straights' but letting the mask down in the company of 'gays'. For some homosexuals, this has meant a virtual retreat from heterosexual society and the formation of 'gay ghettoes'. For others, it has meant living a double life, living – as Wildeblood called it – a lie. For still others, it has been a solitary secret shared only with themselves, and a secret that may accompany them untold to the grave. Only those who could not control the situation revealed their homosexual identity.

Yet, paradoxically, it is this understandable desire for concealment which has probably exacerbated the problem. For while most members of society at large know many homosexuals and daily come into face-to-face contact with them, they are hardly aware of this fact.[15] With little direct face-to-face experience of homosexuality, the 'conventional' society is almost entirely dependent for its knowledge of homosexuals upon the media, stereotypes and lay and scientific imagery. It cannot think about homosexuality in real (i.e. non-stereotyped) terms, because it thinks it has no contact with the *real* phenomenon. It seems possible, at any rate, that if the two million homosexuals in present-day England were able to reveal themselves, did in fact reveal themselves, then some aspects[16] of the social problem of homosexuality may be alleviated. But until recently, homosexuals themselves – for very good reasons – have not been willing (able) to do this. It is this which I have termed the paradox of homosexual secrecy.

Indications of change

There are nevertheless some recent indications that the problem of concealment may be altering, and there are several factors that have influenced this. Most important in this respect was the emergence of the Gay Liberation Front, whose central platform rested upon being publicly identifiable and challenging the accepted orthodoxy. Thus, the movement has produced for the first time in modern history, homosexuals who are willing to go on to the streets, into the parks, and on to the media as 'full-frontal' homosexuals. Wearing 'Gay is Good' badges, holding hands and kissing in the streets, and gathering together in public places has dramatically changed the climate for at least many younger homosexuals, and some older ones too. In addition, the Front has taken up the challenge of being publicly slandered. For example, in their eyes, the sickness theory of homosexuality has been a popular form of slander for thirty years or more – and nobody until recently has ever fought back as a homosexual. It is true, of course, that for some time homosexuals have among themselves attacked such a rhetoric; but they have not been willing to publicly attack it. Now, with the Gay Liberation Front, one hears in England demands to withdraw slanderous books and public meetings at which homosexuals openly contest their right to have a club;[17] while in America, it now appears that any social scientist who ventures a comment upon homosexuality is likely to be the subject of a public demonstration. Teal, for example, in his book the *Gay Militants* (1971: 293–301) describes how Gay and Women's Liberation interrupted the national convention of the American Psychiatric Association on 14 May 1970 where aversion therapy was being discussed, how they 'non-plussed a workshop on "Family Medicine"' organized by the American Medical Association, and how uproar broke out at the 2nd Annual Behavioural Modification Conference on 17 October of the same year when Dr Feldman (of Birmingham University) was publicly attacked for his film on aversion therapy. These events and others are indicative of a changing mood, by which some homosexuals are now quite willing to 'come out' and 'drop the mask'.

Another factor, closely related to this, is the growing possibility for public discussion about homosexuality. Sagarin (1969: 78–110) has commented upon this:

> Few subjects for so long completely enshrouded in silence have
> so quickly become so widely discussed. It strains one's memory
> to recall that the word was literally banned from the pages of the
> *New York Times* in the early 1950's, only to make its appearance
> there a few years later in the headlines.

195

Sagarin, in fact relates this growth largely to the publication of the Kinsey Report – 'a veritable sexual atom bomb' – in 1948, and the concomitant growth of awareness of the extent of the homosexual phenomenon. Whatever the reasons may be, in the 1970s homosexuality is a publicly spoken about issue – in films, plays, books, television, public meetings and so forth, homosexuality if not accepted is at least seen. The structural preconditions of irrelevance and invisibility appear to be breaking down.

Another factor that could be mentioned here is the emergence of what Winick (1968) called the 'Beige Epoch' – the decline in rigid definitions of masculinity and femininity, the blurring of their boundaries. This position should not be overstated, but nevertheless there is some evidence that particularly among the young college life and hippydom there is a less clear demarcation of gender boundaries. It thus becomes possible for a boy to dress in bright clothes, tight trousers, wear colognes and fuss about his hair – and not be perceived as a homosexual. The concomitant of this, of course, is that the homosexual in this instance may be less vulnerable to public attack than he was before.

These factors – the Gay Liberation Front, the increasing public willingness to talk about sexual things and the Beige Epoch – are but three of many possible indicators that rapid change may be taking place in the structure of homosexual awareness. In the past, as I have discussed in the body of this chapter, homosexuals have had to become skilled at dramaturgical stagecraft while the underlying structures of society helped them to conceal their homosexuality by facilitating the existence of closed-awareness contexts. In the immediate future, one may suggest that things are about to change – that homosexuality will become increasingly visible, spoken about and an issue; and that sexuality too will become a more public experience. If this does happen, the interaction patterns analysed in this chapter will become speedily outdated.

part four

Conclusion

10 Conclusion

Within this book, at least four miniature studies may be found. First, it is a study in the interactionist perspective. Broadening the traditional field of symbolic interactionism to embrace phenomenological insights, it has related this perspective to the substantive fields of deviancy, sexuality and sexual deviance.

Second, it is a study in the sociology of sexuality, or rather the neglect of such a sociology. It has argued that while sociologists have seriously ignored the study of sexuality, it would be a profitable area for inquiry in the future. Such inquiry however would be seriously hampered if not guided by a theoretical approach consistent with sociological principles; if, for example, it remained on the Schofield and Kinsey level of social book-keeping. It was suggested that interactionism would provide a fertile theoretical orientation, and a long list of research problems generated from such an orientation have been raised throughout the book.

Third, it is a study in the labelling approach to sexual deviation. Taking as its guiding notion the idea that sexual experiences become qualitatively different when labelled by self or other as deviant, it has sketched the passage of an individual from a situation of random sexual differentiation through to stabilized sexual deviance. It has looked at the questions (causes, characteristics and consequences) and problem areas (action, reaction and interaction) that need to be taken into account in any full study of sexual deviation; discussed points of contrast with traditional clinical theories, in particular developing an alternative typology of deviation to that given in the clinical literature; highlighted the continuity between explanations of becoming sexual and explanations of becoming deviant; and raised a series of research problems encountered along the way.

Fourth, it is a study in the sociology of homosexuality. While there is now a vast literature on homosexuality, most of it is firmly in the clinical tradition and usually concerned with the question of primary aetiology. I have demonstrated some of the drawbacks of such an approach by stressing that homosexuality cannot be adequately understood apart from the meanings constructed around it in a predominantly hostile society. It has gone on to explore four useful areas for subsequent research – the nature and origins of the societal reaction, the homosexual career, the subculture of homosexuality and the management of identity problems in day to day encounters.

Put like this, it may indeed appear that my book contains four studies, not one. But I believe it to be a synthetic whole, guided throughout by the interactionist perspective and moving step by step from the more general to the more specific, at each stage pausing to indicate research tasks arising from the analysis. Indeed, it is wiser to view this study as a research programme, than it is to see it as research. (Almost every paragraph could be expanded to a full length study.) And at each stage the problems that arise may be linked directly back to the three foci of interactionism raised at the outset. Thus, whether the topic is sexuality, deviancy, sexual deviancy in general or homosexuality, I have constantly been raising the following questions:

1 What are the meanings here? How are they built up? How do they persist over time? How may they be transformed, modified, lost, regained? What constraints are placed upon their emergence – by biology, by culture and by the interaction process itself? What are the consequences of bestowing such meanings on a situation?

2 What are the reactions here? Who is reacting – self, significant others, control agents, media, etc.? What are the sources of such reactions? What consequences do they have for action? In particular, how do they constrain action? How may they be transformed or modified?

3 What are the processes here? What are the dynamics involved in a limited situation (encounter) and what are the dynamics involved across the life span, or part of it (career)? What are the significant 'turning-points' and fateful moments in an encounter? What are the outcomes of such moments? How can one account for stability and persistence?

It should be clear that these questions have permeated this book, whether the topic has been sexuality, deviance or homosexuality. Some illustrations may help to make explicit this theoretical unity.

First the issue of meanings is raised throughout. The general discussion of sexuality in part 1 was not concerned with the biological mechanisms of genital sex (as Masters and Johnson tended to emphasize), nor with the overt behavioural sexual acts (as Kinsey tended to), nor even with the emotional foundations of sexuality (as Freud did). Rather, the concern was with the problem of how an actor came to see something as sexual, and what these sexual meanings were. The process of becoming sexual discussed in part 2 was not concerned with the process of physiological maturation or the process of libidinal development through the famous Freudian stages. Rather, the analysis stressed the sensitive turning-points throughout life where some objects were given sexual meanings and where some encounters gave rise to the emergence of sexual meanings. A related concern was the potentiality for widespread variation in such personalized meanings. The discussion of homosexuality in part 3 was not concerned with viewing the homosexual act or person as something which merely emanated from the chromosomes, hormones and familial crisis – but rather as a process by which certain kinds of feelings and situations came to be interpreted as homosexual. Further, the concern was not to analyse homosexuality outside of meaningful contexts, but rather to demonstrate how the hostile meanings in which the homosexual experience is enmeshed tend to affect the very nature of that experience. Thus, throughout the book, the concern has been with the fundamentally problematic nature of sexual meanings and a plea has been raised for a detailed analysis of them.

Likewise, each section raises the problem of reactions. It is indeed a *sine qua non* of labelling theory that deviancy arises through interaction, but it is often overlooked that reactions are also integral to any analysis of social organization. Reactions may thus have been explicit when considering the process of becoming deviant – indeed, the section on homosexuality aimed to show in part how reactions affect the process of becoming homosexual, how they assist in the emergence of a homosexual subculture and how they modify the day to day experiences of the homosexual. But they were also present when considering the process of constructing sexual meanings in chapters 2 and 3. For clearly, sexual meanings do not automatically emerge; rather they are mediated through interaction with other social beings.

While stressing reactions, I hope to have avoided the absurdly crude view put forward by some critics of labelling theory, that the only significant reactions are those made towards deviants by control agents, or at any rate those made by role-partners. This view I explicitly reject. Labelling theory is much more subtle than that. For it includes the highly important self-reaction – the reaction which an individual reflexively makes towards himself and, while it asks key questions about the conditions under which individuals come to accept labels of deviancy, it also asks questions about the manner in which they hold such labels at bay. Thus, to stress the importance of labelling theory to the study of homosexuality is *not* to suggest

201

that homosexuals actually have to be reacted against by members of society, or that when so labelled they will automatically acquiesce. On the contrary, I suspect that most homosexuals are never publicly labelled and that self-labelling is much more important an area for analysis. Likewise, some individuals who are publicly labelled as homosexuals may spend considerable time neutralizing or disavowing such labels.

Finally, each section has stressed the problems of process, both at the level of interactive encounters and over the life span (erotic careers). The book looked not only at the fragile moments of imputing sexual meanings, disavowing deviant labels and 'passing' in hostile contexts; it also analysed the processes of *becoming* sexual, *becoming* sexually different, *becoming* deviant, and *becoming* a homosexual. Yet while process was the constant source for analysis, attempts were made in each section to deal with the factors that led to stability – 'commitments', 'perspectives', 'self-lodging', 'self-stabilization', 'world-taken-for-granted views', and costs and rewards. The dual problem of process and stability was posed throughout.

In sum: while the book has raised a number of discrete problems, it has synthesized each area of analysis with an underlying theoretical continuity. The central commitment of the study has been to the interactionist perspective and a subsidiary one has been to further understanding of sexuality. I believe, and hope to have demonstrated, that the marriage of these two commitments will be a productive one.

Notes

1 Introduction: the problem of sexuality in sociology

1 The interested reader will find useful preliminary statements on the history of sex research in the work of Ellis and Abarbanel (1961), Ehrmann (1964), Brecher (1970) and Sagarin (1971a). A useful compendium of earlier statements is Krich (1963), and a somewhat curious 'Introductory Guide to the Study of Sexual Behaviour' listing thirty-two 'fundamental volumes' is to be found in Marshall and Suggs (1971).

2 The neglect of sociological perspectives on sexuality needs fuller documentation, but in 1967 Reiss could comment that there were only sixteen sociologists in America heavily involved in the field (Reiss, 1967: 2). The number in England is considerably smaller than this. For example, a review of the 1968 BSA Sociological Register in England (with some four hundred entries) showed nobody who specified human sexuality as a research interest. Likewise, an analysis of the major sociological journals published in England revealed few references to sexuality, and a later analysis did not include sexuality as a variable to be considered (Collinson and Webber, 1971). Further, a review of *Sociology in Britain* by Krausz (1969) makes no reference to sex in the contents or index – though it does devote a few pages to Schofield's important but non-sociological work, and makes passing reference to Comfort. Recently, however, productivity in the field of the sociology of sex has increased – a number of members, for instance, of the National Deviancy Conference of York mention sexuality in the handbook of members' interests. And likewise the literature in America seems to have noticeably increased – quantitatively and qualitatively – in the past few years.

3 For documentation on some of the problems involved in sex research, the reader could consult the work of Ehrmann (1964), Bell (1966), Reiss (1967), Marshall and Suggs (1971), Pomeroy (1972) and Douglas (1972).

4 Little has been written on the resolution of practical sexual problems through either social policy or interpersonal intervention, but recent

samples of such analysis may be found in Gochros and Schultz (1972) and Resnik and Wolfgang (1972).

5 See for example the diatribe by Holbrook (1972: esp. ch. 8). While I am in sympathy with the broad principles of phenomenology that pervade this work, much of his analysis is dangerously ill-founded. For example, he condemns the Masters and Johnson research as dehumanizing and objectifying. If his condemnation is accepted, the same charge may be levied at all medicine. Medical research into cancer, subnormality and brain disorders are by the same accounts dehumanizing. As is so frequently the case, Holbrook provides one set of criteria to sex, and another to everything else.

2 Deviance, sexuality and the interactionist perspective

1 There are many other ways of approaching interactionism. Blumer's own technique is to analyse a series of root images about human groups or societies: social interaction, objects, the human being as actor, human action, and the interconnectedness of action (Blumer, 1969). Kuhn approaches the subject as a series of historically developing schools, such as self theory and reference-groups theory (Kuhn, in Manis and Meltzer (1967)). Rose develops an argument around a series of analytic and genetic assumptions that the theory makes (Rose, 1962).

2 I am very much aware that to leave such a vital problem undeveloped is grossly unsatisfactory. To paraphrase Russell, to exclude what you dislike has 'all the advantages of theft over honest toil'. However true that may be, to write about these epistemological problems would require a longer and basically quite different kind of book. I take comfort from the fact that at least two recent proponents of interactionism and the sociology of knowledge have also preferred 'theft over honest toil' in one book, while going on to spell out their epistemologies elsewhere (see Berger and Luckmann (1967: 25), and Berger (1971b), as well as Gouldner (1971) and (1973: 94)).

3 For the contexts of these two short quotes, see Tiryiankin (ch. 7) in Gordon and Gergen (1968) and Lindesmith and Strauss (1968: 8). The discussion of determinism in more general terms can be found in Kuhn (1964), Rose (1962: Introduction), and McCall and Simmons (1966).

4 The argument of Berger and Luckmann (1967) is relevant to an understanding of the manner in which the problematic and emergent nature of interaction becomes institutionalized and habitualized over time. Berger has elsewhere remarked upon the nightmare that awaits those who do not wish to routinize their lives (Berger, 1971a).

5 One of the paradoxes of the interactionist perspective is that simultaneously with viewing society as emergent, problematic, etc., the notion of a solid, stable world is reintroduced through the backdoor with the notion that is central to phenomenology – the 'natural attitude'. Men, in their 'natural attitude', do not find the world as problematic as the sociologist renders it for them.

6 Even this view has been heavily criticized by those sociologists who argue that the 'flexible role-making' approach of Turner and others still

ignores the procedures and 'deep rules' used by the actor in interpreting behavioural displays for the purpose of role-taking and role-making. Such a criticism remains sceptical about the widespread use of the term 'role' without full recognition of the model of the world used by the actor. This view, while provocative, leads into linguistic analyses that would obscure the main routes of this study, and is thus largely neglected (cf. Cicourel, 1973: ch. 1).

7 I have not discussed here the kinds of implications that interactionism has for methodology, although I have elsewhere (Plummer, 1973a). An interactionist methodology may be viewed under two headings: (1) the manner in which interactionism affects the methods of approach to the subject-matter of the research, and (2) the manner in which interactionism affects the researcher's awareness of his own role as social researcher. The key texts on interactionist methodology are: Denzin (1971); Bruyn (1966); Glaser and Strauss (1967); Becker (1971: part 1); Cicourel (1964); Lofland (1971).

8 I give here only the intellectual reasons. It would make an interesting study in the 'sociology of sociology' to ask about the social factors that influenced this growth. Rubington and Weinberg (1971: 167) have seen its growth as akin to social movements, and Gouldner has provided a polemical account of its rise (Gouldner, 1973: ch. 2).

9 I have discussed each of these strands more fully elsewhere (Plummer, 1973c).

10 'Labelling theory' is often treated as synonymous with interactionism, and interactionism is often treated as synonymous with the 'new deviancy perspective'. I have argued in the article cited above that this has led to much conceptual muddling, and in particular has allowed too many critics of the approach to get away lightly by shifting their target too easily. A distinction needs to be drawn between the new deviancy perspectives as (1) a general orientation, (2) a specific theoretical stance and (3) a much narrower concern with problem areas and specific propositions. For clarity, I refer to the first as the 'new deviancy perspectives', the second may refer to any specific stance – in this case the 'interactionist stance' – and the third may refer to any problem area – for example, the labelling problem.

11 Both Sutherland and Waller were graduates of Chicago. Waller wrote on a range of social problem areas, but his key interest was 'marriage and the family'. In particular, he showed in 1930 how 'divorce prejudice' (societal reaction) complicated adjustment problems for the divorcee (see Waller, 1930).

12 Becker's work although published in systematic form in 1963 began to appear in journals around 1953. See the interview with Becker, in Debro (1970).

13 Some recent writers who have stressed the political nature of deviancy analysis are Lofland (1969); Chambliss (1969); Becker (1963); Matza (1969); Quinney (1970); Scheff (1968); Taylor, Walton and Young (1973); Douglas (1971b); Horowitz (1968). Since the growth of the new deviancy perspective most writers have recognized the political nature of deviancy, and the more fruitful question concerning the kind of political processes involved in the creation of deviancy has been posed.

14 For my comments on the aforementioned study by Williams and Weinberg, see my review in *British Journal of Criminology*, 12, 189–92.

15 See, for example, Matza's representation of interactionist theory and especially Becker's work (Matza, 1969: ch. 6). It could be argued however that he overstates the position of Becker, though not that of Blumer.

16 It is also sometimes assumed that once a deviant has been 'imprisoned' in deviancy by labelling processes, it is impossible for him to become 'delabelled'. Lofland makes it quite clear that this is not the case in his discussion of 'the assumption of normal identity' (Lofland, 1969: part 3). See also Trice and Roman (1970).

17 The writings of Jack Douglas make these points frequently. His most systematic statement, in which the traditional perspective is contrasted with the new perspective, is to be found in Douglas (1970c).

18 This is another point of misunderstanding among critics, who argue that labelling theory cannot explain the behaviour in the first place. There are three kinds of answers to this criticism, all complementary. The first answer is simply that Becker and others never intended the theory to answer that question! (Debro, 1970: 167). The second answer, more complex, is that Becker did not see it as important to account for 'deviant impulses' because such things were widespread, and non-problematic to sociologists who were more concerned with how deviance becomes stabilized (Becker, 1963: 26). The third answer is that Becker and others worked from a notion of cumulating causes rather than single causes (Lofland, 1971: 65), and hence preferred sequential models in which the 'initial impulse' was only one small part (Becker, 1963: 22).

19 This dynamic element in deviancy analysis has encouraged fruitful historical studies such as Platt's study of child-saving, Gusfield's study of the temperance movement and Erickson's study of the Puritans of Massachusetts Bay (Gusfield, 1963; Erickson, 1966; Platt, 1969).

20 For example, Chall defined sex as 'the actions of human beings to accomplish sexual union between the male and the female' in 1961 (Ellis and Abarbanel, 1961: 25) and more recently Gebhard defines sexual behaviour as 'those movements, vocalisation, and reactions directly concerned with causing the physiological responses which constitute, in part, sexual arousal and which – if continued – would ordinarily result in orgasm' (Marshall and Suggs, 1971: 251). These may be helpful as operational definitions, but they also obscure the problem of knowing what sex is.

21 Such a problem leads me to the tentative hypothesis that there are deeply regulative rules surrounding sexuality that link it very firmly to the genitals.

22 Skipper and McCaghy (1970; 1971); McCaghy and Skipper (1969) locate homosexuality among 'strippers' in the occupational structure of stripping and not in the personality structure. They write: 'We found that homosexual behaviour was an important aspect of the culture which apparently stemmed less from any predisposition of the participants than from contingencies of the occupation' (1969: 264). Thus, here the occupation gives the meaning to homosexuality; see also Stewart (1972).

23 The following discussion raises a very important research area worthy of much detailed research. My comments are severely limited, and merely exploratory.

24 A useful introduction to this area is Turner (1970: 319–25), though he uses very different categories: physiological, sacred, secular, serious and casual interpersonal meanings.

25 See the discussion on the 'institutional form of autonomous sexuality' by Sprey (1969).

26 Sjvall (1970: 121) writes: 'Human sexuality is a means of expressing and satisfying individual needs for safety and/or intimacy; on rare occasions such behaviour will also fulfil procreative functions.' See also Kinsey's discussion on total sexual outlet and sexual outlet in marriage (Kinsey *et al.*, 1948; 1953). Note that if it is true that 'sex-as-procreation' is statistically rare, then if a statistical definition of deviancy is accepted (Becker, 1963: ch. 1), then sex-as-procreation becomes deviance. It is ironic that those who use the statistical notions of deviancy are also probably those who see procreative sex as the only normal sex!

27 It is notable that these phrases are put into the feminine person. In the past, I suspect for males sexual meanings have meant *erotic meanings* and for females they have meant *romantic meanings*.

28 There may also be interactive constraints set by 'deeply regulative rules'. The notion of 'deep structures' is borrowed here very loosely from Chomsky and Cicourel's work. In the same way as the capacity for grammatical speech is somehow 'in' the brain, and the grammatical patterns of all languages may be reducible to a finite series of rules – a 'universal grammar' – which locate the principles of all particular grammars, it may well be that the capacity for sexuality is somehow 'in' the genitals, and there is only a limited finite range of variations possible: a 'universal sexual grammar'.

3 The social context of sexual deviation

1 This situation is not dissimilar to that described by Scheff (1966: 8) for the field of mental illness. Here there was a similar concern with 'psychologizing', an outpouring of thousands of papers, and a similar lack of progress. Scheff's own statement was one source of a re-orientation in research problems in the field of mental illness, a re-orientation which stressed societal factors. Such a reorientation is imminent in the study of sexual deviance.

2 For some recent considerations of the kinds of questions that should be asked in deviancy research, see Cloward and Ohlin (1960: ch. 2); DeLamater (1968: 446); Phillipson (1971: 53); Box (1971a: 6); Young (1971: chs 4 and 5); Taylor, Walton and Young (1973: ch. 9). In Plummer (1973a) there is a more extended discussion of this problem.

3 I take these three questions of 'causes, characteristics and consequences' from the study by Lofland (1971: 13).

4 The clearest earlier statements on the relevance of interactionism to sexual deviance are contained in Lemert (1951: ch. 8); Schur (1965); Williams and Weinberg (1971); Henslin (1971a). All the writings of Gagnon and Simon remain signally and centrally important. Some

207

rather weak critical comments may be found in Polsky (1967: ch. 5) and Reiss (1970).

5 I am aware of the inherent dangers in presenting a 'finished theoretical product'. Interactionists view the entire research process as ongoing and emergent, and any attempt to finally capture a theory is doomed to failure. Glaser and Strauss (1967) have made much of this point.

6 The framework used here is largely derived from Berger and Luckmann (1967), although it is itself a derivation of Schutz's work. Buckner's (1971) study has also been of value in demonstrating the utility of this framework to deviancy, as has the article by Scott (1972). What follows is only a sketchy outline, and would make an interesting full-length study.

7 Clor suggests that even the notorious Kinsey respondents, while committing widely discrepant behaviour, related their values and attitudes to a wider common moral framework, explaining their differences by reference to these 'wider community standards'. Clor is criticizing the work of the Kronhausens for assuming too much discrepancy, see Clor (1969: ch. 7, esp. p. 175).

8 It is inherent in my argument that any empirical observations that I make are situation-specific. Unless otherwise specified, I refer to the England and the America of the late 1960s. There are, of course, significant differences between the two countries: the racial problem, the pervasiveness of the media, the lack of aristocracy, and the apparent ubiquity of relativism (Douglas, 1971b) in America may well mean real differences which I gloss over throughout this book.

9 On plausibility structures, see the writings of Berger (1971b); and on the way they have been used in the field of sexuality and the family, see Gagnon and Simon (1970: 11) and Skolnick and Skolnick (1971: 5).

10 Overt conflict in the field of sexuality has been manifested in recent years in such events as the *Oz* trial, the 'Festival of Light Campaign', the 'Clean Up Television Campaign', the attack on pornography, and the work of the Women's, Schoolkids' and Gay Liberation movements. However, such conflict is by no means new.

11 On contradictions, see the writings of Ellis on the media portrayal of sexuality in the 1950s and the 1960s (Ellis, 1961), or the comments of Reiss (1966: 127–30). Contradictions in sexual meanings may exist within belief systems and between them.

12 Several recent anthologies have testified to the existence of widespread change, e.g. Skolnick and Skolnick (1971); Streib (1973). Some writers see dramatic and rapid changes in the field of sexuality (e.g. Toffler, 1973), while others note changes but are much more cautious (Gagnon and Simon, 1972; Reiss, 1966; 1967; 1968).

13 All societies provide regulation and organization for sexuality, although such constraints may vary within and between societies. There are some kinds of sexual experience which do seem more or less universally abhorred (although each category has problematic aspects); incest, child-molestation and rape are three areas of high condemnation according to a comparative study by Brown (1952), and Davis has also provided a universal list (Davis, 1971: 319). In our culture, the arena of consensus is now much wider than that associated with Victorianism –

many 'taboo' topics are now more legitimate. But there remain strong limits: few members of this society would hold in high esteem the zoophile, the child-molester, the sex murderer, the rapist or the necrophiliac. On these 'deviations', see the polemical but interesting comments by Ullerstam (1967).

14 See notes 10–13 for some documentation. It is more important for the future that competing and opposing evidence is sought. Evidence of general variation is discussed later in this chapter, but see Kinsey *et al.* (1948; 1953); Schofield (1965b; 1973); Reiss (1967); Gochros and Schultz (1972: ch. 4); Packard (1968).

15 For an expansion of such problems, see Douglas (1971b). Along with the principle of the contextual determination of meanings, he views 'abstract' meanings as 'the basic resources from which concrete meanings must be constructed for the situation at hand' (p. 201).

16 Cf. also Rodman's (1963) concept of 'value-stretch' which attempts to bridge discrepancies in consensual public values and privatized variance. His discussion explicitly deals with illegitimacy in the Caribbean.

17 For an expansion on this point, see Scheff's two essays on consensus and relationships (Scheff, 1967; 1970).

18 The notion of 'deep rules' also seems to be predicated upon a notion of absolutism, which is otherwise anathema to interactional studies. There is a paradox here: sociologists have escaped from a surface world of consensus and absolutism, to a world of emergence and relativism; only to find that this world after all may be bounded by deeply regulative rules.

19 Historical analysis is sometimes considered to be beyond the interactionist (e.g. Lichtman, 1970). But this is a fallacy, for as Strauss – a major interactionist – commented: 'A social psychology without a full focus upon history is a blind psychology' (Strauss, 1959: 173). There may be some difficulties in interactionists conducting historical studies, but it is not in principle beyond them (cf. Gusfield, 1963).

20 An adequate theory ought to be isomorphic – using the same theoretical model to explain action, reaction and interaction in this case. Thus, if one conceives the process of becoming sexual deviant as processual, interactive and ambiguous, then the societal reaction ought to be similarly conceived. It is hardly adequate to see becoming sexually deviant in relativist and interactional terms, while retaining absolutist and functional explanations of the origins of deviant labels.

21 An important source of these ideas is the classic paper on an ecology of games by Long (1958). He writes:

> The local community, whether viewed as a polity, an economy, or a society, presents itself as an order in which expectations are met and functions performed. [The objective reality.] In some cases, as in a new company-planned mining town, the order is the willed product of centralised control, but for the most part the order is the product of a history rather than the imposed effect of any central nervous system of the community. For historical reasons we readily conceive the massive task of feeding New York to be achieved through the unplanned, historically developed

cooperation of thousands of actors largely unconscious of their collaboration to this individually unsought end.

22 Such an analysis is presented by Douglas (1971b); and more specifically in this context by Quinney (1970). While holding to a phenomenological picture of the world, Quinney 'imposes' on it a structural picture of 'interests' as the 'manipulation' of laws, control agencies, media, etc. A lucid exposition of law in harmony with this book is Rock (1973).

23 I discuss some aspects of socialization more fully in chapter 7, with special reference to homosexuality. The theoretical base of this account draws from Rose (1962: 3–20); Lindesmith and Strauss (1968); Berger and Luckmann (1967); Strauss (1959); McCall and Simmons (1966).

24 By 'erotic career', I mean the recurrent problems and contingencies encountered by actors over their life span that are linked with notions of sexuality. This differs slightly from the initial usage by Roth (1963) and others.

25 From Exner to Kinsey and from Schofield to Gorer, a mass of data has been gathered from questionnaire studies that provide detailed descriptions of the stages of sexual growth. Such data are important pragmatically, but because they lack a theoretical basis fail to help us in understanding the complex processes involved in sexual development very adequately. Indeed, in some cases, they may even be misleading – failing to record shifts that have occurred at the level of meaning. Nearly all the studies, for example, that we have of childhood and sexualization simply tell us the age at which a child committed a first act, and other observable, external facts that are easily capable of being quantified. But while it may be well established that children play with their genitals, have orgasms, and conjure up copulatory fantasies (Ramsey, 1943), we cannot automatically assume that such activity represents a sexual meaning to the child. As one correspondent wrote to me: 'At about the age of eight I was coerced by a stranger to masturbate him. My chief understanding at the time was that the stranger urinated. That is, I did not understand either the ejaculation or the sexual meaning of the encounter. It struck me as bizarre, but the sexual meanings were retrospectively imposed when I learnt about orgasms.' Practically nothing is known about the ways in which children come to learn the sexual meanings of these acts.

26 Differential access to varying sexual opportunity structures (cf. Cloward and Ohlin, 1960) will be important in developing a range of sexual meanings. Long ago Freud commented: 'We find with gruesome frequency sexual abuse of children by teachers and servants merely because they have the best opportunity for it' (Freud, 1962). More recently, Kinsey noted the higher frequency of zoophilia among farm boys (Kinsey et al., 1948: 670).

27 It is possible to add a third general process to this list, one perhaps increasingly common: over-labelling. Here, family members may place an exaggerated emphasis on sexuality – encouraging openness and sexual talk, nudity and sexual experimentation. Such a process may have very different implications to those I discuss briefly in the text.

28 Most of my discussion throughout will relate to boys and men – the male culture. This is for analytic convenience, and not for any ideological reasons.

29 Sexual socialization constitutes a vast and critically important research area, currently grossly underexplored. A useful framework to guide work in this field has been provided by Gagnon and Simon (1973).

30 The existence of human variation was one of the guiding notions of Kinsey's philosophy (Christenson, 1971: 3–9), and it was also a guiding principle behind Havelock Ellis's saying that 'everybody is not like you, your loved ones and your friends and neighbours' (Brecher, 1970).

31 In England, one estimate before the Abortion Act, 1967, suggested that there were some 31,000 illegal abortions a year. See the discussion contained in Hindell and Simms (1971: esp. ch. 1, p. 37). Also Henslin (1971c) and Manning (1971).

32 A fourth source of evidence comes from the few existing 'victim studies'. The rate of rape per 100,000 is quadrupled when sample data are compared with the FBI's uniform crime reports (Ennis, 1967).

33 In fairness, some studies display very little variation (e.g. Schofield, 1965b; 1973). However, one may hypothesize that this is more of a consequence of research procedures than the actual situation – the surveys not being designed to tap variations. Also, see the comments by Gebhard on the smallness of many 'deviant' groups (in Karlen, 1971: 281).

4 The emergence of sexually deviant conduct

1 Allen, in his preface to the 2nd edition (1969: vii), comments: 'This book was written in an attempt to collect together psychosexual disorders into a group of psychiatric diseases which should form part of the accepted corpus of reputable medicine.'

2 Storr (1964: 17) comments: 'It is true to say that all sexual deviations are forms of immaturity, childish attitudes which have not been outgrown.' See also Batchelor (1969: 197).

3 This is Freud's term. Freud's writings are, of course, central to this kind of definition.

4 Cf. Storr (1964), who locates two main characteristics: guilt and inferiority.

5 Not all clinicians adopt an absolutist stance on the nature of deviance; many at least pay homage to the cross-cultural variability of values and norms. Chesser's study (1970: 17) suggests that 'perversion and deviation are terms that express individual moral judgments. They do not belong to any scientific language. They do not describe the facts of behaviour but merely how some people react emotionally to the facts.' Having given this definition he then goes on to show how his personal definition of sexual deviance is based on the notion of loveless sex: 'Perhaps loveless sex, whatever form it assumes, is the true and only perversion' (p. 21). This, it seems to me, is a perfectly justified exercise as long as it does not pose as being anything more than one man's view. In this study I have tried to avoid any kind of personal judgment

211

against any form of deviation – but this is not to say that I would condone all sexual variation in my private life. The issue as to what should be considered deviant is an ethical and political one.

6 For example: Mayer-Gross comments (1969: 160): 'A sexual activity is usually regarded as perverse if it has no immediate connection with reproduction and still more so if it tends to replace sexual activity which could lead to reproduction.' Yet the reproductive function is statistically the least important of all sexual functions. The relativist nature of the other comments given here are supported by any standard anthropological work on sexuality, e.g. Westermarck (1917); Ford and Beach 1952); Marshall and Suggs (1971).

7 Consider the findings relating to homosexuality. While many early studies demonstrated psychological malfunctioning among homosexuals the classic study by Hooker (1957) severely challenged this – when 30 homosexual and 30 heterosexual men failed to reveal any significant differences on a Rorschach test. A more recent study by Thompson (1971) failed to differentiate significantly between a larger group of homosexuals and heterosexuals; although one conducted by Loney (1971) using an MMPI found homosexuals to be significantly differentiated on 27 out of 29 items. This whole field has recently been reviewed by Freedman (1971: 87) who concludes: 'Most of the homosexually oriented individuals evaluated in the studies function as well as comparable groups of heterosexually oriented individuals; that their functioning typically could be characterised as normal; and that, in some cases, their functioning even approximates that of self-actualising people.' This raises a paradox: if homosexuals are not psychologically abnormal, they *ought* to be – because my argument stresses that one could expect such abnormalities where there is the violation of proscriptive norms. The point which I stress later is that access to supportive groups, etc., may neutralize the damaging consequences of hostility. One may thus expect some homosexuals to be psychologically 'normal', and others to be psychologically 'abnormal'.

8 Hill and Lloyd-Jones (1970: 2–5) have reviewed forty-two sex education texts on the 'problem' of masturbation, and demonstrated the tendency to link it with 'guilt'.

9 Storr (1964: 18) also notes that guilt permeates our culture with regard to sexuality, but feels 'it is especially characteristic of the sexually deviant'.

10 For earlier discussions on the identification of sexual deviance, see Reiss (1960) and Gagnon and Simon (1973), as well as limited discussions like Amir's writings on rape (1971: 26, *et seq*.). More generally, see Downes and Rock (1971).

11 The terms 'sex-negative' and 'sex-positive' are used by Churchill (1967). Ollendorf provides a detailed account of their contrasting features (Ollendorf, 1966: 52–65). Examples of varying societies are systematically discussed in Ford and Beach (1952). See also the classic study by Seward (1954: ch. 8).

12 Such arguments are however very oversimplified. Wilkins's (1964) discussion of deviance in simple communities, and Karp's (1973) study of behaviour in pornographic bookstores reveal some of the complexities of my observation.

13 See, for example, the case of Russell George, in Parker (1969: 1–36).
14 See the discussion on unmarried mothers by Vincent (1961) which explicitly comments on the importance of visibility, though with reference also to the more general aspect of unwanted pregnancy. On unmarried mothers more generally, see Roberts (1966) and Rains (1971).
15 The Indiana Study of Sex Offenders suggests that suitable fetish materials are not usually to be found from those immediately at hand, that usually a stranger provides a better source for fetish materials. This is not surprising by the arguments above – fetishism among friends and lovers remains undetected. See Gebhard et al. (1965: 413–20).
16 Techniques of denial have been discussed with regard to boy prostitutes (Reiss, 1961); nudists (Weinberg, 1970c); sexually aggressive students (Kanin, 1967); abortion clients (Henslin, 1971c); and sex offenders (Taylor, 1972).
17 See the discussion by Braginsky (1969) in which the 'holiday-camp' image of mental illness is put forward. Here, the argument is advanced that some members of mental hospitals actually seek hospitalization, as a problem-solving device; see also Turner (1972).
18 On the changing belief systems of 'sexual deviants', see Skipper and McGaghy (1970; 1971) on 'strippers'; McGaghy (1968a) on child-molesters; Bryan (1966; 1969) and N. J. Davis (1971) on prostitutes; Gibbons (1968) on sex offenders; Bartell (1971) and Symonds (1971) on wife-swapping; Buckner (1971) on transvestites; Rains (1971) on unmarried mothers; Henslin (1971c) on abortions; Dank (1971) on homosexuals; Weinberg (1965, 1966, 1970c) on nudists; Mohr et al. (1964) on exhibitionism and paedophilia; Amir (1971) on rapists.
19 Even in the extreme case of Christie, there was social organization surrounding the murders (see: Ludovic Kennedy's Ten Rillington Place, and Wilson, 1966: 142).
20 But the rate of sexual differentiation varies from one part of society to another. While there may be no 'zoophiliac subcultures' in towns, there may be such a subculture in some rural areas. Certainly, Kinsey suggested considerable activity in such areas (Kinsey et al., 1948: ch. 22).
21 It is unlikely that there is anything approaching a subculture of child-molesters. Nevertheless, Kutchinsky (1972) has described how some 'child-molesters do hang around together in the same parks'.
22 Much more of course remains to be done. In particular, a theory would need to describe and explain the day to day functioning of the 'deviant' and the 'controllers'. I take up some of the former issues in chapter 9.
23 Grant (1953) writes:

A more typical case concerns a man whose fetish was women's shoes and legs. He was arrested several times for loitering in public places like railroad stations and libraries watching women's legs. Finally, he chanced on a novel solution to his problem. Posing as an agent for a hosiery firm, he hired a large room, advertised for models, and took moving pictures of a number of girls walking and seated with their legs displayed to

213

best advantage. He then used these pictures to achieve sexual satisfaction and found that they continued to be adequate for the purpose.

24 I am suggesting what Hempel (1952) has called an 'ideal typology'. The only sociological typology of which I am aware is that by Gagnon and Simon (1968a) on which I have very loosely based my distinctions. They distinguish between (a) incidence of sexual experience, (b) level of invoked sanctions and (c) the existence of a specialized social structure. Only (c) is explicitly incorporated into my typology, although clearly I regard (b) to be a crucial independent variable. A limitation of their typology is that it structures the traditionally conceived 'types' of deviancy (clinical definitions) into the newer categories, and hence reduces flexibility. Another minor weakness is that they fail to clearly label each cell in their typology; an irritating factor which makes it difficult to use easily.

25 See the comments by Ferdinand on constructing 'synthetic typologies' which articulate the insights of both clinical and social perspectives on deviance (Ferdinand, 1966: ch. 3, 55).

26 See the comments made by Lofland (1971: 7):

A properly conducted social science is itself a highly humanistic enterprise. Properly done, there is no conflict between the humanistic and scientific in the study of human group life. Abstracting, conceptualising and ordering – the activities of the social scientists – are activities we carry on anyway. Through them we understand the world better. Through a detailed rendering of the reality of other people's worlds, we understand other people better. Through the concerted effort self-consciously and explicitly to carry on simultaneously detailed description and careful analysis, we can hope to have even better understanding.

Lofland's own study of *Deviance and Identity* is a prime example of such ordering and clarification. It serves as a useful conceptual framework and orienting system to the further analysis of deviancy (Lofland, 1969).

27 This orienting statement (Homans, 1967: 14–18) is clearly not a theory, it is more like a 'research programme' for the construction of a theory.

5 Introductory: interactionism and the forms of homosexuality

1 There are many statements of this view; for example, Bergler (1957); Bieber *et al.* (1962); Allen (1958); Socarides (1968); Gadpaille (1972). Even sociologists view it as a condition, Schofield (1965a: 203) writes: 'Homosexuality is not a type of conduct, it is a condition characterised by a psychosexual propensity towards others of the same sex.' The view that it is a condition is sometimes equated with the body – for example as 'genetic females with male bodies' – but in general Magee's observation that 'homosexuality is a condition not of the body but of the personality' (1968: 12) is the dominant viewpoint.

3 In 1968, for example, Ellis wrote: 'Although I once believed that

exclusive homosexuals are seriously neurotic, [I now believe that] most fixed homosexuals are borderline psychotic or outright psychotic' (p. 99). Proponents of the 'sickness theory' of homosexuality are many: Bergler's statements (1957) appear to be the most notorious in influencing public opinion, but one suspects they were not well heeded by the academic community. According to Bergler, homosexual men are not just sick – but also narcissistic, irrational, jealous, parasitic, megalomaniacal, supercilious and 'injustice collectors'. More recently, Bieber *et al.* (1962) and Socarides (1968) have become the main proponents of this view. See the discussions on sickness theory in Crompton (1969) and Green (1972); and the forum: 'Are Homosexuals Sick?' in *Time* (31 October 1969: 44). A trenchant critique of the sickness theory is Benson (1965).

4 These observations are only examples. I develop this argument in chapter 8, and elsewhere. In particular, see Plummer (1974a), in which I analyse the male homosexual couple and the role of reactions in inhibiting their development.

5 Cf. the ideas of bisexuality and latent homosexuality. In order to account for the fact that many more people 'dabble' in homosexual behaviour than are exclusively committed to it, bisexual man is announced (cf. Rado, 1964). To give credence to the fact that some people give marginal indications of homosexuality while at the same time refusing to behave homosexually, the 'latent' homosexual is declared (cf. Salzman, 1964). There are also men in prison who wilfully commit homosexual acts together, but who clearly are not 'true' homosexuals – for them the title of 'facultative homosexuals' is invented. Then, there are the numerous typologies that have emerged with no systematic criteria. Hauser, for example, lists over forty differing types, ranging from the 'war queer' and the homosexual alcoholic to the 'toucher', 'body builder' and 'mentally sick homosexual'. One seriously wonders how many 'types' of heterosexual he would be randomly capable of unearthing, ranging possibly from the heterosexual bank clerk to the heterosexual 'virgin chaser' (Hauser, 1962).

6 The clearest statement of the need for role perspectives in the analysis of homosexuality is the important study by McIntosh (1968), although her analysis draws more from a structural approach to roles than an interactionist one. She criticizes the notion of 'condition', analysing some of the functions of such a conception. Reiss (1971) has also stressed the value of the role perspective.

7 As Hooker (1968) says, ' "Who is a homosexual?" and "What is homosexuality?" are very complex questions, clarification of which could be a lasting contribution to the social sciences.' I do not propose to consider these complexities, but provide instead a simple, sensitizing definition.

8 On clinical typologies, see Cappon (1965: 40–60); Scott (in Rosen, 1964: 87–100); Clarke (1965).

9 A more recent listing of 'kinds of homosexual people' is much more theoretically sophisticated, and is geared to a specific problem area. Thus, in Humphreys's study of public sex (1970: ch. 6) he uses two main criteria—occupational autonomy and marital status – and constructs

four types: 'trade', 'ambisexual', 'gay' and 'closet queens'. He modifies this, less successfully, in a subsequent paper (Humphreys, 1971).

10 See Kinsey *et al.* (1948: 638). The rating-scale moves from 0 (exclusively heterosexual with no homosexual) through to 6 (exclusively homosexual) and can be scored on two levels – psychological reactions, and overt experience. See also Gebhard (1966).

11 It should be clear that this is the same typology considered in chapter 4.

12 Perhaps the love of an Aschenbach for a Tadzio is an example of this (cf. Mann's *Death in Venice*).

13 Kinsey, for example, estimates that about 60 per cent of pre-adolescent boys engage in homosexual activities (Kinsey, 1948: 610). Schofield's figures for the English situation are much lower however (1965b: 57–9).

14 See especially the comparative study by Schofield (1965a) of three types of homosexuality.

15 The Albany Survey was a postal-questionnaire survey conducted into the social needs of the homosexual between Summer 1969 and February 1970 ($n = 2,600$). With Michael Schofield and Tom Barratt, I presented a résumé of the analysis of the findings of this survey at the York Conference on Homosexual Needs, July 1970. The findings, however, were generally 'weak', and the survey was crudely quantitative and poorly conducted.

16 On homosexuality in institutional settings, see especially Ward and Kassebaum (1965); Vedder and King (1967); Gagnon and Simon (1968b); Kirkham (1971); Hefferman (1972).

6 Some issues in the societal reactions to homosexuality

1 In saying this, I do not reject the importance of conducting individual medical research concerned solely with organic functioning such as hormonal level (cf. Kolodny *et al.*, 1972). Nor do I reject the importance of psychological/psychodynamic studies that emphasize the micro-family unit – providing they also explicitly recognize the consequences of social hostility to personality functioning (e.g. Kardiner and Ovesey, 1962; Freedman, 1971).

2 Among the controversies here, it should be noted that: (1) most studies are concerned with 'simpler' societies and draw little material from complex, industrial society. They assume the relevance of these societies; (2) in very few, if any, societies does homosexuality become accepted as better than heterosexuality: it may be accepted, but not as equally valid; (3) many of the accounts of societies which validate homosexuality such as Licht and Eglinton's study of Greece are themselves the butt of much criticism (Eglinton, 1971; Churchill, 1967: ch. 7; Karlen, 1971: ch. 2); (4) any attempt to generalize cross-culturally is difficult for the interactionist, since for him 'homosexuality' is endemically linked to situated contests: Homosexuality in Greece is contextually different from that in contemporary California.

3 There is no survey of contemporary attitudes to homosexuality throughout the world, let alone a study of homosexuality in different contemporary cultures. On the former, however, see the brief comments

in Karlen (1971: ch. 13); Churchill (1967); Cappon (1965: 149); the detailed study by Meilof-Oonk (1969) on attitudes among the Dutch population; the attitude survey among police and public in Australia by Wilson (1971: chs. 3, 5 and 6); and the attitude survey among students in Brazil and Canada (Dunbar *et al.*, 1973).

4 Cf. Hauser (1962). As one respondent put it: 'I shared a room with a queer at the university. He knew I had a girl friend and never made any move. He was quite different from the people we hear of who ought to be dealt with so they can't do it again' (1965 paperback edition: 156).

5 At the end of 1969, *New Society* conducted a survey which suggested that the earlier laws on homosexuality (and divorce, abortion, etc.) were highest among the items 'most objected to' by respondents; see Barker and Harvey (1969).

6 A more specific attempt at scaling reactions to deviant groups is the 'aversion scale towards sexually deviant groups' reported by Sigusch (1968). This used a Thurstone technique and applied it to eight groups – prostitutes, homosexuals, lesbians, exhibitionists, sodomites, sadists, paedophiles and criminal sex offenders. Homosexuals and lesbians were placed second and third in rank order of evaluation. Thus, while homosexuals may rank low in general groups of deviants, they may well rank high in groups of sexual deviants. However, the above study was conducted in Germany and this may be a significant factor. For an interesting and polemical discussion on sexual deviance in Sweden which also suggests that homosexuals are the least condemned of sexually deviant groups, see Ullerstam (1967).

7 Although the authors do express some doubts about the validity of this.

8 Schofield's work (1973) does not actually produce the findings concerning homosexuality which was gathered from his sample in 1970. I am very grateful for his permission to draw from this otherwise unpublished material.

9 This is a problem category: females in general are less permissive, but their attitude towards homosexuality is generally shown to be more tolerant.

10 There are few studies of 'homosexuality in the media', the most important of which is that by Pearce, in Cohen and Young (1973), which serves as a useful reference point for further work on the media and social problems. Most of the other areas mentioned have received no attention at all, except in the writings of journalists (e.g. 'The Queer Bash Killers', *Sunday Times*, 7 February 1971), or in hard to obtain Ph.D. theses (e.g. Loeffler (1969), 'An Analysis of the Treatment of the Homosexual Character in Dramas Produced by the New York Theater', *Dissertation Abstracts*, 29: 4599a, 1970). The best source point for starting such work is with the homophile journals, where homosexuals have begun to document their own oppression.

11 For example, Westermarck (1917: 483) writes:

> due to that feeling of aversion or disgust which the idea of homosexual intercourse tends to call forth in normally constituted adult individuals whose sexual instincts have developed under

normal conditions, I assume that nobody will deny the general
prevalence of such a tendency.

12 Hoffman (1968: 181–2) writes:

> Freud held that all individuals had sexual feelings toward
> members of their own scx, but that these had to be repressed in
> our society. Therefore, the dread of homosexuality is a result of,
> and derives its tremendous force from, the wishes for homosexual
> expression which are present in our unconscious minds. In other
> words, the fear is intimately connected with the wish, and the wish
> is only repressed because of the dread which is conjured up by
> the social taboo.

Such ideas are also contained in Gorer's discussion (1948: 69, 96). As
he writes:

> Among the generality of Americans, homosexuality is regarded
> not with distaste, disgust or abhorrence but with panic; it is seen as
> an immediate and personal threat. . . . In America . . . the homo-
> sexual is a threat, not to the young and immature, but above all
> to the mature male, nobody is sure that he might not succumb.

See also the discussion in Cory (1953: ch. 2); Altman (1971: ch. 3); and
Ovesey's (1969) discussion of pseudohomosexuality.

13 Some of these issues and their relationship to mystification are brought
out by Szasz (1971), although he does not use the same language as I do.
Szasz's study is a comparative analysis of the inquisition primarily of
witches, but also of Jews and homosexuals, during the thirteenth and
sixteenth centuries, and the Mental Health Movement in America from
Benjamin Rush onwards. In effect, his analysis is a development of the
more general thesis developed ten years earlier in the *Myth of Mental
Illness*, in which Szasz argued that there was no such thing as mental
illness – only 'problems in living'. In this study, he systematically contrasts the power relationships and ideologies of the middle ages with
those of contemporary mental-health movements in order to demonstrate that, although the rhetoric may have changed, the relationships
are similar (1971: 58):

> My thesis . . . is that the special function of institutional
> psychiatry and the Inquisition lies in the service that each renders
> its society: both provide an intellectually meaningful, morally
> uplifting, and socially well-organised system for the ritualised
> affirmation of the benevolence, glory, and the power of society's
> dominant ethic. From without, to the critical observer, these
> institutions might appear harsh and oppressive; but from within,
> or to the true believer, they are beautiful and merciful,
> flattering at once the masses and their masters. This is the secret
> of their success.

A little later he puts his argument more forcefully. Having shown how
the images of the inquisitions and the mental-health movement are

'badly out of focus', he remarks that they obscure an insight that man has recently acquired at great cost (p. 63):

> The fundamental conflicts in human life are not between competing ideas, one 'true' and the other 'false' – but rather between those who hold power and use it to oppress others, and those who are oppressed by power and seek to free themselves of it.

Quinney (1970) has labelled this phenomenon of authority and reality the 'politics of reality', and has attempted to demonstrate the socially constructed nature of criminality. He comments (p. 303):

> Realities are . . . the most subtle and insidious of our forms of social control. No weapon is stronger than the control of one's world of reality. It is the control of one's mind.

Continuing, he talks of crime in a manner which could equally well be applied to homosexuality:

> By constructing a reality that we are all to believe in, those in positions of power legitimise their authority. That which is believed to be true, to be the real nature of things is good in itself. It is right simply because it *is*, and is not to be questioned or refuted. Believing is accepting. Hence the reality of crime [homosexuality] that is constructed for all of us by those in a position of power is the reality we tend to accept as our own. By doing so, we grant those in power the authority to carry out the actions that best promote their interests . . . this is the politics of reality.

There are, then, two areas of analysis if the tendency to mystify is to be avoided: the concrete political conflict between groups whose interests are different, and the socially constructed canopies of legitimation.

14 Many of the ideas that follow are drawn from Scott's essay, in which he produces a framework for analysing deviance as a property of social order. I have not done his ideas justice – the insights from his essay could provide the basis of a significant analysis of reaction to homosexuality (Scott, 1972).

15 Scott is indebted to Mary Douglas's important work on natural symbols. I draw only marginally from her here; see Mary Douglas (1970). The quotation given by Scott is on p. 52.

16 I am throughout this section implicitly using the functionalist framework and ignoring the problems that this raises. Douglas – who is one of the strongest opponents of functionalism – also adopts this perspective in part. As he comments (1970b: 4–5):

> In our everyday lives morality and immorality, respectability and disrespectability, the otherworldly and this-worldly, the sacred and the secular – each term necessarily implies the existence of its opposite, and depends on its opposite for its own meaning and above all for the force that it exerts on our lives . . . the most general consequence of this necessary linkage in social

meanings between good and evil is that we will always have evil at the same time that – and precisely because – we have good ... the 'good' behaviour cannot exist unless there is also its opposite, the 'evil' behaviour. It is for this reason that immorality in its many forms is a necessary and inevitable part of our social reality. As long as our basic categories, our fundamental criteria for evaluating existence, are relativistic in this way, we will have evil, immorality, disreputability and crime. And there is no indication at all that our basic categories are getting less relativistic. If we do eradicate our present evils, we will simply construct new ones. What really happens is that we eradicate some of our presently worse evils and then we readapt our comparisons: what used to be lesser evils are now worse evils.

7 The individual reaction to homosexuality: the homosexual career

1 The main comments on adult socialization and homosexuality are contained in the work of Dank (1971) and the forthcoming research of the Indiana Institute for Sex Research (Gebhard, 1966). The literature on the 'primary aetiology' of homosexuality is now quite extensive, and it is no task of this book to consider this in detail. Current reviews of this field include Cappon (1965); Churchill (1967); West (1968); Hatterer (1970); Karlen (1971). A recent bibliography by Weinberg and Bell (1972) provides annotated entries on several hundred theories of homosexual aetiology.

2 Reviewer in the *American Journal of Psychotherapy*, quoted on cover of paperback edition.

3 Karlen (1971: 573). Chapter 30 provides a critical analysis of Bieber's work.

4 Marshall and Suggs (1971: 245) describe Bieber in this way in their shortlist of 'fundamental volumes' in sex research.

5 For some general comments on the multifactor approach, see Merton and Nisbett (1971: 116).

6 For a recent statement on biological factors, see Gadpaille (1972). An earlier systematic critique is contained in Ellis (1963).

7 Or as Hooker (1961: 170) writes: 'According to psychoanalytic theory, homosexuality ... may be produced by (1) hostility to the mother (2) excessive affection for the mother (3) hostility to the father (4) excessive affection for the father.'

8 Salzmann (1964) criticizes the notion of 'latent homosexuality' on the grounds that it could sensitize members of society to view very feminine, or very masculine or impotent men as latent homosexuals and thereby to facilitate 'self-fulfilling prophecies'. See also the comments by Wyden (1968). Related difficulties ensue from the idea of 'pre-delinquents'.

9 The evidence on the 'treatment' of homosexuality is as muddled and confusing as the literature on aetiology. But see West (1968: ch. 11); Socarides (1968); Karlen (1971: ch. 30); Hatterer (1970); Feldman and McCullogh (1971).

10 The Task Force on Homosexuality was appointed by the Director of the National Institute of Mental Health, in September 1967, to review carefully the current state of knowledge regarding homosexuality in its mental-health aspects and to make recommendations for Institute programming in this area. The Task Force had Evelyn Hooker as its chairman, and fifteen outstanding members, including Marmor, Ford, Gebhard, Money, Wheeler, Ploscowe and Schur (see Hooker, 1969a).

11 This nice phrase is used by Brim, in Clausen (1968).

12 For parallel discussions, see Scheff (1966) and Scott (1969).

13 I use this term therefore in a way slightly at variance with that of Roth (1963: 94).

14 See the illuminating discussion of man as a dreamer in McCall and Simmons (1966).

15 Schofield had hinted at these stages in one of his earlier publications (Westwood: 1960: 183), and spells it out more fully in Schofield (1965a: 181).

16 Having written this section, I came across a very similar account in a religious anthology. See sections of the first essay in Oberholtzer (1971: 22) which draws – as I do – from Schutz and Lofland.

17 Kagan comments more fully (1964: 161):

> The occurrence of homosexual behaviour or fear of being a homosexual is often related to anxiety over not attaining the masculine ideal. To most adolescents and adults in our society, the term *homosexual* implies ... not interested in girls, slight of build, non-masculine interests. The adolescent or adult male who feels he possesses these attributes is in the precarious position of beginning to believe that he may be a homosexual. The inaccuracy of this belief is no safeguard against its appearance. The boy who has failed to develop masculine interests will be anxious about initiating heterosexual behaviour because of the anticipation of being rejected. This chronic anxiety soon leads to an avoidance of girls and a growing apathy until the individual comes to believe that he is incapable of becoming interested in girls. He does not interpret his apathy and avoidance as the sequelae of long-standing fear. Instead, he interprets them as an indication that he is a homosexual. The panic that results from this realisation leads to a more intense fear of initiating contact with women. For the self-label homosexual often carries with it the expectation of failure in a heterosexual relation.

See also the comment on p. 152, concerning body-build. Money (1963: 34) has commented that 'homosexuality is very much a matter of body morphology and body image'. For some discussion on the 'artistic' homosexual, see Stoller (1968: ch. 10) and the 'effeminate' homosexual, see Green and Money (1966).

18 I have ignored here, and indeed throughout, the important problem of class variations in self-imputation of homosexual labels, but it would make an interesting study. Kagan (1964) in summarizing the literature on class variations on gender identification suggests that lower-class children adopt more rigidly masculine roles than middle-class children,

and that effeminacy serves as a greater threat. If this is so, the experience of homosexual imputation may be much more painful among lower-class groups. The implications of this need exploring.

19 However, one recent study of the 'tribal family' in America suggested that homosexuality was uncommon; see Downing (1970: 126).

20 The most detailed studies of homosexuality in prisons are those of lesbianism and 'jailhouse turnouts' discussed by Giallombardo (1966) and Ward and Kassebaum (1964: 1965).

21 Cf. Matza (1969: 146). Much of the discussion to follow was influenced by Matza's seminal work.

22 Murphy – in a personal statement on homosexuality – describes how he turned to books to discover about homosexuality; and as well as demonstrating the negative imagery in scientific work, he also shows how most of the fictional literature portrays homosexuals in a 'sad' light (see Murphy, 1971: ch. 3).

23 See also the hysterical tones in which homosexuality is discussed by David Reuben in his dangerous and sensational polemic *Everything You Always Wanted to Know about Sex* (1971), which provides an extreme example of a denunciatory attitude towards homosexuality. See also the comments by Wyden (1968), which are given as advice to parents of homosexuals, and Murphy (1971), for experiences of a homosexual who encounters this literature.

24 See Hooker (1967); Burgess (in Hoch and Zubin, 1949); Gebhard (1966); Achilles (1967); Bell (1971).

25 Hall (1966: 146) has suggested with regard to the delinquent subculture that 'delinquents with strong degrees of identification (with the delinquent subculture) tend to have high levels of self evaluation, and delinquents with weak degrees of identification tend to have lower levels of self evaluation'. The same is probably true of the homosexual experience, although firm empirical support for this is lacking. Certainly, much of the recent empirical work with homosexuals in the community at large reveals a high degree of self-evaluation. Williams and Weinberg's study showed that only 20–25 per cent of their samples had hostile or negative self-evaluations (1971: 130–6), and one study suggests that homosexuals in the community at large are more likely to be involved in the subculture and more likely to be better adjusted (Schofield, 1965a: 122–8) than those homosexuals in prison or before psychiatrists. Likewise, when Clarke studied 20 homosexuals under psychiatric treatment for his Master's thesis, he found – using a semantic-differential score – that they had lower self-estimations than non-homosexuals (Clarke, 1965), while when Chang and Block studied 20 male homosexuals in the community they found no significant lowering in self-estimation. Such evidence is suggestive that *homosexuals in the subculture may well have higher self-valuation than those outside the subculture* (Chang and Block, 1960).

26 The problem of neutralizing deviancy has been touched upon at several points. Becker (1963: ch. 4, 72–8) has provided one of the clearest statements of the fashion in which subcultures provide the means of overcoming problems of conventional morality. Within the homosexual subculture, it can be argued that there exist a series of 'accounts'

and 'social motives' available for the homosexual to learn in order to either 'excuse' or 'justify' his behaviour, and which serve to neutralize his deviance. (See in this connection, Mills, 1940; Henslin, 1970; 1971a; Sykes and Matza, 1957; Becker, 1963; Matza, 1964; Lyman and Scott, 1970; Taylor, 1972.) With specific reference to homosexual legitimation, see McIntosh (1965), where an attempt is made to discuss patterns of homosexuality with regard to their techniques of coping with ambivalence. Homosexuals in the bar settings, for example, employ 'partial legitimation' and homosexuals in the homophile movement employ 'total legitimation'. To this pattern now could be added the kind of legitimation sought by the Gay Liberation Front – a radical alternative legitimation.

27 On the 'wonders' of homosexual love, see in particular the literary sources such as those contained in Sutherland and Anderson (1964). It is true however that most of the literature on homosexuality stresses the more painful aspects. Murphy (1971) discusses the way misery and misfortune runs through the literature, and reviews the classic homosexual novels (especially ch. 3).

28 See 'The Positive Sides of Negative Identities', Lemert (1967: 48); Goffman (1961a: 21) on 'secondary gains'; DeLameter (1968: 453). But see also Simmons (1969: 68) on the 'risks' of going deviant.

29 Magee (1968: chs 12 and 13) lists some of the following advantages, although I suspect some are more imaginary than real: (1) a higher standard of living, (2) a greater autonomy and freedom to be irresponsible, (3) a 'feeling of being special', (4) 'comparative absence of hypocrisy about sex', (5) 'freedom from class barriers', (6) greater personal mobility, (7) an in-feeling of 'belonging' to a minority. Magee comments that such advantages accrue more to middle- and upper-class homosexuals.

30 Cf. Hyde (1970: ch. 5); Wildeblood (1955); Harvey (1971).

8 The collective reaction: the subculture of homosexuality

1 I am following here some of the questions urged by Cloward and Ohlin (1960).

2 While used earlier, the first prominent use of the concept of subculture was Cohen's seminal statement about delinquency (1955) which provoked an enormously rich literature (e.g. Miller, 1962; Cloward and Ohlin, 1960; Matza, 1964; Downes, 1966). Since that time the concept has been used to describe, and less frequently explain, all kinds of differential behaviour, ranging from class groups and the poor, to the aged and all manner of 'deviants'. Several recent writers have commented upon its overuse, its ambiguity and its potentiality as a reified concept in the whole process of social control. For useful general comments and criticisms, see Yinger (1960); Wolfgang and Ferrachiut (1967: ch. 3); Arnold (1970); Bell (1971).

3 See for example Westwood's (1952) account of four levels: the street corner, the queer bars, the exclusive clubs and the outsiders. Cory's (1953) study highlights the street corner, the gay bar, and drag (p. 129); and his (1963) study with John LeRoy has a section called 'In the Life'

which deals with bars and 'locales for chance encounters'. Hoffman (1968) describes 'the public place of gay life' as (a) streets, parks and rest-rooms, (b) the baths and (c) the gay bar.

4 I had originally proposed to discuss each of the subcultural elements in some detail, but space precludes this. See, on the *homosexual bar*, Westwood (1952: chs 20 and 21); Westwood (1960: ch. 5); Cory (1953: ch. 11); Cory and LeRoy (1963: chs 9 and 10); Hoffman (1968: chs 1 and 3); Achilles (1967); Hooker (1967); Cavaan (1966). On the *public places of sex*, see Humphreys (1970); Hoffman (1968: ch. 3); Cory and Leroy (1963: ch. 11); Cory (1953: ch. 10). On *male prostitution*, see Benjamin and Masters (1964); Craft (1966); Cory and LeRoy (1963: ch. 8); Harris (1973); Reiss (1961); Ginsburg (1967); Pittman (1971). See also the review of much of this material presented by Mike Brake and myself (Brake and Plummer, 1970), as well as the sensitizing novels by Rechy. On *homophile movements*, see Masters (1964); Sagarin (1969); Weltge (1969: part 4); Teal (1971); McCaffrey (1972: part 2); Altman (1971); Humphreys (1972).

5 I am using here a simple idea put forward by Kameny. He writes (1971: 51):

> Most men have an 'erotic eye'; . . . traditionally, most men are – potentially or actually – 'girl watchers'; most of the remainder are 'boy watchers' (using the term 'boy' in precise parallel with the usage of the term 'girl' to mean an attractive woman and, of course, not in either case to mean a juvenile), while a few are both; and fewer are neither. One has there, in a nutshell, the heterosexuals, the homosexuals, the bisexuals, and the asexuals, which includes just about everybody.

6 Consider Henslin's (1971b) study of taxi-cab drivers where sex seems to permeate much of their working day.

7 The 1972 edition of *Chambers' English Dictionary* includes 'gay' and 'camp'.

8 Some general comments on homosexual language are made by Cory (1953: ch. 5) and Karlen (1971) and glossaries are given by Cory and LeRoy (1963); Hauser (1962); Westwood (1960); Sonenschein (1969); Rodgers (1973). The only detailed study of homosexual language is the preliminary paper by Sonenschein (1969), although there are also comments in McIntosh and Young (1970).

9 For example, one Gay Liberation pamphlet for public display read: 'Are we a load of screaming queens? Yes! Are we a load of butch dykes? Yes! Filthy Reds? Yes! Cocksuckers? Yes! Freaks. Beautiful People? Right On!' (London GLF, 1971).

10 See Ackerley's comments on the difficulties involved in fellatio (Ackerley, 1971: 113).

11 Very little is at present known about the class distribution of homosexual experiences – popular stereotypes that it is found more in the upper classes notwithstanding. Certainly it arises in all classes, but whether the rate of occurrence is the same is an unknown quantity awaiting research. Given the overwhelming importance of class variations in other areas of life, and also the differences known to occur in

the sexual sphere, it would be surprising if there were not in fact some class differences in the rate of homosexuality. The subculture is also likely to manifest variations, and I suspect they are variations continuous with the dominant culture. This means that some bars are likely to cater for more pronounced working-class groups (the 'skinhead' gay bar) and others are more likely to cater for upper-class groups (the 'pisselegant' bar). However, the entire sphere of class variations and homosexuality is one about which practically nothing is known.

12 See Hooker's statement of the four main kinds of areas where gay bars are likely to arise (Hooker, 1967); and Mileski and Black's short account of the social basis of homosexual organization (Mileski and Black, 1972).

13 The Mattachine Society of New York conducted a campaign called 'Trees for Queens', in which funds were raised to restore trees and shrubbery that had been pulled down by a gang of homosexual vigilantes concerned about homosexuals using an enclosed park surrounded by trees for their activities!

14 It is unlikely that many homosexuals become homosexual because of direct socialization into homosexuality – a socialization or reinterpretative process is more probable (cf. DeLameter, 1968). However, some fringe home experiences (a mother who wishes her son to be a bohemian or a homosexual), and institutional experiences (cf. Irwin, 1970: 28), may be nearer direct socialization.

15 See Schur's (1965) discussion on these points. He suggests the homosexual subculture may decline if the law is not so hostile (1965: 173).

16 See Bloch (1965); Taylor, in Marmor (1965); Pearsall (1969: ch. 10); Hyde (1970). Thus, as illustrative in 1709, Ward writes (Bloch, 1965: 228):

> There is a curious band of fellows who call themselves 'Mollies' (effeminates; weaklings) who are so totally destitute of all masculine attributes that they prefer to behave as women. They adopt all the small vanities natural to the feminine sex to such an extent that they try to speak, walk, chatter, shriek and scold as women do, aping them as well in other respects. In a certain tavern in the city . . . they hold parties and regular gatherings. As soon as they arrive there they begin to behave exactly as women do, carrying on light gossip as is the custom of a merry company of real women.

In 1729 (Taylor):

> They also have their walks and appointments to meet and pick up one another, and their particular houses of resort to go to because they dare not trust themselves in an open tavern. About twenty of these sorts of houses have been discovered beside the Nocturnal Assemblies of great numbers of the like vile persons, which are the Royal Exchange, Lincoln's Inn Bog Houses, the South Side of St. James's Park, the Piazzas in Covent Garden, St. Clement's Churchyard [and so forth].

In the 1890s: Havelock Ellis writes (quoted in Brecher, 1970: 130):

> The world of sexual inverts is indeed, a large one in any American city, and it is a community distinctly organized with words, customs, traditions of its own; and every city has its numerous meeting places; certain churches where inverts congregate; certain cafés well known for the inverted character of their patrons; certain streets where, at night, every fifth man is an invert. . . . You will probably infer that the police know of these places and endure their existence for a consideration; it is not unusual for the inquiring stranger to be directed there by a policeman.

And, more recently, a respondent of Humphreys (1971: 38) commented:

> Back around 1930, when I was a very young man, I had sex with a really old fellow who was nearly 80. He told me that when he was younger – around the end of the Civil War – he would make spending money by hustling in that very park. Wealthy men would come down from the Hills in their carriages to pick up boys who waited in the shadows of the tree-lined walks at night.

17 Coffee bars were one of the first signs of a marked youth culture, and they emerged in the gay world to cater for young people especially in the late 1950s and early 1960s. Some interesting side-lights on this and the immediate post-war period are given by Hunter Davies, in *The New London Spy* (1966: 221–31).

18 On the 'swinging London' scene in general, see Aitken (1967). My first brief experiences of the homosexual world came as an undergraduate in 1966 and were very greatly shaded by the 'swinging' 'sixties' era, which was most firmly located around the Carnaby Street area in Soho and the King's Road area in Chelsea. Most of the boys selling and buying clothes in these shops would be found dancing and raving to the latest records in the Soho and Chelsea clubs. My impression was almost of a complete overlap between the two scenes, although the changes that have since taken place are marked.

19 The literature on Gay Liberation and the Homophile Movement is now quite extensive. The most significant accounts include those by Teal (1971); Altman (1971); Murphy (1971); McCaffrey (1972); Humphreys (1972); Fernbach (1973). Analyses of the earlier forms of the Gay Movement include Masters (1964); Sagarin (1969); Weltge (1969: part 4). The interested reader, however, is advised to go to the primary documents produced by these groups for a clearer understanding of the matters involved. In England, this means consulting the London GLF's *Gay Manifesto* (1971), its *Psychiatry and the Homosexual*, and the major journals which include: *Come Together, Gay News, Lunch, Gay Marxist* and *Quorum* – all of which help to demonstrate the diversity within the movement. Indeed, whether GLF itself still exists at the time I am writing this note (1973) is a moot point: it is more likely that the Gay Movement has now become another diversified form of 'being gay'. A useful short account of these changes in England has been provided by Fernbach (1973).

9 Some interaction problems of the homosexual

1 A revised and shortened version of this chapter has been published as 'Awareness of Homosexuality', in Bailey and Young (1973).

2 The homosexual thus becomes what Garfinkle has called a 'dramaturgical methodologist'. See the discussion of this in Williams and Weinberg (1971) and in my revised version (Plummer, 1973b: 116–17).

3 Goffman (1957) suggests that self-conscious role-playing can lead to alienation. If this is so, homosexuals could well be more alienated. See the general discussion by Hoffman (1968: 192–8).

4 Such skills may not be equally available to all men. Ford, Young and Box (1967) have discussed class variations in role-playing – suggesting such skills are less often found among working-class groups. This could suggest that the interaction problems of working-class homosexuals are much greater than their middle-class counterparts.

5 For example, in the Albany Survey, respondents were asked: 'Do your employers know that you are a homosexual?' Of the 1,822 men who replied, 1,152 said their employers did not know, 233 said they did, and 447 were not sure. See also Westwood (1960: ch. 9). Both these studies, however, do not necessarily indicate closed awareness – as neither were concerned with discovering the perceptions of employers.

6 On 'accounts' in general, see Lyman and Scott (1970: ch. 5). For the context of the two examples given, see Westwood (1960: 37), and Reiss, in Becker (1964: 181).

7 See the general discussion of this by Pearce (1973) and more specifically the accounts by Wildeblood (1955), Hyde (1970) and Harvey (1971).

8 Most accounts suggest that no more than 15 per cent of the homosexual population are recognizable as homosexuals. Pomeroy suggests that 15 per cent of men and 5 per cent of women may be recognizable. Sonenschein (1971) after ethnographic fieldwork concluded that 95 per cent are invisible. Westwood (1960: 92), who assessed the stereotypical traits of his respondents during his interviews, commented that only 13 per cent were recognizable as homosexuals. Magee (1968: 40) also comments: 'At a very rough guess I would hazard that something like one twentieth of homosexuals are to be heterosexual eyes recognizably homosexual.'

9 'Into the Twilight World', News of the World, 27 July 1964. See also 'How to Spot a Possible Homo', Sunday Mirror, 28 April 1963, and Wyden (1968). I give a longer list from Wilkinson in Plummer (1973b: 107).

10 Ellis (1963: 173) has suggested how sometimes an effeminate-looking male or a masculine-looking female may be handicapped in social sex-relationships:

> Such a person will actually have a hard time attracting suitable members of the other sex; or else, believing that he or she will have a hard time, such a person may easily develop severe feelings of social-sexual inadequacy and may refrain from active heterosexual participation. The more an effeminate man or a masculine-looking female shies away from heterosexual participation, the less practice in such affairs he or she will get

and the greater his or her feelings of social inadequacy will usually become. In time, such a person frequently feels estranged from the other sex and is then an easy prey for homosexual proselytising.

11 Here I restrict my observation to only one aspect of the gay world: the 'gay bar'.

12 In this section I am adopting a fairly conventional approach, involving the listing of factors. An alternative model would have been to employ the 'game model' described by Lyman and Scott. Here, in an information game, a series of control moves, covering moves, uncovering moves and recovering moves employed by both the homosexual and his partner could have been employed. See Lyman and Scott (1970: 58–66; and 1968).

13 Page reference refers to the 1968 Penguin ed.

14 It must be recognized that here I am talking about role distance from a heterosexual role, not a homosexual one.

15 In the Kitsuse survey of 700 students, 75 'had known a homosexual' (Kitsuse, 1962). Schofield, ten years later and in England, however, found that 48 per cent of his sample of 376 young adults from all classes had known at least one homosexual. Such contradictions may have been transitory.

16 Certainly not all: the Negro is highly visible but he is none the less oppressed.

17 I have material, not included here, which documents a public meeting in Burnley in 1971 where well over half the audience in a large overcrowded hall stood up as homosexuals to challenge the 'priestly' orthodoxy. A few years before such a situation would have been impossible.

Bibliographical index

Figures in square brackets refer to page numbers in the present book.

ABARBANEL, A. and ABARBANEL, W. G. B. (1961), 'Phallicism and Sexual Symbolism', in ELLIS, A. and ABARBANEL, A. (1961), *op. cit.*, pp. 819–26. [36]

ACHILLES, N. (1967), 'The Development of the Homosexual Bar as an Institution', in GAGNON, J. H. and SIMON, W. S. (1967a), *op. cit.*, pp. 228–44. [222, 224]

ACKERLEY, J. R. (1971), *My Father and Myself*, Penguin Books, Harmondsworth, [224]

AITKEN, J. (1967), *The Young Meteors*, Secker & Warburg, London. [226]

AKERS, R. L. (1968), 'Problems of Definition and Behaviour in the Sociology of Deviance', *Social Forces*, 46, 455–65. [22]

ALLEN, C. (1958), *Homosexuality: Its Nature, Causation and Treatment*, Staples Press, London.

ALLEN, C. (1969), *A Textbook of Psychosexual Disorders*, (2nd ed.), Oxford University Press. [45, 67, 88, 97, 181, 211]

ALLPORT, F. M. (1924), *Social Psychology*, Houghton Mifflin Co., Boston. [50]

ALLPORT, G. W. (1955), *Becoming: Basic Considerations for a Psychology of Personality*, Yale University Press. [131]

ALTMAN, D. (1971), *Homosexual Oppression and Liberation*, Outerbridge & Dienstfrey, New York. [6, 115, 118, 173, 218, 224, 226]

AMIR, M. (1971), *Patterns in Forcible Rape*, University of Chicago Press. [76, 212]

ARNOLD, D. O. (1970), *The Sociology of Subcultures*, Glendessary Press, Berkeley, California. [171, 223]

ASHWORTH, A. E. and WALKER, W. M. (1972), Social Structure and Homosexuality: A Theoretical Appraisal', *British Journal of Sociology*, 23, 146–58. [128]

AUBERT, V. (1965), *The Secret Society*, Bedminster Press, New Jersey. [35]

BAILEY, D. S. (1955), *Homosexuality and the Western Christian Tradition*, Longmans, London. [117]

BAILEY, R. V. and YOUNG, W. S. (1973), *Contemporary Social Problems in Britain*, D. C. Heath, London. [227]

BALDWIN, J. (1963), *Giovanni's Room*, Corgi ed., London. [142]

BALL, D. W. (1966), 'An Abortion Clinic Ethnography', *Social Problems*, 14, 293–301. [86]

BANDYOPADHAY, P. (1971), 'One Sociology or Many: Some Issues in Radical Sociology', *Sociological Review*, 19, 5–29. [28]

BARKER, P. and HARVEY, J. (1969), 'Facing Two Ways: Between the 60's and the 70's', *New Society*, 27 November, 847–50. [217]

BARNES, K. C. (1962), *He and She*, Penguin, Harmondsworth. [143]

BARTELL, G. D. (1971), *Group Sex: A Scientist's Eyewitness Account of the American Way of Swinging*, P. H. Wyden, New York. [32, 64, 213]

BATCHELOR (1969), *Henderson and Gillespie's Textbook of Psychiatry*, (10th ed.), Oxford University Press. [211]

BEACH, F. (ed.) (1965), *Sex and Behaviour*, John Wiley, New York. [56]

BECKER, H. S. (1963), *Outsiders: Studies in the Sociology of Deviance*, Macmillan, London. [21, 66, 67, 130, 179, 205, 206, 207, 222]

BECKER, H. S. (ed.) (1964), *The Other Side: Perspectives on Deviance*, Macmillan, London. [25, 110, 227]

BECKER, H. S. (1971), *Sociological Work*, Allen Lane: Penguin Press, London. [16, 21, 205]

BECKER, H. S., GREER, B., RIESMAN, D. and WEISS, R. S. (1968), *Institution and The Person; Papers presented to E. C. Hughes*, Aldine, Chicago. [14]

BECKER, H. S. and HOROWITZ, I. L. (1970), 'The Culture of Civility', *Trans-Action*, April, 12–19. [40]

BEIGEL, H. (ed.) (1963), *Advances in Sex Research*, Harper & Row, New York.

BELL, R. (1971), *Social Deviance: A Substantive Analysis*, Dorsey Press, London. [222, 223]

BELL, R. R. (1966) *Premarital Sex in a Changing Society*, Prentice-Hall, New Jersey. [203]

BENDER, L. and BLAU, A. (1937), 'The Reaction of Children to Sexual Relations with Adults', *American Journal of Orthopsychiatry*, 27, 500–18.

BENE, E. (1965), 'On the Genesis of Male Homosexuality: An Attempt at Clarifying the Role of the Parents', *British Journal of Psychiatry*, 3, 803–13. [125]

BENJAMIN, H. (1966), *The Transexual Problem*, Julian Press, New York.

BENJAMIN, H. and MASTERS, R. E. L. (eds) (1964), *The Prostitute in Society*, Julian Press, New York. [224]

BENSON, R. O. D. (1965), *In Defence of Homosexuality: Male and Female: A Rational Evaluation of Social Prejudice*, Julian Press, New York. [215]

BERGER, B. (1963), 'On the Youthfulness of Youth Cultures', *Social Research*, 30, 319–42. [161]

BERGER, P. L. (1965), 'Toward a Sociological Understanding of Psychoanalysis', *Social Research*, 32, 26–41. [108]

BERGER, P. L. (1966), *Invitation to Sociology: A Humanistic Perspective*, Penguin Books, Harmondsworth. [43]

BERGER, P. L. (1971a), 'Sociology and Freedom', *American Sociologist*, 6, 1–5. [204]

BERGER, P. L. (1971b), *A Rumour of Angels: Modern Society and the Rediscovery of the Supernatural*, Penguin Books, Harmondsworth. [204, 208]

BERGER, P. L. and KELLER, H. (1964), 'Marriage and The Construction of Reality', reprinted from *Diogenes* (1964) in DREIZEL, H. P. (ed.), *op. cit.* [49]

BERGER, P. L. and LUCKMANN, T. (1967), *The Social Construction of Reality*, Allen Lane: Penguin Press, London. [39, 47, 48, 53, 56, 61, 114, 116, 122, 204, 208, 210]

BERGLER, E. (1957), *Homosexuality: Disease or Way of Life*, Hill & Warg, New York, [214, 215]

BERNSTEIN, B (1971), *Class, Codes and Control*, Routledge & Kegan Paul, London [59]

BERSANI, C. A. (ed.) (1970), *Crime and Delinquency: A Reader*, Macmillan, London. [28]

BIEBER, I. *et al.* (1962), *Homosexuality: A Psychoanalytic Study of Male Homosexuality*, Basic Books, New York. [69, 123, 214, 215, 220]

BLOCH, I. (1965), *Sexual Life in England*, Corgi, London. [225]

BLUMER, H. (1969), *Symbolic Interactionism: Perspective and Method*, Prentice-Hall, New Jersey. [1, 10, 17, 112, 204]

BORDUA, D. J. (1967a), 'Recent Trends: Deviant Behaviour and Social Control', in BERSANI, C. A. (ed.), *op. cit.* [28]

BORDUA, D. J. (1967b), *The Police; Six Sociological Essays*, John Wiley & Sons, New York. [79]

BOX, S. (1971a), *Deviance, Reality and Society*, Holt, Rinehart & Winston, London. [127, 207]

BOX, S. (1971b), 'Review of Matza's *Becoming Deviant*', *Sociology*, 4, 403–4. [19]

BRAGINSKY, B. M. and BRAGINSKY, D. D. (1969), *Methods of Madness: The Mental Hospital as Last Resort*, Holt, Rinehart & Winston, London. [213]

BRAKE, M. and PLUMMER, K. (1970), *Bent Boys and Rent Boys*, paper presented at York Deviancy Symposium, 1–3 January 1970. [224]

BRECHER, E. M. (1970), *The Sex Researchers*, André Deutsch, London. [203, 211, 226]

BRECHER, R. and BRECHER, E. (1967), *An Analysis of Human Sexual Response*, André Deutsch, London. [204]

BRIM, O. G. JR and WHEELER, S. (1966), *Socialisation after Childhood: Two Essays*, John Wiley & Sons, London.

BRINTON, C. (1959), *A History of Western Morals*, Harcourt, New York.

BRITISH MARKET RESEARCH BUREAU (1963), *Report on Answers to Public Opinion Questions*, B.M.R.B./48032, November 1963 [105]

BRODERICK, C. B. (1966), 'Sexual Behaviour of Pre-Adolescents', *Journal of Social Issues*, 22, 6–12. [31]

BRODERICK, C. B. and BARNARD, J. (eds) (1969), *Individual, Sex and Society*, Johns Hopkins, Baltimore. [49]

BROWN, F. and KEMPTON, R. T. (1970), *Sex Questions and Answers*, (2nd ed.), McGraw-Hill, London.

BROWN, J. (1952), 'A Comparative Study of Deviations from Sexual Mores', *American Sociological Review*, 17, 135–46. [208]

BROWN, N. O. (1969), *Life Against Death*, Sphere Books, London.

BRUYN, S. T. (1966), *The Human Perspective in Sociology: The Methodology of Participant Observation*, Prentice-Hall, New Jersey. [205]

BRYAN, J. H. (1966), 'Occupational Ideologies and Individual Attitudes of Call Girls', *Social Problems*, 13, 441–50. [213]

BRYAN, J. H. (1969), 'Occupational Socialisation and Interpersonal Attitudes: A Partial Failure in the Acculturation of High Class Prostitutes', in PLOG S. C. and EDGERTON, R. B., *op cit.* [213]

BUCKNER, H. T. (1971), *Deviance, Reality and Change*, Random House, New York. [117, 118, 171, 208, 213]

BULLOUGH, V. L. (1972), 'Sex in History: A Virgin Field', *Journal of Sex Research*, 8, 101–16.

CAPON, J. (1972), *And there was Light: the Story of the Nationwide Festival of Light*, Lutterworth paperback, London. [208]

CAPPON, D. (1965), *Toward an Understanding of Homosexuality*, Prentice-Hall, New Jersey. [103, 215, 217, 220]

CAVAAN S. (1966), *Liquor License: An Ethnography of Bar Behaviour*, Aldine, Chicago. [160, 166, 187, 188]

CHAMBLISS, W. J. (1969), *Crime and the Legal Process*, McGraw-Hill, London. [53, 88, 205]

CHANG, J. and BLOCK, J. (1960), 'A study of identification in male homosexuality', *Journal of Consulting Psychology*, 24, 307–10. [222]

CHAPMAN, D. (1968), *Sociology and the Stereotype of the Criminal*, Tavistock, London. [79]

CHESSER, E. (1970), *The Human Aspects of Sexual Deviation*, Arrow Books, London. [211]

CHRISTENSEN, H. T. (1960) 'Cultural Relativism and Premarital Sex Norms', *American Sociological Review*, 25, 31–9. [71]

CHRISTENSEN, H. T. (ed.) (1964), *Handbook of Marriage and the Family*, Rand McNally, Chicago. [203]

CHRISTENSEN, H. T. (1966), 'Scandinavian and American Sex Norms: Some Comparisons with Sociological Implications', *Journal of Social Issues*, 22, 60–75 [71]

CHRISTENSEN, H. T. and CARPENTER, G. R. (1962), 'Value–Behaviour Discrepancies Regarding Pre-Marital Coitus in Three Western Cultures', *American Sociological Review*, 27, 66–74. [71]

CHRISTENSEN, H. T. and GREGG, C. F. (1970), 'Changing Sex Norms in America and Scandinavia'; *Journal of Marriage and Family Living*, 32, 611–28. [7, 71]

CHRISTENSON, C. V. (1971), *Kinsey: A Biography*, Indiana University Press, Bloomington. [4, 211]

CHURCHILL, W. (1967), *Homosexuality in the Male Species—A Cross Cultural Approach*, Hawthorn, New York. [97, 103, 212, 216–17, 220]

CICOUREL, A. V. (1964), *Method and Measurement in Sociology*, Free Press, New York. [205]

CICOUREL, A. V. (1968), *Social Organisation of Juvenile Justice*, John Wiley & Sons, New York. [61]

CICOUREL, A. V. (1973), *Cognitive Sociology*, Penguin Books, Harmondsworth. [51, 205, 207]

232

CLARKE, R. V. G. (1965), *An Investigation by Conceptual Analytic Methods of Attitudes to Homosexuality in Normal and Homosexual Males*, University of London M.A. thesis, unpublished. [215, 222]

CLAUSEN, J. A. (ed.) (1968), *Socialization and Society*, Little, Brown, Boston. [133, 221]

CLINARD, M. B. (1968), *Sociology of Deviant Behaviour*, (3rd ed.) Holt, Rinehart & Winston, London. [98]

CLINARD, M. B. (1972), *Deviance, Socialisation and Social Structure: The Place of the Labelling Perspective*; Unpublished Paper Presented at 'Ethnomethodology Labelling Theory and Deviance', Conference, Edinburgh University, 28–30 June 1972. [22]

CLINARD, M. B. and QUINNEY, R. (1967), *Criminal Behaviour Systems: A Typology*; Holt, Rinehart & Winston, London. [213]

CLINARD, M. B. (ed.) (1964), *Anomie and Deviant Behaviour*; Macmillan, London, Free Press, New York.

CLOR, H. M. (1969), *Obscenity and Public Morality: Censorship in a Liberal Society*, University of Chicago Press. [208]

CLOWARD, R. and OHLIN, L. E. (1960), *Delinquency and Opportunity*, Free Press, Chicago. [149, 167, 207, 210, 223]

COCHRAN, W. G., MOSTELLER, F. and TUKEY, J. W. (1953), 'Statistical Problems of the Kinsey Report', reprinted in LIEBERMAN, B. (ed.), *op. cit.*, pp. 397–420. [62]

COCKBURN, A. and BLACKBURN, R. (1969), *Student Power: Problems, Diagnosis, Action*, Penguin Books, Harmondsworth.

COHEN, A. K. (1955), *Delinquent Boys: The Culture of the Gang*, Collier-Macmillan, London. [86, 167, 168, 173, 223]

COHEN, A. K. (1965), 'The Sociology of the Deviant Act: Anomie Theory and Beyond', *American Sociological Review*, 30, 1–14.

COHEN, A. K., LINDESMITH, A. and SCHUESSLER, K. (eds.) (1956), *The Sutherland Papers*, Indiana University Press, Bloomington.

COHEN, S. (ed.) (1971), *Images of Deviance*, Penguin Books, Harmondsworth.

COHEN, S. (1972), *Folk Devils and Moral Panics: The Creation of Mods and Rockers*, MacGibbon & Kee, London. [183]

COHEN, S. (1974), *Criminology and the Sociology of Deviance in Britain: A Recent History and a Current Report*, in ROCK, P. and MACINTOSH, M., *op. cit.* [19, 45]

COHEN, S. and YOUNG, J. (eds) (1973), *The Manufacture of News: Deviance, Social Problems and the Mass Media*, Constable, London. [217]

COLEMAN, J. C. (1964), *Abnormal Psychology and Modern Life*, (3rd ed.), Scott, Foresman & Co, London. [67, 76, 88]

COLLINSON, P. and WEBBER, S. (1971), 'British Sociology, 1950–1970: A Journal Analysis', *Sociological Review*, 19, 521–41. [203]

COMFORT, A. (1963), *Sex in Society*, Penguin Books, Harmondsworth. [203]

COMFORT, A. (1968), *The Anxiety Makers: Some Curious Sexual Preoccupations of the Medical Profession*, Panther Modern Society, London.

COOPER, D. (1971), *The Death of the Family*, Allen Lane: Penguin Press, London.

CORY, D. W. (1953), *The Homosexual Outlook: A Subjective Approach*, Nevill, London. [115, 218, 223, 224]

CORY, D. W. and LEROY, J. P. (1963), *The Homosexual and His Society: A View from Within*, Citadel Press, New York. [142, 186, 223, 224]

CRAFT, M. (1966), 'Boy Prostitutes and their Fate', *British Journal of Psychiatry*, 112, 1,111–14. [224]

CRESSEY, D. R. and WARD, D. A. (eds) (1969), *Delinquency, Crime and Social Process*, Harper & Row, London.

CROMPTON, L. (1969), *Homosexuality and the Sickness Theory*, Albany Trust Talking Point, London. [94, 215]

CROWLEY, M. (1968), *The Boys in the Band*, Secker & Warburg, New York. [140]

CROWTHER, R. M. (1960), 'Homosexual Culture', *Homophile Studies*, 9, 176–82. [170]

CUBER, J. and HARROFF, P. B. (1965), *The Significant Americans: A Study of Sexual Behaviour Among the Affluent*, Appleton-Century-Crofts, New York. [49]

CUMMINS, M. (1971), 'Police and Petting: Informal Enforcement of Sexual Standards', in HENSLIN, J. M. (ed.) (1971a), *op. cit.*, pp. 225ff. [79]

DAHRENDORF, R. (1968), *Essays in the Theory of Society*, Routledge & Kegan Paul, London. [18]

DANK, B. M. (1971), 'Coming out in the Gay World', *Psychiatry*, 34, 180–97. [100, 147, 148, 213, 220]

DAVIES, H. (1966), *The New London Spy*, Blond & Briggs, London. [226]

DAVIS, A. J. (1968), 'Sexual Assaults in the Philadelphia Prison System and Sheriff's Vans', *Trans-Action*, 6, 8–16. [216]

DAVIS, F. (1961), 'Deviance Disavowal: The Management of Strained Interaction Amongst the Visibly Handicapped', *Social Problems*, 9, 120–32. [28]

DAVIS, F. (1963), *Passage Through Crisis: Polio Victims and their Families*, Hobbs Merrill, New York. [175]

DAVIS, F. (1968), 'Professional Socialisation as Subjective Experience: The Process of Doctrinal Conversion Amongst Student Nurses', in BECKER, *et al.*, *op. cit.*, ch. 17. [14, 134]

DAVIS, K. (1936), 'Jealousy and Sexual Property', *Social Forces*, 14, 395–405.

DAVIS, K. (1937), 'The Sociology of Prostitution', *American Sociological Review*, 2, 744–55.

DAVIS K. (1939), 'Illegitimacy and the Social Structure', *American Journal of Sociology*, 14, 215–33.

DAVIS, K. (1971), 'Sexual Behaviour', in MERTON, R. and NISBETT, R., *op. cit.* [38, 52, 115, 208]

DAVIS, N. J. (1971), 'The Prostitute: Developing a Deviant Identity', in HENSLIN, J. M. (ed.) (1971a), *op. cit.*, p. 297. [213]

DAVIS, N. J. (1972), 'Labelling Theory in Deviance Research', *Sociological Quarterly*, 13, 447–74. [28]

DAWKINS, J. (1967), *A Textbook of Sex Education*, Blackwell, Oxford. [144]

DE BECKER, R. (1967), *The Other Face of Homosexuality: The Definitive Study of Homosexuality*, Neville Spearman, London. [103]

DEBRO, J. (1970), 'Dialogue with Howard S. Becker', *Issues in Criminology*, 5, 159–79. [19, 205, 206]

DELAMETER, J. (1968), 'On the Nature of Deviance', *Social Forces*, 46, 445–55. [167, 207, 223, 225]

DENZIN, N. K. (1969), 'Symbolic interactionism and ethnomethodology', *American Sociological Review*, 34, 922–34. [16]

DENZIN, N. K. (1970), 'Rules of Conduct and the Study of Deviant Behaviour: Some Notes on the Social Relationship', in MCCALL, G. J. (1971), *op. cit.*, and DOUGLAS, J. D. (ed.) (1970a), *op. cit.* [25, 76]

DENZIN, N. K. (1971), *The Research Act in Sociology: A Theoretical Introduction to Sociological Methods*, Butterworth, London. [205]

DEUTSCHER, I. (1966), 'Words and Deeds: Social Science and Social Policy', *Social Problems*, 13, 235–54. [104]

DEVEREUX, G. (1937), 'Institutionalised Homosexuality of the Mohave Indians', *Human Biology*, 9, 498–527; and reprinted in RUITENBECK, H. M., *op. cit.* [94]

DICKSON, D. T. (1968), 'Bureaucracy and Morality: An Organisational Perspective on a Moral Crusade, *Social Problems*, 16, 143–56. [53]

DOUGLAS, J. D. (ed.) (1970a), *Observations of Deviance*, Random House, London. [19]

DOUGLAS, J. D. (ed.) (1970b), *Deviance and Respectability: The Social Construction of Moral Meanings*, Basic Books, London. [219]

DOUGLAS, J. D. (1970c), 'Deviance and Order in a Pluralistic Society', in MCKINNEY, J. C. and TIRYAKIAN, E. A. *op. cit.* [206]

DOUGLAS, J. D. (ed.) (1971a) *Understanding Everyday Life*, Routledge & Kegan Paul, London. [11]

DOUGLAS, J. D. (1971b), *American Social Order: Social Rules in a Pluralistic Society*, Collier-Macmillan, London. [7, 48, 50, 61, 118, 205, 208, 209, 210]

DOUGLAS, J. D. (ed.) (1972), *Research on Deviance*, Random House, London, [203]

DOUGLAS, M. (1970), *Purity and Danger: An Analysis of Concepts of Pollution and Taboo*, Routledge & Kegan Paul, London. [16, 219]

DOWNES, D. (1966), *The Delinquent Solution: A Study in Subcultural Theory*, Routledge & Kegan Paul, London. [223]

DOWNES, D. and ROCK, P. (1971), 'Social reaction to deviance and its effects on crime and criminal careers', *British Journal of Sociology*, 22, 351–64. [212]

DOWNING, J. (1970), 'The tribal family and the society of awakening', in OTTO, H. A. (ed.), *The Family in Search of a Future*, Appleton-Century-Crofts, New York, 119–35. [222]

DREITZEL, H. P. (ed.) (1970), *Recent Sociology No. 2: Patterns of Communicative Behaviour*, Collier-Macmillan, London.

DUNBAR, J., BROWN, M. and VUORINEN, S. (1973), 'Attitudes Toward Homosexuality among Brazilian and Canadian College Students', *Journal of Social Psychology*, 90, 173–83. [105, 217]

DUSTER, T. (1970), *The Legislation of Morality: Law, Drugs and Moral Judgement*, Macmillan, London.

EDGERTON, R. B. (1967), *The Cloak of Competence: Stigma in the Lives of the Mentally Retarded*, University of California Press, Berkeley. [25, 49]

235

EGLINTON, J. (1971), *Greek Love*, (2nd ed.) Neville Spearman, London. [32, 94, 216]

EHRMANN, W. W. (1964), 'Marital and Non-Marital Sexual Behaviour', in CHRISTENSEN, H. T. (ed.) (1964), *op. cit.* [203]

ELLIS, A. (1961), *The Folklore of Sex*, Grove Press, New York. [208]

ELLIS, A. (1963), 'Constitutional Factors in Homosexuality: a Re-Examination of the Evidence', in BIEGEL, H. (ed.), *op. cit.* [125, 220, 227]

ELLIS, A. (1968), 'Homosexuality: The Right to be Wrong', *Journal of Sex Research*, 4, 96–107. [215]

ELLIS, A. and ABARBANEL, A. (1961), *The Encyclopaedia of Sexual Behaviour*, (2 vols), Hawthorn Books, New York. [36, 203, 206]

EMERSON, J. P. (1970), 'Behaviour in Private Places: Sustaining Definitions of Reality and Gynaecological Examinations', in DREITZEL, H. P. (ed.), *op. cit.* [31, 52]

ENNIS, P. H. (1967), *Criminal Victimization in the United States: A Report of a National Survey*, report of a research study submitted to the President's Commission on Law Enforcement and Criminal Justice, US Government Printing Office, Washington. [211]

ERICKSON, K. T. (1966), *Wayward Puritans*, Wiley, London. [116, 120, 152, 206]

EVANS, R. B. (1969), 'Childhood Parental Relationships of Homosexual Men', *Journal of Consulting and Clinical Psychology*, 33, 129–35. [123]

EVANS, R. I. and ROSELL, R. M. (1970), *Social Psychology in Life*, Allyn & Bacon, London.

EYSENCK, H. J. (1953), *Uses and Abuses of Psychology*, Penguin Books, Harmondsworth.

EYSENCK, H. J. (1972) *Psychology is about People*, Allen Lane: Penguin Press, London. [56]

FARBEROW, N. L. (ed.) (1963), *Taboo Topics*, Atheling Books, Atherton Press, New York. [4]

FARIS, R. E. L. (1967), *Chicago Sociology 1920–1932*, University of Chicago Press.

FELDMAN, M. P and MACCULLOGH, M. J. (1971), *Homosexual Behaviour – Therapy and Assessment*, Experimental Psychology, 14, Pergamon, London. [195, 220]

FERDINAND, T. N. (1966), *Typologies of Delinquency: A Critical Analysis*, Random House, New York. [214]

FERNBACH, D. (1973), *The Rise and Fall of the Gay Liberation Front*, London Gay Culture Pamphlet, London School of Economics. [226]

FILMER, P. PHILLIPSON, M., SILVERMAN, D. and WALSH, D. (1972), *New Directions in Sociological Theory*, Collier-Macmillan, London. [28, 51, 94]

FILSTEAD, W. J. (1972), *An Introduction to Deviance: Readings in the Process of Making Deviants*, Markham Publishing Co., Chicago.

FIRESTONE, S. (1971), *The Dialectic of Sex: The Case for Feminist Revolution*, Cape, London.

FOOTE, N. N. (1954), 'Sex as Play', *Social Problems*, 1, 159–63. [36]

FORD, C. S. and BEACH, F. (1952), *Patterns of Sexual Behaviour*, Methuen, London. [103, 212]

FORD, J., YOUNG, D. and BOX, S. (1967), 'Functional Autonomy, Role Distance and Social Class', *British Journal of Sociology*, 18, 370–81. [59, 227]

FORT, J., STEINER, C. M. and CONRAD, F. (1971), 'Attitudes of Mental Health Professionals Towards Homosexuality and its Treatment', *Psychological Report*, 29, 347–51. [109]

FREEDMAN, M. (1971), *Homosexuality and Psychological Functioning*, Brooks/Cole Publishing, California. [212, 216]

FREUD, S. (trans. by James Strachey) (1962), *Sigmund Freud: Three Essays on the Theory of Sexuality*, Hogarth Press, London. [56, 88, 97, 210]

GADPAILLE, W. J. (1972), 'Research into the Physiology of Maleness and Femaleness: Its Contributions to the Aetiology and Psychodynamics of Homosexuality', *Archives of General Psychiatry*, 26, 193–206. [69, 214, 220]

GAGNON, J. H. (1965a), 'Sexuality and Sexual Learning in the Child', *Psychiatry*, 28, 212–28. [31, 57]

GAGNON, J. H. (1965b), 'Female Child Victims of Sex Offences', *Social Problems*, 13, 176–92. [64]

GAGNON, J. H. and SIMON, W. S. (eds) (1967a), *Sexual Deviance*, Harper & Row, London.

GAGNON, J. H. and SIMON, W. S. (1967b), 'Pornography: Raging Menace or Paper Tiger', *Trans-Action*, 4, July–August 1967, 41–8.

GAGNON, J. H. and SIMON, W. S. (1968a), 'Sexual Deviance in Contemporary America', *Annals of the American Academy of Political and Social Science*, 376, 107–22. [6, 43, 98, 214]

GAGNON, J. H. and SIMON, W. S. (1968b), 'The Social Meaning of Prison Homosexuality', *Federal Probation 1968*, 32, 23–9. [33, 216]

GAGNON, J. H. and SIMON, W. S. (1970), *The Sexual Scene*, Aldine, Chicago. [208]

GAGNON J. H. and SIMON, W. S. (1972), 'Prospects for Change in American Sexual Patterns', in STREIB, G. F., *op. cit.* [7, 208]

GAGNON, J. H. and SIMON, W. S. (1973), *Sexual Conduct: The Social Sources of Human Sexuality*, Aldine, Chicago. [57, 79, 132, 207, 211, 212]

GALLO, J. J., MASON, S. M. *et. al.* (1966), 'The Consenting Adult Homosexual and the Law: An Empirical Study of Enforcement and Administration in Los Angeles County', *U.C.L.A. Law Review*, 13, 643–832. [113]

GARFINKLE, H. (1956), 'The Conditions of Successful Degradation Ceremonics', *American Journal of Sociology*, 61, 420–24. [152]

GARFINKLE, H. (1967), *Studies in Ethnomethodology*, Prentice-Hall, New Jersey. [35, 52, 120, 160, 227]

GAY LIBERATION FRONT (1971), *Gay Liberation Front Manifesto*, Pamphlet, London. [226]

GEBHARD, P. H. (1965), 'Situational Factors Affecting Human Sexual Behaviour', in BEACH, F. (ed.), *op. cit.*

GEBHARD, P. H. (1966), 'Homosexual Socialisation', *Excerpta Medica Found.* (Amsterdam), International Congress Serv. No. 117, paper at fourth World Congress. [216, 220, 222]

GEBHARD, P. H., GAGNON, J., POMEROY, W. and CHRISTENDEN, C. (1965), *Sex Offenders: An Analysis of Types*, Harper & Row, London. [59, 213]

GERASSI, J. (1966), *Boys of Boise: Furor, Vice and Folly in an American City*, Macmillan, New York. [113, 183, 184]

GIALLOMBARDO, R. (1966), *A Study of a Women's Prison*, Wiley & Sons, London. [222]

GIBBENS, T. C. N. and PRINCE, J. (1963), *Child Victims of Sex Offences*, Institute for the Study and Treatment of Delinquency, London.

GIBBONS, D. C. (1968), *Society, Crime and Criminal Careers*, Prentice-Hall, New Jersey. [213]

GIBBONS, D. C. and JONES, J. F. (1971), 'Some Critical Notes on Current Definition of Deviance', *Pacific Sociological Review*, 14, 20–37.

GIBBS, J. P. (1972), 'Issues in Defining Deviant Behaviour', in SCOTT, R. A. and DOUGLAS, J. D., *op. cit.*, pp. 39–68. [25, 28]

GIGEROFF, A. K. (1969), *Sexual Deviance in the Criminal Law: Homosexual, Exhibitive and Paedophiliac Offences in Canada*, Oxford University Press, London.

GINSBURG, K. N. (1967), 'The Meat Rack: A Study of the Male Homosexual Prostitute', *American Journal of Psychotherapy*, 21, 170–85. [224]

GLASER, B. G. and STRAUSS, A. L. (1965), *Awareness of Dying: A Sociological Study of Attitudes towards the Patient Dying in Hospital*, Weidenfeld & Nicolson, London. [90, 177]

GLASER, B. G. and STRAUSS, A. L. (1967), *The Discovery of Grounded Theory: Strategies for Qualitative Research*, Weidenfeld & Nicolson, London. [205, 208]

GLASER, B. G. and STRAUSS, A. (1971), *Status Passage: A Formal Theory*, Routledge & Kegan Paul, London. [133]

GOCHROS, H. and SCHULTZ, L. G. (1972), *Human Sexuality and Social Work*, Association Press, New York. [204, 209]

GOFFMAN, E. (1952), 'On Cooling the Mark Out: Some Aspects of Adaption to Failure', *Psychiatry*, 15, 451–63.

GOFFMAN, E. (1956a), *The Presentation of Self in Everyday Life*, University of Edinburgh Monograph; Penguin ed., 1971. [19]

GOFFMAN, E. (1956b), 'Embarrassment and Social Organisation', *American Journal of Sociology*, 62, 264–71.

GOFFMAN, E. (1957), 'Alienation From Interaction', *Human Relations*, 10, 47–60. [227]

GOFFMAN, E. (1961a), *Asylums: Essays on the Social Situation of Mental Patients and Other Inmates*, Anchor Books, Doubleday, New York, and Penguin Books, Harmondsworth. [24, 83, 96, 223]

GOFFMAN, E. (1961b), *Encounters: Two Studies on the Sociology of Interaction*, Bobbs-Merrill, Indiana. [193]

GOFFMAN, E. (1963a), *Stigma: Notes on the Management of Spoiled Identity*, Prentice-Hall, New Jersey, and Penguin Books, Harmondsworth. [28, 160, 175, 189, 193]

GOFFMAN, E. (1963b), *Behaviour in Public Places*, Collier-Macmillan, London.

GOODE, E. (1968), 'Multiple Drug Use Among Marijuana Smokers', *Social Problems*, 17, 48–64. [158]

GOODE, E. (1969), 'Marijuana and the Politics of Reality', *Journal of Health and Social Behaviour*, 10, 83–94. [69]

GORDON, C. and GERGEN, K. J. (1968), *The Self in Social Interaction* (vol. 1), Wiley & Sons, London. [17, 204]

GORER, G. (1948), *The Americans: A Study in National Character*, Cresset Press, London. [103, 218]

GORER, G. (1971), *Sex and Marriage in England Today*, Thomas Nelson & Sons, London. [108]

GOSLIN, D. A. (1969), *Handbook of Socialisation Theory and Research*, Rand McNally, Chicago.

GOULDNER, ALVIN, W. (1971), *The Coming Crisis of Western Sociology*, Heinemann, London. [28, 90, 204]

GOULDNER, ALVIN W. (1973), *For Sociology: Renewal and Critique in Sociology Today*, Allen Lane: Penguin Press, London. [28, 204, 205]

GOVE, W. R. (1970), 'Societal Reaction as an Explanation of Mental Illness', *American Sociological Review*, 35, 873–84. [28]

GRANT, N. W. (1953), 'A Case Study of Fetishism', *Journal of Abnormal Social Psychology*, 48, 142–9. [213]

GREEN, R. (1972), 'Homosexuality as a Mental Illness', *International Journal of Psychiatry*, 10, 77–128. [94, 215]

GREEN, R. and MONEY, J. (1966), 'Stage Acting, Role Taking and Effeminate Impersonation During Boyhood', *Archives of General Psychiatry*, 15, 535–8. [221]

GRUNWALD, H. (ed.) (1964), *Sex In America*, Bantam Books, New York. [113]

GUNDLACH, R. H. (1969), 'Childhood Parental Relationships and the Establishment of Gender Roles of Homosexuals', *Journal of Consulting and Clinical Psychology*, 33, 136–9. [123]

GUSFIELD, J. R. (1963), *Symbolic Crusade: Status Politics and The American Temperance Movement*, University of Illinois Press, London. [115, 206, 209]

HABENSTEIN, R. W. (1971), *Pathways to Data: Field Methods for Studying Ongoing Social Organisations*; Aldine, Chicago. [123]

HACKER, H. M. (1971), 'Homosexuals: Deviant or Minority Group', in SAGARIN, E. (ed.), (1971a), *op. cit.*, pp. 65–90. [104]

HALL, P. M. (1966), 'Identification With the Delinquent Subculture and the Level of Self-Evaluation', *Sociometry*, 29, 146–58. [164, 222]

HAMMOND, B. E. and LADNER, J. A. (1969), 'Socialisation into Sexual Behaviour in a Negro Slum Ghetto', in BRODERICK C. B. and BARNARD, J. (eds), *op. cit.* [49]

HAMPSON, J. L. (1965), 'Determinants of Psychosexual Orientation', in BEACH, F. (ed.), *op. cit.*

HARDY, K. R. (1964), 'An Appetitional Theory of Sexual Motivation', *Psychological Review*, 71, 1–18. [37, 56]

HARLOW, H. F. (1965), 'Sexual Behaviour in the Rhesus Monkey', in BEACH, F. (ed.) *op. cit.*, pp. 234–65. [56]

HARRIS, M. (1973), *The Dilly Boys: Male Prostitution in Piccadilly*, Croom-Helm, London. [224]

HARVEY, I. (1971), *To Fall Like Lucifer*, Sidgwick & Jackson, London. [223, 227]

HATTERER, L. J. (1970), *Changing Homosexuality in the Male*, McGraw-Hill, London. [126, 220]

HAUSER, R. (1962), *The Homosexual Society*, Bodley Head, London. Page references are to the 1965 Mayflower-Dell paperback edition. [97, 136, 215, 217, 224]

HAVELIN, A. (1970), 'Political Attitudes Towards Homosexuals and Homosexuality', *Sociological Abstracts*, 1195.

HEFFERMAN, E. (1972), *Making it in Prisons: The Square, the Cool and the Life*, Wiley & Sons, London. [216]

HEISS, J. (ed.) (1968), *Family Roles and Interaction: An Anthology*, Rand McNally, Chicago. [19]

HEMPEL, C. G. (1952), 'Symposium: Problems of Concept and Theory Formation in the Social Sciences', reprinted in BRODBECK, MAY (1968), *Readings in the Philosophy of Science*, Macmillan Co., New York. [214]

HENRIQUES, F. (1959), *Love in Action: The Sociology of Sex*, MacGibbon & Kee, London.

HENSLIN, J. M. (1970), 'Guilt and Guilt Neutralisation: Response and Adjustment to Suicide', in DOUGLAS, J. D. (ed.) (1970a), *op. cit.* [223]

HENSLIN, J. M. (ed.) (1971a), *Studies in the Sociology of Sex*, Appleton-Century-Crofts, New York. [207, 223]

HENSLIN, J. M. (1971b), 'Sex and Cabbies' in HENSLIN, J. M., *ibid.* [49, 64, 224]

HENSLIN, J. M. (1971c), 'Criminal Abortion: Making the Decision and Neutralising the Act', in HENSLIN, J. M., *ibid.* [28, 211, 213]

HENSLIN, J. M. and BIGGS, M. A. (1971), 'Dramaturgical Desexualisation: The Sociology of the Vaginal Examination', in HENSLIN, J. M. (1971a), *op. cit.*, pp. 243–72. [31, 52]

HILL, M. and LLOYD-JONES, M. (1970), *Sex Education: The Erroneous Zone*, National Secular Society, London. [143, 212]

HINDELL, K. and SIMMS, M. (1971), *Abortion Law Reformed*, Peter Owen, London. [211]

HINDESS, B. (1973), *The Use of Official Statistics in Sociology*, Macmillan, London. [12]

HIRSCHI, T. (1962), 'The Professional Prostitute', *Berkeley Journal of Sociology*, 7, 33–49.

HIRSCHI, T. (1969), *Causes of Delinquency*, University of California Press. [127]

HOCH, P. H. and ZUBIN, J. (eds) (1949), *Psychosexual Development in Health and Disease*, Grune & Stratton, New York. [222]

HOFFMAN, M. (1966), 'Review of Schofield', *Issues in Criminology*, 313–16. [123]

HOFFMAN, M. (1968), *The Gay World: Male Homosexuality and the Social Creation of Evil*, Basic Books, New York. [103, 151, 161, 218, 223, 224, 226, 227]

HOLBROOK, D. (1972), *Sex and Dehumanization*, Pitman, London. [204]

HOMANS, G. C. (1967), *The Nature of Social Science*, Harbinger Book, Harcourt, Brace & World, New York. [214]

HOOD, R. and SPARKS, R. (1970), *Key Issues in Criminology*, Weidenfeld & Nicolson, London. [61]

240

HOOKER, E. (1957), 'The Adjustment of the Male Overt Homosexual', *Journal of Protective Techniques*, 21, 18–31 [91, 212]

HOOKER, E. (1958), 'Male Homosexuality in the Rorschach', *Journal of Projective Techniques*, 22, 33–54. [212]

HOOKER, E. (1961), 'Homosexuality – Summary of Studies', in DUVALL, E. M., *et al.*, *Sex Ways – In Fact and Faith*, Association Press, London. [220]

HOOKER, E. (1963), 'Male Homosexuality', in FARBEROW, N. L. (ed.), *op. cit.* [4]

HOOKER, E. (1967), 'The Homosexual Community', in GAGNON, J. H. and SIMON, W. S. (eds.) (1967a), *op. cit.*, pp. 167–84. [155, 222, 224, 225]

HOOKER, E. (1968), 'Homosexuality', in *International Encyclopaedia of Social Sciences*, 14, 222–32. [215]

HOOKER, E. (1969a), 'Final Report of the Task Force on Homosexuality', *Homophile Studies*, 8, 5–12. [131, 221]

HOOKER, E. (1969b), 'Parental Relations and Male Homosexuality in Patient and Non-Patient Samples', *Journal of Consulting and Clinical Psychology*, 33, 140–2. [123]

HORNITRA, L. (1967), 'Homosexuality', *International Journal of Psycho-Analysis*, 48, 394–401. [124]

HOROWITZ, I. L. (1968), *Professing Sociology: Studies in the Life Cycle of Social Science*, Aldine, Chicago, [115, 173, 205]

HUMPHREYS, L. (1970), *Tea-room Trade: A Study of Homosexual Encounters in Public Places*, Duckworth, London. [24, 65, 78, 82, 100, 140, 159, 167, 168, 180, 182, 193, 215, 224]

HUMPHREYS, L. (1971), 'New Styles in Homosexual Manliness', *Trans-Action*, March–April, 38–46. [171, 216, 226]

HUMPHREYS, L. (1972), *Out of the Closets: The Sociology of Homosexual Liberation*, Prentice-Hall, Spectrum Book, New Jersey. [224, 226]

HYDE, H. M. (1970), *The Other Love: An Historical and Contemporary Survey of Homosexuality in Britain*, Heinemann, London. [117, 223, 227]

IRWIN, J. (1970), *The Felon*, Prentice-Hall, New Jersey. [225]

JELLINEK, E. M. (1960), *The Disease Concept of Alcoholism*, Hillhouse Press, New Haven, Connecticut. [71]

KAGAN, J. (1964), 'Acquisition and Significance of Sex Typing and Sex Role Identity', in HOFFMAN M. L. and HOFFMAN L. W. (eds), *Child Development Research*, (vol. 1), Russell Sage Foundation, New York. [36, 221]

KALLMAN, F. J. (1952), 'Comparative Twin Study on the Genetic Aspects of Male Homosexuality', *Journal of Nervous Mental Disorders*, 115, 283–98. [125]

KAMENY, F. E. (1969), 'Gay is Good', in WELTGE, R. W. (ed.), *op. cit.* [224]

KAMENY, F. E. (1971), 'Homosexuals as a Minority Group', in SAGARIN, E., (ed.) (1971a), *op. cit.*, pp. 50–64. [224]

KANIN, E. J. (1967), 'Reference Groups and Sex Conduct Norm Violation', *Sociological Quarterly*, 8, 495–505. [59, 75, 213]

KARDINER, A. (1963), 'The Flight from Masculinity', in RUITENBECK, H. M., *op. cit.* [128]

KARDINER, A. and OVESEY, L. (1962), *The Mark of Oppression*, Meridian Books, New York. [216]

241

KARLEN, A. (1971), *Sexuality and Homosexuality: The Complete Account of Male and Female Sexual Behaviour and Deviation*, Macdonald, London. [103, 165, 211, 216, 217, 220, 224]

KARP, D. A. (1973), 'Hiding in Pornographic Bookstores', *Urban Life and Culture*, 1, 427–5. [212]

KIMBALL-JONES, H. (1967), *Towards a Christian Understanding of the Homosexual*, SCM Press, London. [76]

KINCH, J. W. (1963), 'A Formalised Theory of the Self-Concept, *American Journal of Sociology*, 68, 481–6. [164]

KINSEY, A. C., GEBHARD, P. POMEROY, W. B. and MARTIN, C. E. (1953), *Sexual Behaviour in the Human Female*, W. B. Saunders, Philadelphia. [56, 59, 62, 103, 207, 209]

KINSEY, A. C., POMEROY W. B., and MARTIN, C. E. (1948), *Sexual Behaviour in the Human Male*, W. B. Saunders, Philadelphia. [38, 59, 62, 63, 91, 97, 137, 196, 207, 209, 210, 213, 216]

KIRKENDALL, L. A. (1960), 'Circumstances Associated with Teenage Boys' Prostitution', *Marriage and Family Living*, 22, 145–50. [75]

KIRKHAM, G. L. (1971), 'Homosexuality in Prison', in HENSLIN, J. M. (ed.) (1971a), *op. cit.*, p. 325. [139, 216]

KITSUSE, J. I. (1962), 'Societal Reaction to Deviant Behaviour: Problems of Theory and Method', *Social Problems*, 9, 247–56. [105, 109, 110, 179, 181, 182, 228]

KITSUSE, J. I. (1972), 'Deviance, Deviant Behaviour and Deviants: Some Conceptual Issues', in FILSTEAD, W. J., *op. cit.* [28]

KLAPP, O. E. (1958), 'Social Types: Process and Structure', *American Sociological Review*, 23, 674–8.

KNUPFER, G. and ROOM, R. (1964), 'Age, Sex and Social Class as Factors in Amount of Drinking in a Metropolitan Community', *Social Problems*, 12, 226. [166]

KOLODNY, R. C., MASTERS, W. H., HENDRYX, J. and TURO, G. (1972), 'Plasma Testosterone and Semen Analysis in Male Homosexuals', *New England Journal of Medicine*, 18 November, 1170–4. [216]

KRAUSZ, E. (1969), *Sociology in Britain*, Batsford, London. [203]

KRICH, A. (ed.) (1963), *The Sexual Revolution* (2 vols), Delta Paperbacks, New York. [203]

KUHN, M. H. (1954), 'Kinsey's View on Human Behaviour', *Social Problems*, 1, 119–25. [29]

KUHN, M. H. (1964), 'Major Trends in Symbolic Interaction Theory in the Past Twenty-Five Years', *Sociological Quarterly*, 5, 61–84. [204]

KUHN, T. S. (1970), *The Structure of Scientific Revolution*, University of Chicago Press.

KUTCHINSKY, B. (1972), 'Deviance and Criminality: The Case of Voyeur in a Peeper's Paradise', paper presented at 'Ethnomethodology, Labelling Theory and Deviance' Conference, Edinburgh University, 28–30 June 1972. [213]

LAING, R. D., PHILLIPSON, H. and LEE, A. R. (1966), *Interpersonal Perception: A Theory and A Method of Research*, Tavistock Publications, London. [177]

LAKATOS, I. and MUSGRAVE, A. (ed.) (1970), *Criticism and The Growth of Knowledge*, Cambridge University Press, London.

LAMBERT, R. (1968), *The Hothouse Society*, Weidenfeld & Nicolson, London.

LEE, N. H. (1969), *The Search for an Abortionist*, University of Chicago Press. [64, 65]

LEISER, R. M. (1973), *Liberty, Justice and Morals: Contemporary Value in Conflict*, Macmillan, London. [106]

LEMERT, E. M. (1951), *Social Pathology*, McGraw-Hill, London. [74, 78, 98, 165, 207]

LEMERT, E. M. (1967) (1972), *Human Deviance, Social Problems and Social Control*, (2nd ed.), Prentice-Hall, New Jersey. [21, 27, 72, 134, 150, 223]

LEMERT, E. M. (1972), 'The Societal Reaction to Deviance', paper delivered at 'Ethnomethodology, Labelling Theory and Deviance' Conference, Edinburgh University, 28–30 June 1972. [116]

LERMAN, P. (1967), 'Gangs, Networks and Subcultural Delinquency', *American Journal of Sociology*, 73, 63–72. [162]

LEWIS, L. S. and BRISSETT, D. (1967), 'Sex as Work: A Study of Avocational Counselium', *Social Problems*, 13, 8–18. [36]

LEZNOFF, M. and WESTLEY, W. A. (1956), 'The Homosexual Community', *Social Problems*, 3, 257–63.

LIAZOS, A. (1972), 'The Poverty of the Sociology of Deviance: Nuts, Sluts and Perverts', *Social Problems*, 20, 103–19. [25, 28]

LICHTMAN, R. (1970), 'Symbolic Interactionism and Social Reality: Some Marxist Queries', *Berkeley Journal of Sociology*, 15, 75–94. [12, 209]

LIEBERMAN, B. (1971), *Human Sexual Behaviour*, Wiley & Sons, London.

LINDESMITH, A. R. (1947), *Opiate Addiction*, Principia Press, Bloomington, Indiana. [20]

LINDESMITH, A. R. and STRAUSS, A. L. (1968), *Social Psychology*, (3rd ed.) Holt, Rinehart & Winston, London. [11, 204, 210]

LOFLAND, J. (with assistance of LYN LOFLAND) (1969), *Deviance and Identity*, Prentice-Hall, New Jersey. [23, 81, 82, 105, 142, 205, 206, 213]

LOFLAND, J. (1970), 'Interactionist Imagery and Analytic Interruptus', in SHIBUTANI, T. (ed.), *op. cit.* [28]

LOFLAND, J. (1971), *Analyzing Social Settings: A Guide to Qualitative Observation and Analysis*, Wadsworth Publishing Co., California. [205, 206, 207, 214]

LONEY, J. (1971), 'An MMPI Measure of Maladjustment in a Sample of "Normal" Homosexual Men', *Journal of Clinical Psychology*, 27, 486–8. [212]

LONG, N. E. (1958), 'The Local Community as an Ecology of Games', *American Journal of Sociology*, 44, 251–61. [116, 117, 209]

LONGFORD, EARL OF (1972), *Pornography: The Longford Report*, Hodder Paperbacks, London. [6, 208]

LORBER, J. (1967), 'Deviance as Performance: The Case of Illness', *Social Problems*, 14, 302–10. [22]

LYMAN, S. M. and SCOTT, M. B. (1970), *A Sociology of the Absurd*, New York, Appleton-Century-Crofts, New York. [21, 25, 81, 176, 184, 191, 223, 227, 228]

MCCAFFREY J. A. (ed.) (1972), *The Homosexual Dialectic*, Prentice-Hall, Spectrum, New Jersey. [224, 226]

243

MCCAGHY, C. M. (1968a), 'Child Molesters: A Study of their Careers as Deviants', in CLINARD, M. B. and QUINNEY, R., *op. cit.* [213]

MCCAGHY, C. M. (1968b), 'Drinking and Deviance Disavowal: The Case of Child Molesters', *Social Problems*, 16, 43–9. [81]

MCCAGHY, C. M. and SKIPPER, J. K. (1969), 'Lesbian Behaviour as an Adaptation to the Occupation of Stripping', *Social Problems*, 17, 262–70. [206]

MCCAGHY, C. M., SKIPPER, J. K. and LEFTON, M. (1968), *In Their Own Behalf: Voices from the Margin*, Appleton-Century-Crofts, London.

MCCALL, G. J., *et al.* (1971), *Social Relationships*, Aldine, Chicago.

MCCALL, G. J. and SIMMONS, J. L. (1966), *Identities and Interactions: An Examination of Human Associations in Everyday Life*, Collier–Macmillan, London. [1, 11, 14, 15, 157, 204, 210, 221]

MCINTOSH, M. (1965), 'The Homophile Movement and the Homosexual's Dilemma', Leicester University staff seminar paper, unpublished. [223]

MCINTOSH, M. (1968), 'The Homosexual Role,' *Social Problems*, 16, 182–92. [215]

MCINTOSH, M. and YOUNG, J. (1970), 'Wide, Cool and Camp: A Study of Argot in Three Deviant Groups', paper presented at National Deviancy Conference, 3–4 January 1970, York, unpublished. [224]

MCKINNEY, J. and TIRYAKIAN, E. A. (1970), *Theoretical Sociology: Perspectives and Developments*, Appleton-Century-Crofts, New York. [206]

MAGEE, B. (1968), *One in Twenty: A Study of Homosexuality in Men and Women* (2nd ed.), Secker & Warburg, London. [151, 214, 223, 227]

MALINOWSKI, B. (1929), *The Sexual Life of Savages in North Western Melanesia*, Liveright, New York. [33, 70]

MANIS, J. G. and MELTZER, B. N. (1967, 1972), *Symbolic Interaction: A Reader in Social Psychology* (2nd ed.), Allyn & Bacon, Boston. [204]

MANKOFF, M. (1971), 'Societal Reaction and Career Deviance: A Critical Analysis, *Sociological Quarterly*, 12, 204–18. [22, 28]

MANNING, P. K. (1971), 'Fixing What you Feared: Notes on the Campus Abortion Search', in HENSLIN, J. M. (1971a), *op. cit.* [211]

MARCUS, S. (1966), *The Other Victorians: A Study of Sexuality and Pornography in Mid 19th Century England*, Weidenfeld & Nicolson, London.

MARCUSE, H. (1969), *Eros and Civilisation*, Sphere Books, London. [6, 115]

MARMOR, J. (ed.) (1965), *Sexual Inversion: The Multiple Roots of Homosexuality*, Basic Books, New York. [225]

MARMOR, J. (1971), ' "Normal" and "Deviant" sexual behaviour', *Journal of the American Medical Association*, 217, 165–70. [69]

MARSHALL, D. S. and SUGGS, R. C. (1971), *Human Sexual Behaviour: Variation Across the Ethnographic Spectrum*, Basic Books, London. [74, 203, 206, 212, 220]

MASTERS, R. E. L. (1964), *The Homosexual Revolution*, Belmont Books, New York. [224, 226]

MATZA, D. (1961), 'Subterranean Traditions of Youth', *The Annals of the American Academy of Political and Social Science*, 338, 102–18. [157]

MATZA, D. (1964), *Delinquency and Drift*, Wiley, London. [113, 130, 223]

MATZA, D. (1969), *Becoming Deviant*, Wiley & Sons, London. [19, 45, 85, 95, 130, 142, 144, 184, 205, 206, 222]

MAYER-GROSS, ELLIOTT, *et al.* (1969), *Clinical Psychiatry* (3rd ed.), Baillière Tindall and Cassell, London. [212]

MEAD, G. H. (1928), 'The Psychology of Punitive Justice', *American Journal of Sociology*, 23, 577–602. [20]

MEAD, G. H. (1934), *Mind, Self and Society*, Chicago Press. [17]

MEILOF-OONK, S. (1969), *Opinions on Homosexuality: A Study on Image Formation and Attitudes in the Adult Dutch Population*, Minterheden, Amsterdam. [217]

MELTZER, B. N. and PETRAS, J. W. (1970), 'The Chicago and Iowa Schools of Symbolic Interactionism', in SHIBUTANI, T., *op. cit.*

MERTON, R. K. (1967), *Social Theory and Social Structure*, Free Press, Collier-Macmillan, London.

MERTON, R. and NISBETT, R. (1971), *Contemporary Social Problems*, (3rd ed.), Harcourt, Brace & World, New York. [220]

MESSENGER, J. C. (1971), 'Sex and Repression in an Irish Folk Community', in MARSHALL, D. S. and SUGGS, R. C., *op. cit.* [40, 74]

MESSINGER, S., *et al.* (1962), 'Life as Theatre: Some Notes on the Dramaturgic Approach to Social Reality', *Sociometry*, 25, 98–110. [176]

MILESKI, M. and BLACK, D. J. (1972), 'The Social Organisation of Homosexuality', *Urban Life and Culture*, 1, 187–202. [225]

MILLER, W. B. (1962), 'Lower Class Culture as a Generating Milieu of Gang Delinquency', in WOLFGANG, M. E., *et al.*, *op. cit.* [167, 223]

MILLETT, K. (1970), *Sexual Politics*, Doubleday, New York.

MILLIGAN, D. (1973), *The Politics of Homosexuality*, Pluto Press Pamphlet, London. [6]

MILLS, C. W. (1940), 'Situated Actions and Vocabularies of Motive', *American Sociological Review*, 5, 904–13. [32, 81, 223]

MILLS, C. W. (1943), 'Professional Ideology of Social Pathologists', *American Journal of Sociology*, 49, 165–80. [25]

MILLS, C. W. (1970), *The Sociological Imagination*, Penguin Books, Harmondsworth. [4]

MIZRUCHI, E. and PERUCCI, R. (1962), 'Norm Qualities and Differential Effects of Deviant Behaviour', *American Sociological Review*, 27, 391–9. [70]

MOHR, J. W., TURNER, R. E. and JERRY, M. B. (1964), *Paedophilia and Exhibitionism*, University of Toronto Press. [213]

MONEY, J. (1963), 'Factors in the Genesis of Homosexuality', in WINOKUR, G., *op. cit.*, pp. 19–43. [221]

MONEY, J. (ed.) (1965), *Sex Research: New Developments*, Holt, New York.

MURPHY, J. (1971), *Homosexual Liberation: A Personal View*, Praeger Publishers, London. [222, 223, 226]

NIEDERHOFFER, A. (1969), *Behind the Shield: The Police in Urban Society*, Anchor Books, New York. [109]

NOBILE, P. (ed.) (1970), *The New Eroticism*, Random House, New York.

NORTH, M. (1970), *The Outer Fringe of Sex: A Study in Sexual Fetishism*, Odyssey, London. [64, 76, 86]

OBERHOLTZER, W. D. (ed.) (1971), *Is Gay Good? Ethics, Theology and Homosexuality*, Westminster Press, Philadelphia. [105, 109, 221]

OLIVER, B. J. Jr (1967), *Sexual Deviation in American Society: A Social–*

Psychological Study of Sexual Non-Conformity, College & University Press, New York. [68]

OLLENDORF, R. (1966), *The Juvenile Homosexual Experience and its Effects on Adult Homosexuality*, Julian Press, New York. [58, 74, 212]

OTTO, H. A. (1970), *The Family in Search of a Future: Alternate Models for Moderns*, Appleton-Century-Crofts, New York.

OVESEY, L. (1969), *Pseudohomosexuality and Homosexuality*, Science House, New York. [218]

PACKARD, V. (1968), *The Sexual Wilderness*, Longmans, London. [209]

PARKER, T. (1969), *The Twisting Lane*, Hutchinson, London. [67, 213]

PARSONS, T. (1951), *The Social System*, Routledge & Kegan Paul, London. [18]

PARSONS, T. (1964), *Essays in Sociological Theory*, Free Press, New York. [129]

PEARCE, F. (1973), 'How to be Immortal and Ill, Pathetic and Dangerous, All at the Same Time: Mass Media Homosexuality', in COHEN S. and YOUNG, J. (eds), *op. cit.* [217, 227]

PEARSALL, R. (1969), *The Worm in the Bud: The World of Victorian Sexuality*, Weidenfeld & Nicolson, London. [225]

PETRAS, J. W. and MELTZER, B. (1973), 'Theoretical and Ideological Variations', in 'Contemporary Interactionism', *Catalyst*, 7, 1–8. [10]

PHILLIPSON, M. (1971), *Sociological Aspects of Crime and Delinquency*, Routledge & Kegan Paul, London.

PITTMAN, D. J. (1971), 'The Male House of Prostitution', *Trans-Action* (March–April) 21–7. [159, 224]

PITTMAN, D. J. and SNYDER, C. R. (1962), *Society, Culture and Drinking Patterns*, Wiley, New York. [166]

PLATT, A. M. (1969), *The Child-Savers: The Invention of Delinquency*, University of Chicago Press. [206]

PLOG, S. C. and EDGERTON, R. B. (1969), *Changing Perspectives in Mental Illness*, Holt, Rinehart & Winston, London.

PLUMMER, K. J. (1973a), 'Deviance, Sexuality and the Interactionist Perspective: The Case of Male Homosexuality', University of London, Ph.D. thesis. [90, 207]

PLUMMER, K. J. (1973b), 'Awareness of Homosexuality', in BAILEY and YOUNG (1973) *op. cit.* [227]

PLUMMER, K. J. (1973c), 'The Rise of the New Deviancy Perspectives', (mimeo.), Middlesex Polytechnic. [205]

PLUMMER, K. J. (1974), 'Men in Love: Observations on the Gay Couple', in CORBIN, M. (ed.), *The Couple*, Penguin, Harmondsworth. [102, 156, 215]

POLSKY, N. (1967), *Hustlers, Beats and Others*, Aldine, Chicago. [24, 38, 52, 123, 138–9, 208]

POMEROY, W. B. (1972), *Dr Kinsey and the Institute for Sex Research*, Thomas Nelson, London. [4, 62, 203]

QUINNEY, R. (1970), *The Social Reality of Crime*, Little, Brown & Co., Boston. [122, 205, 210, 219]

RADO, S. (1964), 'A Critical Examination of the Concept of Bisexuality', in MARMOR, J. (ed.) (1965), *op. cit.* [215]

RAINS, P. (1971), *Becoming an Unwed Mother: A Sociological Account*, Aldine, Atherton, Chicago. [76, 81, 87, 213]

RAINWATER, L. (1966), 'Some Aspects of Lower Class Sexual Behaviour', *Journal of Social Issues*, 22, 96–108. [49]

RAMSEY, G. (1943), 'The Sexual Development of Boys', *American Journal of Psychology*, 56, 217–33. [210]

RAY, M. B. (1964), 'The Cycle of Abstinence and Relapse Among Heroin Addicts', in BECKER, H. S. (ed.) (1964), *op. cit.* [152]

REICH, W. (1969), *The Sexual Revolution: Toward a Self Governing Character Structure* (4th rev. ed.), Farrar, Straus & Giroux, New York. [6, 52, 115]

REICHE, R. (1970), *Sexuality and Class Struggle*, New Left Books, London.

REISS, A. J. JR (1960), 'Sex Offences: The Marginal Status of the Adolescent', *Law and Contemporary Problems*, 25, p. 310–33. [59, 212]

REISS, A. J. JR (1961), 'The Social Integration of Queers and Peers', *Social Problems*, 9, 102–19. [75, 100, 138, 159, 213, 224, 227]

REISS, I. L. (1966), 'The Sexual Renaissance: A Summary and Analysis', *Journal of Social Issues*, 22, 123–37. [208]

REISS, I. L. (1967), *The Social Context of Premarital Sexual Permissiveness*, Holt, Rinehart & Winston, New York. [4, 7, 75, 203, 208, 209]

REISS, I. L. (1968), 'How and Why American's Sex Standards are Changing', *Trans-Action*, March, 26–32. [208]

REISS, I. L. (1970), 'Premarital Sexual Behaviour and Deviance Theory', *American Sociological Review*, 35, 78–87. [208]

REISS, I. L. (1971), *The Family System in America*, Holt, Rinehart & Winston, New York. [215]

RESNIK, N. L. P. and WOLFGANG, M. E. (1972), *Sexual Behaviours*, Little, Brown & Co., Boston. [204]

REUBEN, D. R. (1971), *Everything You Always Wanted to Know About Sex*, Pan Books, London. [45, 222]

ROBERTS, R. W. (ed.) (1966), *The Unwed Mother*, Harper & Row, London. [213]

ROBINSON, K. (1964), 'Parliament and Public Attitudes', in ROSEN, I. (ed.) (1964), *op. cit.* [117]

ROBINSON, P. Z. (1969), *The Sexual Radicals*, Temple Smith, London.

ROCK, P. (1973), *Deviant Behaviour*, Hutchinson University Library, London. [22, 210]

ROCK, P. and MCINTOSH, M. (eds.) (1974), *Deviance and Social Control*, Tavistock, London.

RODGERS, B. (1973), *The Queen's Vernacular: A Gay Lexicon*, Blond & Briggs, London. [224]

RODMAN, H. (1963), 'The Lower Class Value Stretch', *Social Forces*, 42, 205–15. [209]

ROONEY, E. A. and GIBBONS D. G. (1966), 'Social Reactions to "Crimes with Victims" ', *Social Problems*, 13, 400–10. [105, 107]

ROSE, A. M. (1962), *Human Behaviour and Social Process: An Interactionist Approach*, Routledge & Kegan Paul, London. [204, 210]

ROSEN, I. (ed.) (1964), *The Pathology and Treatment of Sexual Deviation*, Oxford University Press, London. [215]

ROSS, H. L. (1971), 'Modes and Adjustments of Married Homosexuals', *Social Problems*, 18, 385–93. [136, 190]

247

ROTH, J. A. (1963), *Timetables – Structuring the Passage of Time in Hospital Treatment and Other Careers*, Bobbs-Merrill, New York. [210, 221]

RUBIN, I. (1965), *Sexual Life After Sixty*, Allen & Unwin, London. [49]

RUBINGTON, E. and WEINBERG, M. S. (1968), *Deviance: The Interactionist Perspective*, Collier-Macmillan, London. [24]

RUBINGTON, E. and WEINBERG, M. S. (1971), *The Study of Social Problems: Five Perspectives*, Oxford University Press, London. [205]

RUITENBECK, H. M. (ed.) (1963), *The Problems of Homosexuality in Modern Society*, Dutton Paperback Original, New York. [106, 192]

RUNCIMAN, W. G. (1972), *Relative Deprivation and Social Justice*, Penguin Books, Harmondsworth. [172]

SAGARIN, E. (1968a), 'Ideology as a Factor in the Consideration of Deviance', *Journal of Sex Research*, 4, 84–94.

SAGARIN, E. (1968b), 'Taking Stock of Studies of Sex', *Annals of the American Academy of Political and Social Science*, 376, 1–5.

SAGARIN, E. (1969), *Odd Man In: Societies of Deviants in America*, Quadrangle Books, Chicago. [155, 189, 195, 224, 226]

SAGARIN, E. (1971a), 'An Overview of Sex Research', in HENSLIN, J. M. (ed.) (1971), *op. cit*. [10, 203]

SAGARIN, E. (ed.) (1971b), *The Other Minorities: Nonethnic Collectivities Conceptualised as Minority Groups*, Waltham, Massachusetts; Ginn & Co., London.

SAGARIN, E. and MACNAMARA, D. E. J. (1968), *Problems of Sex Behaviour*, Cromwell, New York.

SALAMAN, G., WEEKS, D. and BOSWELL, D. (1972), *Social Interaction*, Open University Press, Portsmouth; Eyre & Spottiswoode, London.

SALZMANN, L. (1964), 'Latent Homosexuality', in MARMOR, J. (ed.) (1965), ch. 13. [215, 220]

SCHEFF, T. J. (1966), *Being Mentally Ill: A Sociological Theory*, Weidenfeld & Nicolson, London. [61, 83, 207, 221]

SCHEFF, T. J. (1967), 'Towards A Sociological Model of Consensus', *American Sociological Review*, 32, 32–46. [177, 209]

SCHEFF, T. J. (1968), 'Negotiating Reality: Notes on Power in the Assessment of Responsibility', *Social Problems*, 16, 3–17. [28, 55, 205]

SCHEFF, T. J. (1970), 'On the Concepts of Identity and Social Relationship', in SHIBUTANI, T. (ed.) (1970), *op. cit*. [177, 209]

SCHERVISH, P. G. (1973), 'The Labeling Perspective', *American Sociologist*, 8, 7–57. [22, 28]

SCHOFIELD, M. (1965a), *Sociological Aspects of Homosexuality*, Longmans, London. [91, 123, 136, 214, 216, 221, 222]

SCHOFIELD, M. (1965b), *Sexual Behaviour of Young People*, Longmans, London. [143, 209, 211]

SCHOFIELD, M. (1973), *Sexual Behaviour of Young Adults*, Allen Lane: Penguin Press, London. [108, 182, 209, 211, 217]

SCHUR, E. M. (1965), *Crimes Without Victims: Deviant Behaviour and Public Policy*, Prentice-Hall, Englewood Cliffs, New Jersey. [87, 92, 129, 207, 225]

SCHUR, E. M. (1969a), *Sociocultural Factors in Homosexual Behaviour*, Working Paper of Hooker Report (*op. cit.*), unpublished. [123, 129]

SCHUR, E. M. (1969b), 'Reactions to Deviance: A Critical Assessment', *American Journal of Sociology*, 75, 309. [26]

SCHUR, E. M. (1971), *Labelling Deviant Behaviour: Its Sociological Implications*, Harper & Row, London. [25, 72]

SCHUTZ, A. (1962), *Collected Papers* (2 vols), Martinus Nijhoff, The Hague. [16, 208]

SCOTT, J. E. and FRANKLIN, S. L. (1973), 'Sex References in the Mass Media', *Journal of Sex Research*, 9, 196–209. [49]

SCOTT, P. D. (1964), 'Definition, Classification, Prognosis and Treatment', in ROSEN, I. (ed.), *op. cit.* [88, 215]

SCOTT, R. (1969), *The Making of Blind Men*, Russell Sage, New York. [221]

SCOTT, R. A. (1972), 'A Proposed Framework for Analysing Deviance as a Property of Social Order', SCOTT and DOUGLAS, *op cit.* [118, 208, 219]

SCOTT, R. A. and DOUGLAS, J. D. (1972), *Theoretical Perspectives on Deviance*, Basic Books, London. [28]

SEWARD, G. H. (1954), *Sex and the Social Order*, Penguin Books, Harmondsworth. [212]

SHAW, C. R. (1930), *The Jack-Roller: A Delinquent Boy's Own Story*, University of Chicago Press. [24]

SHIBUTANI, T. (ed.) (1970), *Human Nature and Collective Behaviour: Essays in Honour of Herbert Blumer*, Prentice-Hall, New Jersey.

SIGUSCH, V. (1968), 'The Aversion Scale Towards Sexually Deviant Groups', *Excerpta Criminologica*, 9, 2. [217]

SIMMEL, G. (1906), 'Friendship, Love and Secrecy', *American Journal of Sociology*, 11, 457–66. [144]

SIMMONS, J. L. (1965), 'Public Stereotypes of Deviants', *Social Problems*, 13, 223–32. [105, 106, 107, 181]

SIMMONS, J. L. (1969), *Deviants*, Glendessary Press, California. [106, 107, 223]

SIMON, W. and GAGNON, J. H. (1967a). 'Homosexuality: The Formulation of a Sociological Perspective', *Journal of Health and Social Behaviour*, 8, 177–85. [91, 127, 147, 166]

SIMON, W. and GAGNON, J. H. (1967b), 'Femininity in the Lesbian Community', *Sexual Problems*, 15, 212–21. [166]

SIMON, W. and GAGNON J. H. (1967c) 'The Lesbians: A Preliminary Overview', in GAGNON and SIMON (1967a), *op. cit.*

SIMON, W. and GAGNON, J. H. (1969), 'Psychosexual Development', *Trans-Action*, March, 9–17. [5, 29, 36, 39, 57, 58, 70]

SJVALL, I. (1970), 'Reproduction and Sexuality', in Ciba Foundation Symposia, ed. ELLIOT, K., *The Family and Its Future*, Churchill, London. [207]

SKIPPER, J. K. and MCCAGHY, C. H. (1970), 'Stripteasers: The Anatomy and Career Contingencies of a Deviant Occupation', *Social Problems*, 17, 391–405. [206, 213]

SKIPPER, J. K. and MCCAGHY, C. H. (1971), 'Stripteasing: A Sex-Oriented Occupation', in HENSLIN, J. M. (ed.) (1971a) *op. cit.* [206, 213]

SKOLNICK, A. S. and J. H. (eds) (1971), *Family in Transition: Rethinking Marriage, Sexuality, Child Rearing and Family Organisation*, Little, Brown & Co., Boston [208]

SKOLNICK, J. H. (1966), *Justice Without Trial*, Wiley, London. [76]

249

SKOLNICK, J. H. and WOODWORTH, J. R. (1967), 'Bureaucracy, Information and Social Control: A Study of a Moral Detail', in BORDUA, D. J. (1967b), *op. cit.*, [79]

SMITH, K. T. (1971), 'Homophobia: A Tentative Personality Profile, *Psychological Reports*, 29, 1091–4. [103, 111]

SOCARIDES, C. W. (1968), *The Overt Homosexual*, Grune & Stratton, New York. [214, 215, 220]

SONENSCHEIN, D. (1968), 'The Ethnography of Male Homosexual Relationships', *Journal of Sex Research*, 4, 69–83. [156]

SONENSCHEIN, D. (1969), 'The Homosexual's Language, *Journal of Sex Research*, 5, 281–91. [162, 163, 224]

SONENSCHEIN, D. (1971), 'How do Homosexuals Identify Each Other As Such?', *Sexual Behaviour*, 49. [227]

SOROKIN, P. (1956), *The American Sex Revolution*, Porter Sargent – Extending Horizons, Massachusetts. [6]

SPITZER, S. P. and DENZIN, N. K. (1968) (eds), *The Mental Patient: Studies in the Sociology of Deviance*, McGraw-Hill, London. [22]

SPREY, J. (1969), 'On the Institutionalisation of Sexuality', *Journal of Marriage and Family*, 31, 432–40. [207]

STEBBINS, R. A. (1969), 'Role Distance, Role Distance Behaviour and Jazz Musicians', *British Journal of Sociology*, 20, 406–15. [193]

STEFFENSMEIER, D. J. (1970), 'Factors Affecting Reactions Toward Homosexuals', Department of Sociology and Anthropology, Iowa University, M.A. thesis, unpublished. [105, 107, 112, 181]

STEWART, G. L. (1972), 'On First Being a John', *Urban Life and Culture*, 1, 225–74. [206]

STINCHCOMBE, A. L. (1963), 'Institutions of Privacy in the Determination of Police Administrative Practice', *American Journal of Sociology*, 64, 150, *et seq.*

STOLLER, R. J. (1964), 'Passing and the Continuum of Gender Identity', in MARMOR, J. (ed.) (1965), *op. cit.*, 190–210. [189]

STOLLER, R. J. (1968), *Sex and Gender*, Science House, New York. [221]

STONE, G. P. (1962), 'Appearance and the Self', in ROSE, A. M. (1962), *op. cit.*, 86–118. [59]

STONE, G. P. and FARBERMAN, H. A. (eds) (1970), *Social Psychology Through Symbolic Interaction*, Xerox Publishing, Massachusetts; Ginn & Co., London.

STORR, A. (1964), *Sexual Deviation*, Penguin Books, Harmondsworth. [211, 212]

STRAUSS, A. L. (1959), *Mirrors and Masks*, Free Press, Chicago. [133, 148, 209, 210]

STREIB, G. F. (1973), *The Changing Family: Adaptation and Diversity*, Addison-Wesley, New York. [208]

SUDNOW, D. (1965), 'Normal Crimes: Sociological Features of the Penal Code', *Social Problems*, 12, 255–70. [76]

SUTHERLAND, A. and ANDERSON, P. (eds) (1964), *Eros: An Anthropology of Friendship*, Blond, London. [223]

SUTHERLAND, E. H. (1937), *The Professional Thief*, University of Chicago Press.

SUTHERLAND, E. H. (1950a), 'The Diffusion of Sexual Psycopath Laws', *American Journal of Sociology*, 56, 142–8. [53, 78]

SUTHERLAND, E. H. (1950b), 'The Sexual Psycopath Laws', *Journal of Criminal Law, Criminology and Police Science*, 40, 543–54. [53]

SUTHERLAND, E. H. and CRESSEY, D. R. (1966), *Principle of Criminology* (7th ed.), J. B. Lippincott Co., Philadelphia. [20]

SYKES, G. M. and MATZA, D. (1957), 'Techniques of Neutralisation: A Theory of Delinquency', *American Sociological Review*, 22, 664–70. [28, 81, 223]

SYMONDS, C. (1971), 'Sexual Mate-swapping: Violation of Norms and Reconciliation of Guilt', in HENSLIN, J. M. (1971a). [213]

SZASZ, T. S. (1971), *The Manufacture of Madness*, Routledge & Kegan Paul, London; pages quoted are from 1970 Harper & Row ed. [23, 218–219]

TANNENBAUM, F. (1938), *Crime and the Community*, Columbia University Press, New York. [20]

TAPPAN, P. W. (1950), *The Habitual Sex Offender: Report to State Commissioner*, New Jersey.

TASK FORCE ON PORNOGRAPHY AND OBSCENITY, *The Obscenity Report*, Stein & Day, New York. [64]

TAYLOR, G. R. (1965a), *Sex in History*, Panther Books, London. [52]

TAYLOR, G. R. (1965b), 'Historical and Mythological Aspects of Homosexuality', in MARMOR, J. (ed.) (1965), *op. cit.* [94, 115, 225]

TAYLOR, I., WALTON, P. and YOUNG, J. (1973), *The New Criminology*, Routledge & Kegan Paul, London. [23, 25, 28, 45, 205, 207]

TAYLOR, L. (1972), 'The Significance and Interpretation of Replies to Motivational Questions: The Case of Sex Offenders', *Sociology*, 6, 23–39. [25, 213, 223]

TEAL, D. (1971), *The Gay Militants*, Stein & Day, New York. [55, 173, 195, 224, 226]

THOMPSON, N. L., MCCANDLESS, B. R. and STRICKLAND, B. R. (1971), 'Personal Adjustment of Male and Female Homosexuals and Heterosexuals', *Journal of Abnormal Psychology*, 78, 237–40. [212]

TOFFLER, A. (1973), *Future Shock*, Bodley Head, London. [7, 208]

TRICE, H. M. and ROMAN, P. M. (1970), 'Delabelling, Relabelling and Alcoholics Anonymous', *Social Problems*, 17, 538–46. [206]

TRUZZI, M. (ed.) (1968), *Sociology and Everyday Life*, Prentice–Hall, Englewood Cliffs, New Jersey. [176]

TURK, A. T. (1969), *Criminality and Legal Order*, Rand McNally, Chicago.

TURNER, R. H. (1962), 'Role-Taking: Process Versus Conformity', in ROSE, A. M., *op. cit.* [18, 96, 204]

TURNER, R. H. (1970), *Family Interaction*, Wiley & Sons, London. [185, 207]

TURNER, R. H. (1972), 'Deviance Avowal as Neutralisation of Commitment', *Social Problems*, 19, 308–21. [96, 213]

ULLERSTAM, L. (1967), *The Erotic Minorities: A Swedish View*, Calder & Boyars, London. [209, 217]

UNWIN, J. D. (1934), *Sex and Culture*, Oxford University Press, London. [6]

VEDDER, C. B. and KING, P. G. (1967), *Problems of Homosexuality in Corrections*, Charles Thomas, Springfield, Illinois. [216]

VINCENT, C. E. (1961), *Unmarried Mothers*, Collier-Macmillan, London. [213]

VIVONA, C. M. and GOMILLION, M. (1972), 'Situational Morality of Bathroom Nudity', *Journal of Sex Research*, 8, 128–35. [52]

WAGNER, H. R. (1970), *Alfred Schutz: On Phenomenology and Social Relations*, University of Chicago Press. [179]

WALKER, N. and ARGYLE, M. (1964), 'Does the Law Affect Moral Judgements, *British Journal of Criminology*, 4, 6, 570–81. [106]

WALLER, W. (1930), *The Old Love and The New: Divorce and Resentment*, Horace Wright, New York. [20, 205]

WALLER, W. (1936), 'Social Problems and the Mores', *American Sociological Review*, 924–30.

WALLIS, R. (1972), 'Dilemma of a Moral Crusade', *New Society*, 13 July, 69–72.

WALSHOK, M. L. (1971), 'The Emergence of Middle-Class Deviant Subcultures: The Case of Swingers', *Social Problems*, 18, 488–95.

WARD, D. A. and KASSEBAUM, G. G. (1964), 'Homosexuality: A Mode of Adaption for Women in a Prison', *Social Problems*, 12, 150–77. [128, 222]

WARD, D. A. and KASSEBAUM, G. G. (1965), *Women's Prison: Sex and Social Structure*, Weidenfeld & Nicolson, London. [216, 222]

WARREN, C. A. B. (1972), 'Observing the Gay Community', in DOUGLAS, J. (ed.) (1972), *op. cit.* [123]

WATTS, A. W. (1958), *Nature, Man and Woman: A New Approach to Sexual Experience*, Thames & Hudson, London. [36]

WEINBERG, G. (1973), *Society and the Healthy Homosexual*, Anchor Books, New York. [103]

WEINBERG, M. S. and BELL, A. P. (1972), *Homosexuality: An Annotated Bibliography*, Harper & Row, London. [220]

WEINBERG, M. S. (1965), 'Sexual Modesty and the Nudist Camp', *Social Problems*, 12, 311–18. [52, 87, 213]

WEINBERG, M. S. (1966), 'Becoming a Nudist', *Psychiatry*, 29, 15–24. [213]

WEINBERG, M. S. (1967), 'The Nudist Camp: Way of Life and Social Structure', *Human Organisation*, 26, 91–9.

WEINBERG, M. S. (1969), 'The Ageing Male Homosexual', *Medical Aspects of Human Sexuality*, 3, 66–72. [152]

WEINBERG, M. S. (1970a), 'The Male Homosexual: Age Related Variations in Social and Psychological Characteristics', *Social Problems*, 17, 527–37. [152]

WEINBERG, M. S. (1970b), 'Homosexual Samples: Differences and Similarities', *Journal of Sex Research*, 6, 312–25. [123]

WEINBERG, M. S. (1970c), 'The Nudist Management of Respectability: Strategy for and Consequences of the Construction of a Situated Morality', in DOUGLAS, J. D. (ed.) (1970b), *op. cit.* [52, 213]

WELTGE, R. W. (ed.) (1969), *The Same Sex: An Appraisal of Homosexuality*, Pilgrim Press, Boston. [103, 224, 226]

WEST, D. J. (1968), *Homosexuality* (2nd ed.), Penguin Books, Harmondsworth. [97, 220]

WESTERMARCK, E. (1917), *Origins and Development of the Moral Ideas*, Macmillan, London. [103, 212, 217]

WESTWOOD, G. (MICHAEL SCHOFIELD), (1952), *Society and the Homosexual* Gollancz, London. [223, 224]

WESTWOOD, G. (MICHAEL SCHOFIELD) (1960), *A Minority: A Report on the Life of the Male Homosexual in Great Britain*, Longmans, London. [124, 145, 146, 188, 189, 221, 224, 227]

WHALEN, R. E. (1966), 'Sexual Motivation', *Psychological Review*, 73, 151–63. [37, 56]

WHEELER, S. (1962), 'Sex Offences: A Sociological Critique', *Law and Contemporary Problems*, 25, 258–69.

WHITEHOUSE, M. (1967), *Cleaning Up T.V.*, Blandford Press, London. [208]

WHYTE, W. F. (1943a), 'A Slum Sex Code', *American Journal of Sociology*, 49, 24–31.

WHYTE, W. F. (1943b), *Street Corner Society*, University of Chicago Press, London.

WILDEBLOOD, P. (1955), *Against the Law*, Weidenfeld & Nicolson, London. [136, 175, 182, 189, 223, 227]

WILKINS, L. T. (1964), *Social Deviance: Social Policy, Action and Research*, Tavistock, London. [167, 169, 212]

WILLIAMS, C. J. and WEINBERG, M. S. (1971), *Homosexuals and the Military: A Study of Less than Honourable Discharge*, Harper & Row, New York. [22, 81, 113, 160, 206, 207, 222, 227]

WILLIAMS, R. (1960), *American Society*, A. A. Knopf, New York. [51]

WILLMOTT, P. (1969), *Adolescent Boys of East London*, Penguin Books, Harmondsworth. [185]

WILSON, C. (1966), *Origin of the Sexual Impulse*, Panther, London. [213]

WILSON, P. (1971), *The Sexual Dilemma: Abortion, Homosexuality, Prostitution and the Criminal Threshold*, University of Queensland Press. [217]

WINICK, C. (1968), *The New People: Desexualisation in American Life*, Pegasus Press, New York. [196]

WINOKUR, G. (1963), *Determinants of Human Sexual Behaviour*, Charles Thomas, Springfield, Illinois.

WOLFF, C. (1971), *Love Between Women*, Duckworth, London. [166]

WOLFF, K. (1950), *The Sociology of Georg Simmel*, Glencoe, London. [144]

WOLFGANG, M. E., *et al.* (eds) (1962), *The Sociology of Crime and Delinquency*, Wiley & Sons, London.

WOLFGANG, M. E. and FERRACUTI, F. (1967), *The Subculture of Violence: Towards an Integrated Theory in Criminology*, Tavistock, London. [223]

WRIGHT, D. (1970), – 'Sex Instinct or Appetite', reprinted from *New Society*, in NOBILE, P. (ed.), *op. cit.* [37, 38]

WRIGHT, D. (1971), *The Psychology of Moral Behaviour*, Penguin Books, Harmondsworth.

WRONG, DENNIS (1961), 'The Oversocialised Conception of Man in Modern Sociology', *American Sociological Review*, 26, 183–92.

WYDEN, P. and WYDEN, B. (1968), *Growing up Straight: What Every Thoughtful Parent Should Know About Homosexuality*, Stein & Day, New York. [220, 222, 227]

253

YINGER, J. M. (1960), 'Contraculture and Subculture', *American Sociological Review*, 625–835. [223]

YOUNG, J. (1971), *The Drugtakers: The Social Meaning of Drug Use*, MacGibbon & Kee, London. [23, 69, 207]

YOUNG, J. (1974), 'New Directions in Subcultural Theory', in REX, J. (ed.) (1974), *Contributions to Sociology*, Routledge & Kegan Paul, London. [170]

YOUNG, W. (1965), *Eros Denied*, Weidenfeld & Nicolson, London. [185]

ZETTERBERG, H. L. (1966), 'The Secret Ranking', *Journal of Marriage and Family Life*, 28, 134–42. [34, 35]

ZIMMERMAN, D. H. and WEIDER, D. L. (1971), 'Ethnomethodology and the Problem of Order, Comment on Denzin', in DOUGLAS, J. (ed.) (1971a), *op. cit.*

ZURCHER, L. A., KIRKPATRICK, R. G., CUSHING, R. G. and BOWMAN, C. K. (1971), 'The Anti-Pornography Campaign: A Symbolic Crusade', *Social Problems*, 19, 217–38. [55]

Subject index

Routledge Social Science Series

Routledge & Kegan Paul   London and Boston

68–74 Carter Lane   London EC4V 5EL

9 Park Street   Boston   Mass 02108

Contents

*Authors wishing to submit manuscripts for any series in
this catalogue should send them to the Social Science Editor,
Routledge & Kegan Paul Ltd, 68–74 Carter Lane,
London EC4V 5EL*

● *Books so marked are available in paperback*
All books are in Metric Demy 8vo format (216 × 138mm approx.)

International Library of Sociology

General Editor John Rex

GENERAL SOCIOLOGY

Barnsley, J. H. The Social Reality of Ethics. *464 pp.*
Belshaw, Cyril. The Conditions of Social Performance. *An Exploratory Theory. 144 pp.*
Brown, Robert. Explanation in Social Science. *208 pp.*
● Rules and Laws in Sociology. *192 pp.*
Bruford, W. H. Chekhov and His Russia. *A Sociological Study. 244 pp.*
Cain, Maureen E. Society and the Policeman's Role. *326 pp.*
Gibson, Quentin. The Logic of Social Enquiry. *240 pp.*
Glucksmann, M. Structuralist Analysis in Contemporary Social Thought. *212 pp.*
Gurvitch, Georges. Sociology of Law. *Preface by Roscoe Pound. 264 pp.*
Hodge, H. A. Wilhelm Dilthey. *An Introduction. 184 pp.*
Homans, George C. Sentiments and Activities. *336 pp.*
Johnson, Harry M. Sociology: *a Systematic Introduction. Foreword by Robert K. Merton. 710 pp.*
Mannheim, Karl. Essays on Sociology and Social Psychology. *Edited by Paul Keckskemeti. With Editorial Note by Adolph Lowe. 344 pp.*
  Systematic Sociology: *An Introduction to the Study of Society. Edited by J. S. Erös and Professor W. A. C. Stewart. 220 pp.*
Martindale, Don. The Nature and Types of Sociological Theory. *292 pp.*
●**Maus, Heinz.** A Short History of Sociology. *234 pp.*
Mey, Harald. Field-Theory. *A Study of its Application in the Social Sciences. 352 pp.*
Myrdal, Gunnar. Value in Social Theory: *A Collection of Essays on Methodology. Edited by Paul Streeten. 332 pp.*
Ogburn, William F., and **Nimkoff, Meyer F.** A Handbook of Sociology. *Preface by Karl Mannheim. 656 pp. 46 figures. 35 tables.*
Parsons, Talcott, and **Smelser, Neil J.** Economy and Society: *A Study in the Integration of Economic and Social Theory. 362 pp.*
●**Rex, John.** Key Problems of Sociological Theory. *220 pp.*
  Discovering Sociology. *278 pp.*
  Sociology and the Demystification of the Modern World. *282 pp.*
●**Rex, John** (Ed.) Approaches to Sociology. *Contributions by Peter Abell, Frank Bechhofer, Basil Bernstein, Ronald Fletcher, David Frisby, Miriam Glucksmann, Peter Lassman, Herminio Martins, John Rex, Roland Robertson, John Westergaard and Jock Young. 302 pp.*
Rigby, A. Alternative Realities. *352 pp.*
Roche, M. Phenomenology, Language and the Social Sciences. *374 pp.*
Sahay, A. Sociological Analysis. *220 pp.*
Urry, John. Reference Groups and the Theory of Revolution. *244 pp.*
Weinberg, E. Development of Sociology in the Soviet Union. *173 pp.*

3

FOREIGN CLASSICS OF SOCIOLOGY

●**Durkheim, Emile.** Suicide. *A Study in Sociology. Edited and with an Introduction by George Simpson. 404 pp.*
Professional Ethics and Civic Morals. *Translated by Cornelia Brookfield. 288 pp.*

●**Gerth, H. H., and Mills, C. Wright.** From Max Weber: *Essays in Sociology. 502 pp.*

●**Tönnies, Ferdinand.** Community and Association. (*Gemeinschaft und Gesellschaft.) Translated and Supplemented by Charles P. Loomis. Foreword by Pitirim A. Sorokin. 334 pp.*

SOCIAL STRUCTURE

Andreski, Stanislav. Military Organization and Society. *Foreword by Professor A. R. Radcliffe-Brown. 226 pp. 1 folder.*

Coontz, Sydney H. Population Theories and the Economic Interpretation. *202 pp.*

Coser, Lewis. The Functions of Social Conflict. *204 pp.*

Dickie-Clark, H. F. Marginal Situation: *A Sociological Study of a Coloured Group. 240 pp. 11 tables.*

Glaser, Barney, and Strauss, Anselm L. Status Passage. *A Formal Theory. 208 pp.*

Glass, D. V. (Ed.) Social Mobility in Britain. *Contributions by J. Berent, T. Bottomore, R. C. Chambers, J. Floud, D. V. Glass, J. R. Hall, H. T. Himmelweit, R. K. Kelsall, F. M. Martin, C. A. Moser, R. Mukherjee, and W. Ziegel. 420 pp.*

Jones, Garth N. Planned Organizational Change: *An Exploratory Study Using an Empirical Approach. 268 pp.*

Kelsall, R. K. Higher Civil Servants in Britain: *From 1870 to the Present Day. 268 pp. 31 tables.*

König, René. The Community. *232 pp. Illustrated.*

●**Lawton, Denis.** Social Class, Language and Education. *192 pp.*

McLeish, John. The Theory of Social Change: *Four Views Considered. 128 pp.*

Marsh, David C. The Changing Social Structure of England and Wales, 1871-1961. *288 pp.*

Mouzelis, Nicos. Organization and Bureaucracy. *An Analysis of Modern Theories. 240 pp.*

Mulkay, M. J. Functionalism, Exchange and Theoretical Strategy. *272 pp.*

Ossowski, Stanislaw. Class Structure in the Social Consciousness. *210 pp.*

Podgórecki, Adam. Law and Society. *About 300 pp.*

SOCIOLOGY AND POLITICS

Acton, T. A. Gypsy Politics and Social Change. *316 pp.*

Hechter, Michael. Internal Colonialism. *The Celtic Fringe in British National Development, 1536–1966. About 350 pp.*

Hertz, Frederick. Nationality in History and Politics: *A Psychology and Sociology of National Sentiment and Nationalism. 432 pp.*

Kornhauser, William. The Politics of Mass Society. *272 pp. 20 tables.*
Laidler, Harry W. History of Socialism. *Social-Economic Movements: An Historical and Comparative Survey of Socialism, Communism, Co-operation, Utopianism; and other Systems of Reform and Reconstruction. 992 pp.*
Lasswell, H. D. Analysis of Political Behaviour. *324 pp.*
Mannheim, Karl. Freedom, Power and Democratic Planning. *Edited by Hans Gerth and Ernest K. Bramstedt. 424 pp.*
Mansur, Fatma. Process of Independence. *Foreword by A. H. Hanson. 208 pp.*
Martin, David A. Pacifism: *an Historical and Sociological Study. 262 pp.*
Myrdal, Gunnar. The Political Element in the Development of Economic Theory. *Translated from the German by Paul Streeten. 282 pp.*
Wootton, Graham. Workers, Unions and the State. *188 pp.*

FOREIGN AFFAIRS: THEIR SOCIAL, POLITICAL AND ECONOMIC FOUNDATIONS

Mayer, J. P. Political Thought in France from the Revolution to the Fifth Republic. *164 pp.*

CRIMINOLOGY

Ancel, Marc. Social Defence: *A Modern Approach to Criminal Problems. Foreword by Leon Radzinowicz. 240 pp.*
Cain, Maureen E. Society and the Policeman's Role. *326 pp.*
Cloward, Richard A., and **Ohlin, Lloyd E.** Delinquency and Opportunity: *A Theory of Delinquent Gangs. 248 pp.*
Downes, David M. The Delinquent Solution. *A Study in Subcultural Theory. 296 pp.*
Dunlop, A. B., and **McCabe, S.** Young Men in Detention Centres. *192 pp.*
Friedlander, Kate. The Psycho-Analytical Approach to Juvenile Delinquency: *Theory, Case Studies, Treatment. 320 pp.*
Glueck, Sheldon, and **Eleanor.** Family Environment and Delinquency. *With the statistical assistance of Rose W. Kneznek. 340 pp.*
Lopez-Rey, Manuel. Crime. *An Analytical Appraisal. 288 pp.*
Mannheim, Hermann. Comparative Criminology: *a Text Book. Two volumes. 442 pp. and 380 pp.*
Morris, Terence. The Criminal Area: *A Study in Social Ecology. Foreword by Hermann Mannheim. 232 pp. 25 tables. 4 maps.*
Rock, Paul. Making People Pay. *338 pp.*
● **Taylor, Ian, Walton, Paul,** and **Young, Jock.** The New Criminology. *For a Social Theory of Deviance. 325 pp.*

SOCIAL PSYCHOLOGY

Bagley, Christopher. The Social Psychology of the Epileptic Child. *320 pp.*
Barbu, Zevedei. Problems of Historical Psychology. *248 pp.*
Blackburn, Julian. Psychology and the Social Pattern. *184 pp.*

●**Brittan, Arthur.** Meanings and Situations. *224 pp.*

Carroll, J. Break-Out from the Crystal Palace. *200 pp.*

●**Fleming, C. M.** Adolescence: Its Social Psychology. *With an Introduction to recent findings from the fields of Anthropology, Physiology, Medicine, Psychometrics and Sociometry. 288 pp.*

● The Social Psychology of Education: *An Introduction and Guide to Its Study. 136 pp.*

Homans, George C. The Human Group. *Foreword by Bernard DeVoto. Introduction by Robert K. Merton. 526 pp.*

● Social Behaviour: *its Elementary Forms. 416 pp.*

●**Klein, Josephine.** The Study of Groups. *226 pp. 31 figures. 5 tables.*

Linton, Ralph. The Cultural Background of Personality. *132 pp.*

●**Mayo, Elton.** The Social Problems of an Industrial Civilization. *With an appendix on the Political Problem. 180 pp.*

Ottaway, A. K. C. Learning Through Group Experience. *176 pp.*

Ridder, J. C. de. The Personality of the Urban African in South Africa. *A Thematic Apperception Test Study. 196 pp. 12 plates.*

●**Rose, Arnold M.** (Ed.) Human Behaviour and Social Processes: *an Interactionist Approach. Contributions by Arnold M. Rose, Ralph H. Turner, Anselm Strauss, Everett C. Hughes, E. Franklin Frazier, Howard S. Becker, et al. 696 pp.*

Smelser, Neil J. Theory of Collective Behaviour. *448 pp.*

Stephenson, Geoffrey M. The Development of Conscience. *128 pp.*

Young, Kimball. Handbook of Social Psychology. *658 pp. 16 figures. 10 tables.*

SOCIOLOGY OF THE FAMILY

Banks, J. A. Prosperity and Parenthood: *A Study of Family Planning among The Victorian Middle Classes. 262 pp.*

Bell, Colin R. Middle Class Families: *Social and Geographical Mobility. 224 pp.*

Burton, Lindy. Vulnerable Children. *272 pp.*

Gavron, Hannah. The Captive Wife: *Conflicts of Household Mothers. 190 pp.*

George, Victor, and **Wilding, Paul.** Motherless Families. *220 pp.*

Klein, Josephine. Samples from English Cultures.
  1. Three Preliminary Studies and Aspects of Adult Life in England. *447 pp.*
  2. Child-Rearing Practices and Index. *247 pp.*

Klein, Viola. Britain's Married Women Workers. *180 pp.*

The Feminine Character. *History of an Ideology. 244 pp.*

McWhinnie, Alexina M. Adopted Children. *How They Grow Up. 304 pp.*

● **Myrdal, Alva,** and **Klein, Viola.** Women's Two Roles: *Home and Work. 238 pp. 27 tables.*

Parsons, Talcott, and **Bales, Robert F.** Family: Socialization and Interaction Process. *In collaboration with James Olds, Morris Zelditch and Philip E. Slater. 456 pp. 50 figures and tables.*

SOCIAL SERVICES

Bastide, Roger. The Sociology of Mental Disorder. *Translated from the French by Jean McNeil. 260 pp.*

Carlebach, Julius. Caring For Children in Trouble. *266 pp.*

Forder, R. A. (Ed.) Penelope Hall's Social Services of England and Wales. *352 pp.*

George, Victor. Foster Care. *Theory and Practice. 234 pp.*
Social Security: *Beveridge and After. 258 pp.*

George, V., and **Wilding, P.** Motherless Families. *248 pp.*

● **Goetschius, George W.** Working with Community Groups. *256 pp.*

Goetschius, George W., and **Tash, Joan.** Working with Unattached Youth. *416 pp.*

Hall, M. P., and **Howes, I. V.** The Church in Social Work. *A Study of Moral Welfare Work undertaken by the Church of England. 320 pp.*

Heywood, Jean S. Children in Care: *the Development of the Service for the Deprived Child. 264 pp.*

Hoenig, J., and **Hamilton, Marian W.** The De-Segregation of the Mentally Ill. *284 pp.*

Jones, Kathleen. Mental Health and Social Policy, 1845-1959. *264 pp.*

King, Roy D., Raynes, Norma V., and **Tizard, Jack.** Patterns of Residential Care. *356 pp.*

Leigh, John. Young People and Leisure. *256 pp.*

Morris, Mary. Voluntary Work and the Welfare State. *300 pp.*

Morris, Pauline. Put Away: *A Sociological Study of Institutions for the Mentally Retarded. 364 pp.*

Nokes, P. L. The Professional Task in Welfare Practice. *152 pp.*

Timms, Noel. Psychiatric Social Work in Great Britain (1939-1962). *280 pp.*

● Social Casework: *Principles and Practice. 256 pp.*

Young, A. F. Social Services in British Industry. *272 pp.*

Young, A. F., and **Ashton, E. T.** British Social Work in the Nineteenth Century. *288 pp.*

SOCIOLOGY OF EDUCATION

Banks, Olive. Parity and Prestige in English Secondary Education: a Study in Educational Sociology. *272 pp.*

Bentwich, Joseph. Education in Israel. *224 pp. 8 pp. plates.*

● **Blyth, W. A. L.** English Primary Education. *A Sociological Description.*
1. Schools. *232 pp.*
2. Background. *168 pp.*

Collier, K. G. The Social Purposes of Education: *Personal and Social Values in Education. 268 pp.*

Dale, R. R., and **Griffith, S.** Down Stream: *Failure in the Grammar School.* *108 pp.*

Dore, R. P. Education in Tokugawa Japan. *356 pp. 9 pp. plates.*

Evans, K. M. Sociometry and Education. *158 pp.*

●**Ford, Julienne.** Social Class and the Comprehensive School. *192 pp.*

Foster, P. J. Education and Social Change in Ghana. *336 pp. 3 maps.*

Fraser, W. R. Education and Society in Modern France. *150 pp.*

Grace, Gerald R. Role Conflict and the Teacher. *About 200 pp.*

Hans, Nicholas. New Trends in Education in the Eighteenth Century. *278 pp. 19 tables.*

● Comparative Education: *A Study of Educational Factors and Traditions.* *360 pp.*

Hargreaves, David. Interpersonal Relations and Education. *432 pp.*

● Social Relations in a Secondary School. *240 pp.*

Holmes, Brian. Problems in Education. *A Comparative Approach. 336 pp.*

King, Ronald. Values and Involvement in a Grammar School. *164 pp.*

School Organization and Pupil Involvement. *A Study of Secondary Schools.*

●**Mannheim, Karl,** and **Stewart, W. A. C.** An Introduction to the Sociology of Education. *206 pp.*

Morris, Raymond N. The Sixth Form and College Entrance. *231 pp.*

●**Musgrove, F.** Youth and the Social Order. *176 pp.*

●**Ottaway, A. K. C.** Education and Society: An Introduction to the Sociology of Education. *With an Introduction by W. O. Lester Smith. 212 pp.*

Peers, Robert. Adult Education: *A Comparative Study. 398 pp.*

Pritchard, D. G. Education and the Handicapped: *1760 to 1960. 258 pp.*

Richardson, Helen. Adolescent Girls in Approved Schools. *308 pp.*

Stratta, Erica. The Education of Borstal Boys. *A Study of their Educational Experiences prior to, and during, Borstal Training. 256 pp.*

Taylor, P. H., Reid, W. A., and **Holley, B. J.** The English Sixth Form. *A Case Study in Curriculum Research. 200 pp.*

SOCIOLOGY OF CULTURE

Eppel, E. M., and **M.** Adolescents and Morality: *A Study of some Moral Values and Dilemmas of Working Adolescents in the Context of a changing Climate of Opinion. Foreword by W. J. H. Sprott. 268 pp. 39 tables.*

●**Fromm, Erich.** The Fear of Freedom. *286 pp.*

● The Sane Society. *400 pp.*

Mannheim, Karl. Essays on the Sociology of Culture. *Edited by Ernst Mannheim in co-operation with Paul Kecskemeti. Editorial Note by Adolph Lowe. 280 pp.*

Weber, Alfred. Farewell to European History: *or The Conquest of Nihilism. Translated from the German by R. F. C. Hull. 224 pp.*

SOCIOLOGY OF RELIGION

Argyle, Michael and **Beit-Hallahmi, Benjamin.** The Social Psychology of Religion. *About 256 pp.*

Nelson, G. K. Spiritualism and Society. *313 pp.*

Stark, Werner. The Sociology of Religion. *A Study of Christendom.*
Volume I. *Established Religion. 248 pp.*
Volume II. *Sectarian Religion. 368 pp.*
Volume III. *The Universal Church. 464 pp.*
Volume IV. *Types of Religious Man. 352 pp.*
Volume V. *Types of Religious Culture. 464 pp.*

Turner, B. S. Weber and Islam. *216 pp.*

Watt, W. Montgomery. Islam and the Integration of Society. *320 pp.*

SOCIOLOGY OF ART AND LITERATURE

Jarvie, Ian C. Towards a Sociology of the Cinema. *A Comparative Essay on the Structure and Functioning of a Major Entertainment Industry. 405 pp.*

Rust, Frances S. Dance in Society. *An Analysis of the Relationships between the Social Dance and Society in England from the Middle Ages to the Present Day. 256 pp. 8 pp. of plates.*

Schücking, L. L. The Sociology of Literary Taste. *112 pp.*

Wolff, Janet. Hermeneutic Philosophy and the Sociology of Art. *About 200 pp.*

SOCIOLOGY OF KNOWLEDGE

Diesing, P. Patterns of Discovery in the Social Sciences. *262 pp.*

●**Douglas, J. D.** (Ed.) Understanding Everyday Life. *370 pp.*

●**Hamilton, P.** Knowledge and Social Structure. *174 pp.*

Jarvie, I. C. Concepts and Society. *232 pp.*

Mannheim, Karl. Essays on the Sociology of Knowledge. *Edited by Paul Kecskemeti. Editorial Note by Adolph Lowe. 353 pp.*

Remmling, Gunter W. (Ed.) Towards the Sociology of Knowledge. *Origin and Development of a Sociological Thought Style. 463 pp.*

Stark, Werner. The Sociology of Knowledge: *An Essay in Aid of a Deeper Understanding of the History of Ideas. 384 pp.*

URBAN SOCIOLOGY

Ashworth, William. The Genesis of Modern British Town Planning: *A Study in Economic and Social History of the Nineteenth and Twentieth Centuries. 288 pp.*

Cullingworth, J. B. Housing Needs and Planning Policy: *A Restatement of the Problems of Housing Need and 'Overspill' in England and Wales. 232 pp. 44 tables. 8 maps.*

Dickinson, Robert E. City and Region: *A Geographical Interpretation* *608 pp. 125 figures.*
The West European City: *A Geographical Interpretation. 600 pp. 129 maps. 29 plates.*
● The City Region in Western Europe. *320 pp. Maps.*
Humphreys, Alexander J. New Dubliners: *Urbanization and the Irish Family. Foreword by George C. Homans. 304 pp.*
Jackson, Brian. Working Class Community: *Some General Notions raised by a Series of Studies in Northern England. 192 pp.*
Jennings, Hilda. Societies in the Making: *a Study of Development and Redevelopment within a County Borough. Foreword by D. A. Clark. 286 pp.*
●**Mann, P. H.** An Approach to Urban Sociology. *240 pp.*
Morris, R. N., and **Mogey, J.** The Sociology of Housing. *Studies at Berinsfield. 232 pp. 4 pp. plates.*
Rosser, C., and **Harris, C.** The Family and Social Change. *A Study of Family and Kinship in a South Wales Town. 352 pp. 8 maps.*

RURAL SOCIOLOGY

Chambers, R. J. H. Settlement Schemes in Tropical Africa: *A Selective Study. 268 pp.*
Haswell, M. R. The Economics of Development in Village India. *120 pp.*
Littlejohn, James. Westrigg: *the Sociology of a Cheviot Parish. 172 pp. 5 figures.*
Mayer, Adrian C. Peasants in the Pacific. *A Study of Fiji Indian Rural Society. 248 pp. 20 plates.*
Williams, W. M. The Sociology of an English Village: *Gosforth. 272 pp. 12 figures. 13 tables.*

SOCIOLOGY OF INDUSTRY AND DISTRIBUTION

Anderson, Nels. Work and Leisure. *280 pp.*
●**Blau, Peter M.,** and **Scott, W. Richard.** Formal Organizations: *a Comparative approach. Introduction and Additional Bibliography by J. H. Smith. 326 pp.*
Eldridge, J. E. T. Industrial Disputes. *Essays in the Sociology of Industrial Relations. 288 pp.*
Hetzler, Stanley. Applied Measures for Promoting Technological Growth. *352 pp.*
Technological Growth and Social Change. *Achieving Modernization. 269 pp.*
Hollowell, Peter G. The Lorry Driver. *272 pp.*
Jefferys, Margot, *with the assistance of Winifred Moss.* Mobility in the Labour Market: *Employment Changes in Battersea and Dagenham. Preface by Barbara Wootton. 186 pp. 51 tables.*

Millerson, Geoffrey. The Qualifying Associations: *a Study in Professionalization. 320 pp.*

Smelser, Neil J. Social Change in the Industrial Revolution: *An Application of Theory to the Lancashire Cotton Industry, 1770-1840. 468 pp. 12 figures. 14 tables.*

Williams, Gertrude. Recruitment to Skilled Trades. *240 pp.*

Young, A. F. Industrial Injuries Insurance: *an Examination of British Policy. 192 pp.*

DOCUMENTARY

Schlesinger, Rudolf (Ed.) Changing Attitudes in Soviet Russia.
2. The Nationalities Problem and Soviet Administration. *Selected Readings on the Development of Soviet Nationalities Policies. Introduced by the editor. Translated by W. W. Gottlieb. 324 pp.*

ANTHROPOLOGY

Ammar, Hamed. Growing up in an Egyptian Village: *Silwa, Province of Aswan. 336 pp.*

Brandel-Syrier, Mia. Reeftown Elite. *A Study of Social Mobility in a Modern African Community on the Reef. 376 pp.*

Crook, David, and **Isabel.** Revolution in a Chinese Village: *Ten Mile Inn. 230 pp. 8 plates. 1 map.*

Dickie-Clark, H. F. The Marginal Situation. *A Sociological Study of a Coloured Group. 236 pp.*

Dube, S. C. Indian Village. *Foreword by Morris Edward Opler. 276 pp. 4 plates.*

India's Changing Villages: *Human Factors in Community Development. 260 pp. 8 plates. 1 map.*

Firth, Raymond. Malay Fishermen. *Their Peasant Economy. 420 pp. 17 pp. plates.*

Firth, R., Hubert, J., and **Forge, A.** Families and their Relatives. *Kinship in a Middle-Class Sector of London: An Anthropological Study. 456 pp.*

Gulliver, P. H. Social Control in an African Society: a Study of the Arusha, Agricultural Masai of Northern Tanganyika. *320 pp. 8 plates. 10 figures.*

Family Herds. *288 pp.*

Ishwaran, K. Shivapur. *A South Indian Village. 216 pp.*

Tradition and Economy in Village India: *An Interactionist Approach. Foreword by Conrad Arensburg. 176 pp.*

Jarvie, Ian C. The Revolution in Anthropology. *268 pp.*

Jarvie, Ian C., and **Agassi, Joseph.** Hong Kong. *A Society in Transition. 396 pp. Illustrated with plates and maps.*

Little, Kenneth L. Mende of Sierra Leone. *308 pp. and folder.*

Negroes in Britain. *With a New Introduction and Contemporary Study by Leonard Bloom. 320 pp.*

11

Lowie, Robert H. Social Organization. *494 pp.*

Mayer, Adrian. C. Caste and Kinship in Central India: *A Village and its Region. 328 pp. 16 plates. 15 figures. 16 tables.*

Peasants in the Pacific. *A Study of Fiji Indian Rural Society. 248 pp.*

Smith, Raymond T. The Negro Family in British Guiana: *Family Structure and Social Status in the Villages. With a Foreword by Meyer Fortes. 314 pp. 8 plates. 1 figure. 4 maps.*

SOCIOLOGY AND PHILOSOPHY

Barnsley, John H. The Social Reality of Ethics. *A Comparative Analysis of Moral Codes. 448 pp.*

Diesing, Paul. Patterns of Discovery in the Social Sciences. *362 pp.*

●**Douglas, Jack D.** (Ed.) Understanding Everyday Life. *Toward the Reconstruction of Sociological Knowledge. Contributions by Alan F. Blum. Aaron W. Cicourel, Norman K. Denzin, Jack D. Douglas, John Heeren, Peter McHugh, Peter K. Manning, Melvin Power, Matthew Speier, Roy Turner, D. Lawrence Wieder, Thomas P. Wilson and Don H. Zimmerman. 370 pp.*

Jarvie, Ian C. Concepts and Society. *216 pp.*

Pelz, Werner. The Scope of Understanding in Sociology. *Towards a more radical reorientation in the social humanistic sciences. 283 pp.*

Roche, Maurice. Phenomenology, Language and the Social Sciences. *371 pp.*

Sahay, Arun. Sociological Analysis. *212 pp.*

Sklair, Leslie. The Sociology of Progress. *320 pp.*

International Library of Anthropology

General Editor Adam Kuper

Brown, Paula. The Chimbu. *A Study of Change in the New Guinea Highlands. 151 pp.*

Lloyd, P. C. Power and Independence. *Urban Africans' Perception of Social Inequality. 264 pp.*

Pettigrew, Joyce. Robber Noblemen. *A Study of the Political System of the Sikh Jats. 284 pp.*

Van Den Berghe, Pierre L. Power and Privilege at an African University. *278 pp.*

International Library of Social Policy

General Editor Kathleen Jones

Bayley, M. Mental Handicap and Community Care. *426 pp.*

Butler, J. R. Family Doctors and Public Policy. *208 pp.*

Holman, Robert. Trading in Children. *A Study of Private Fostering. 355 pp.*

12

Jones, Kathleen. History of the Mental Health Service. *428 pp.*
Thomas, J. E. The English Prison Officer since 1850: *A Study in Conflict.* *258 pp.*
Woodward, J. To Do the Sick No Harm. *A Study of the British Voluntary Hospital System to 1875. About 220 pp.*

International Library of Welfare and Philosophy

General Editors Noel Timms and David Watson

● **Plant, Raymond.** Community and Ideology. *104 pp.*

Primary Socialization, Language and Education

General Editor Basil Bernstein

Bernstein, Basil. Class, Codes and Control. *2 volumes.*
   1. *Theoretical Studies Towards a Sociology of Language. 254 pp.*
   2. *Applied Studies Towards a Sociology of Language. About 400 pp.*
Brandis, W., and **Bernstein, B.** Selection and Control. *176 pp.*
Brandis, Walter, and **Henderson, Dorothy.** Social Class, Language and Communication. *288 pp.*
Cook-Gumperz, Jenny. Social Control and Socialization. *A Study of Class Differences in the Language of Maternal Control. 290 pp.*
● **Gahagan, D. M.,** and **G. A.** Talk Reform. *Exploration in Language for Infant School Children. 160 pp.*
Robinson, W. P., and **Rackstraw, Susan D. A.** A Question of Answers. *2 volumes. 192 pp. and 180 pp.*
Turner, Geoffrey J., and **Mohan, Bernard A.** A Linguistic Description and Computer Programme for Children's Speech. *208 pp.*

Reports of the Institute of Community Studies

Cartwright, Ann. Human Relations and Hospital Care. *272 pp.*
●   Parents and Family Planning Services. *306 pp.*
   Patients and their Doctors. *A Study of General Practice. 304 pp.*
● **Jackson, Brian.** Streaming: *an Education System in Miniature. 168 pp.*
Jackson, Brian, and **Marsden, Dennis.** Education and the Working Class: *Some General Themes raised by a Study of 88 Working-class Children in a Northern Industrial City. 268 pp. 2 folders.*
Marris, Peter. The Experience of Higher Education. *232 pp. 27 tables.*
   Loss and Change. *192 pp.*

Marris, Peter, and Rein, Martin. Dilemmas of Social Reform. *Poverty and Community Action in the United States. 256 pp.*

Marris, Peter, and Somerset, Anthony. African Businessmen. *A Study of Entrepreneurship and Development in Kenya. 256 pp.*

Mills, Richard. Young Outsiders: *a Study in Alternative Communities. 216 pp.*

Runciman, W. G. Relative Deprivation and Social Justice. *A Study of Attitudes to Social Inequality in Twentieth-Century England. 352 pp.*

Willmott, Peter. Adolescent Boys in East London. *230 pp.*

Willmott, Peter, and Young, Michael. Family and Class in a London Suburb. *202 pp. 47 tables.*

Young, Michael. Innovation and Research in Education. *192 pp.*

●Young, Michael, and McGeeney, Patrick. Learning Begins at Home. *A Study of a Junior School and its Parents. 128 pp.*

Young, Michael, and Willmott, Peter. Family and Kinship in East London. *Foreword by Richard M. Titmuss. 252 pp. 39 tables.*
The Symmetrical Family. *410 pp.*

Reports of the Institute for Social Studies in Medical Care

Cartwright, Ann, Hockey, Lisbeth, and Anderson, John L. Life Before Death. *310 pp.*

Dunnell, Karen, and Cartwright, Ann. Medicine Takers, Prescribers and Hoarders. *190 pp.*

Medicine, Illness and Society

General Editor W. M. Williams

Robinson, David. The Process of Becoming Ill. *142 pp.*

Stacey, Margaret, *et al.* Hospitals, Children and Their Families. *The Report of a Pilot Study. 202 pp.*

Monographs in Social Theory

General Editor Arthur Brittan

●Barnes, B. Scientific Knowledge and Sociological Theory. *About 200 pp.*

Bauman, Zygmunt. Culture as Praxis. *204 pp.*

● Dixon, Keith. Sociological Theory. *Pretence and Possibility. 142 pp.*

●Smith, Anthony D. The Concept of Social Change. *A Critique of the Functionalist Theory of Social Change. 208 pp.*

Routledge Social Science Journals

The British Journal of Sociology. *Edited by Terence P. Morris. Vol. 1, No. 1, March 1950 and Quarterly. Roy. 8vo. Back numbers available. An international journal with articles on all aspects of sociology.*

Economy and Society. *Vol. 1, No. 1. February 1972 and Quarterly. Metric Roy. 8vo. A journal for all social scientists covering sociology, philosophy, anthropology, economics and history. Back numbers available.*

Year Book of Social Policy in Britain, The. *Edited by Kathleen Jones. 1971. Published annually.*

Printed in Great Britain by Unwin Brothers Limited
The Gresham Press Old Woking Surrey
A member of the Staples Printing Group